ABOUT JIM WILLIS

Having earned his master's degree in theology from Andover Newton Theological School, **Jim Willis** has been an ordained minister for over 40 years. He has also taught college courses in comparative religion and cross-cultural studies. In addition, Jim has been a professional musician, high school orchestra and band teacher, arts council director, and even a drive-time radio show host. His background in theology and education led to his writings on religion, the apocalypse, cross-cultural spirituality, and the mysteries of the unknown. His books include Visible Ink Press's *The Religion Book: Places, Prophets, Saints, and Seers; Censoring God: The History of the Lost Books (and Other Excluded Scriptures); Armageddon Now: The End of the World A to Z;* and *Ancient Gods: Lost Histories, Hidden Truths, and the Conspiracy of Silence.* He has also published *Faith, Trust & Belief: A Trilogy of the Spirit; Savannah: A Bicycle Journey through Space and Time;* and *The Dragon Awakes.* Jim resides in the woods of South Carolina and can be found online at jimwillis.net.

ALSO FROM VISIBLE INK PRESS

Ancient Gods: Lost Histories, Hidden Truths, and the Conspiracy of Silence
by Jim Willis
ISBN: 978-1-57859-614-0

Angels A to Z, 2nd edition
by Evelyn Dorothy Oliver and James R. Lewis
ISBN: 978-1-57859-212-8

Armageddon Now: The End of the World A to Z
by Jim Willis and Barbara Willis
ISBN: 978-1-57859-168-8

The Astrology Book: The Encyclopedia of Heavenly Influences, 2nd edition
by James R. Lewis
ISBN: 978-1-57859-144-2

Censoring God: The History of the Lost Books (and Other Excluded Scriptures)
by Jim Willis
ISBN: 978-1-57859-732-1

Demons, the Devil, and Fallen Angels
by Marie D. Jones and Larry Flaxman
ISBN: 978-1-57859-613-3

The Dream Encyclopedia, 2nd edition
by James R. Lewis and Evelyn Dorothy Oliver
ISBN: 978-1-57859-216-6

The Dream Interpretation Dictionary: Symbols, Signs and Meanings
by J.M. DeBord
ISBN: 978-1-57859-637-9

Earth Magic: Your Complete Guide to Natural Spells, Potions, Plants, Herbs, Witchcraft, and More
by Marie D. Jones
ISBN: 978-1-57859-697-3

The Encyclopedia of Religious Phenomena
by J. Gordon Melton, PhD
ISBN: 978-1-57859-209-8

The Fortune-Telling Book: The Encyclopedia of Divination and Soothsaying
by Raymond Buckland
ISBN: 978-1-57859-147-3

The Handy Bible Answer Book
by Jennifer R. Prince
ISBN: 978-1-57859-478-8

The Handy Christianity Answer Book
by Stephen A Werner, PhD
ISBN: 978-1-57859-686-7

The Handy Islam Answer Book
by John Renard, PhD
ISBN: 978-1-57859-510-5

The Handy Mythology Answer Book
by David Leeming, PhD
ISBN: 978-1-57859-475-7

The Handy Religion Answer Book,
2nd edition
by John Renard, PhD
ISBN: 978-1-57859-379-8

The New Witch: Your Guide to
Modern Witchcraft, Wicca, Spells,
Potions, Magic, and More
by Marie D. Jones
ISBN: 978-1-57859-716-1

Real Miracles, Divine
Intervention, and Feats of
Incredible Survival
by Brad Steiger and Sherry
Hansen Steiger
ISBN: 978-1-57859-214-2

Real Visitors, Voices from Beyond,
and Parallel Dimensions
by Brad Steiger and Sherry
Hansen Steiger
ISBN: 978-1-57859-541-9

The Religion Book: Places,
Prophets, Saints, and Seers
by Jim Willis
ISBN: 978-1-57859-151-0

The Spirit Book: The Encyclopedia
of Clairvoyance, Channeling, and
Spirit Communication
by Raymond Buckland
ISBN: 978-1-57859-790-1

Supernatural Gods: Spiritual Mys-
teries, Psychic Experiences, and
Scientific Truths
by Jim Willis
ISBN: 978-1-57859-660-7

Time Travel: The Science and
Science Fiction
by Nick Redfern
ISBN: 978-1-57859-723-9

The Vampire Almanac: The Com-
plete History
by J. Gordon Melton, PhD
ISBN: 978-1-57859-719-2

The Witch Book: The Encyclopedia
of Witchcraft, Wicca, and Neo-pa-
ganism
by Raymond Buckland
ISBN: 978-1-57859-114-5

Please visit us at visibleinkpress.com

AMERICAN CULTS

AMERICAN CULTS

CABALS, CORRUPTION, AND CHARISMATIC LEADERS

Jim Willis

Most Visible Ink Press books are available at special quantity discounts when purchased in bulk by corporations, organizations, or groups. Customized printings, special imprints, messages, and excerpts can be produced to meet your needs. For more information, contact Special Markets Director, Visible Ink Press, www.visibleink.com, or 734-667-3211.

Managing Editor: Christa Gainor
Art Director: Alessandro Cinelli, Cinelli Design
Cover Design: John Gouin, Graphikitchen, LLC
Typesetting: Marco Divita
Image Editor: Gregory Hayes
Proofreader: Larry Baker
Indexer: Shoshana Hurwitz

ISBN: 978-1-57859-800-7 (paperback)
ISBN: 978-1-57859-825-0 (hardcover)
ISBN: 978-1-57859-826-7 (eBook)

Cataloging-in-Publication Data is on file at the Library of Congress.

10 9 8 7 6 5 4 3 2 1

AMERICAN CULTS

CABALS, CORRUPTION, AND CHARISMATIC LEADERS

Jim Willis

CONTENTS

INTRODUCTION: CRYSTAL BALLS AND CONSPIRACIES ... XIII

PROLOGUE: WHAT MAKES A CULT POSSIBLE? ... 1

IN THE BEGINNING: WHY IS AMERICA SUCH A FERTILE FIELD FOR CULTS? ... 13

Lip-Service Religion

Rebelliousness

Entrepreneurship

Religious Freedom

Evolving Social Media

Infatuation with Conspiracy Theory

Living on "The Eve of Destruction"

OFFSHOOTS: BREAKING AWAY FROM TRADITIONAL RELIGIONS ... 35

Cyrus Teed and the Koreshan Unity

Father Divine and the Peace Mission

Jim Jones and the Peoples Temple Full Gospel Church

Jim Bakker, *The PTL Club*, and the Return of Jesus

The Evangelical Church, Politics, and the NRA

Joshua, Jesus, Muhammad, and the Implications of Jihad

David Berg and the Family International: From Teens for Christ to Grown-up Cult

The Watchtower Society and Jehovah's Witnesses

Westboro Baptist Church

Jane Whaley, the Word of Faith Fellowship, and the Gospel of Prosperity

David Koresh and the Branch Davidians

SCIENCE, POLITICS, ECONOMICS, AND METAPHYSICS: A TRICKY LINK ... 113

The Cult of Scientism

The Dogma of Politics

Multi-Level Marketing Cults (MLMs): Pyramids, Ponzis, and Profits

The World of Metaphysics: "It Seems to Me ..."

Sun Myung Moon and the Unification Church

Eckankar: Discovering God

THE UNIVERSE AND BEYOND: ANSWERS FROM THE FINAL FRONTIER ... 151

The Christian Rapture, Carl Jung, and Flying Saucers

The Church of Scientology

Raëlians and the Elohim: Intelligent Design for Atheists

Into the Universe: Latter-day Saints and the Colonization of the Cosmos

Heaven's Gate: Help from Above?

PROPHETS OF THE END TIMES: TELLING THE FUTURE FOR FUN AND PROFIT ... 191

From 666 to the "Seventy Sevens": What Does the Bible Really Say about THE END?

From Nostradamus to Edgar Cayce and Beyond

The Doomsday Clock

Roch Thériault and the Ant Hill Kids

THE RISE OF RACIAL RELIGION CULTS AND SOCIAL MEDIA ... 231

From the Ku Klux Klan to White Nationalism

The New Militia Movement

Nuwaubian Nation: From Black Supremacists to UFOs

Social Media and the Rise of Hate Groups

Spoofing the Movement: Fun with Cults

QAnon: Political Conspiracy and Religious Icons

SEX IN THE CITY: THE DARK POTENCY OF CULTS ... 277

Bhagwan Shree Rajneesh: Coming to America

Keith Raniere and NXIVM: The Case of the Self-Styled Revered One

Sullivanians: Sex as a Way of Life

CONCLUSIONS: WHAT'S AHEAD FOR INDIVIDUAL FREEDOM? ... 293

Is Every Organization a Cult?

Leaders, Followers, and Pathology

What's Ahead for Individual Freedom?

EPILOGUE: HOW DO I GET OUT? ... 305
FURTHER READING ... 313
IMAGE CREDITS ... 317
INDEX ... 323

INTRODUCTION

CRYSTAL BALLS AND CONSPIRACIES

Cult: A system of religious veneration and devotion directed toward a particular figure or object; a relatively small group of people having religious beliefs or practices regarded by others as strange or sinister; a misplaced or excessive admiration for a particular person or thing. (*Oxford Language Dictionary*)

What is a cult, really?

"Cult" is a word that has long been bandied about to describe organizations of quite disparate views and values. During the 1960s and '70s, it was often applied to the Manson Family, a communal gang based in California and led by Charles Manson. About 100 followers, most of whom were habitual users of LSD and other hallucinogenic drugs, became convinced that Manson was a reincarnated manifestation of Jesus Christ. He prophesied that America would soon become immersed in an apocalyptic race war. The group might have escaped public notoriety had members not broken into the home of actress Sharon Tate in 1969. In a gruesome manner, they killed her and four other people, and they committed similar atrocities in other locations. Manson died in prison in 2017 while serving a lifetime sentence for murder, among other crimes.

If all it takes to define a cult is to identify a charismatic leader and enthusiastic followers with evil intentions, there is no greater example than that of Japan's Shoko Asahara and the group that became known as Aum Shinrikyō.

Asahara was born into a very poor family. He was partially blind, and as a child he attended a boarding school that worked with students whose sight was impaired. While there, he gained a reputation as a bully who dominated other students and was involved in a series of scams. The scams continued after he left the school. For a while he ran an acupuncture salon that specialized in dubious cures, but by 1986 he was traveling throughout the Himalayas, searching for enlightenment.

Aum Shinrikyō was behind one of the most chilling and memorable news stories of the mid-1990s: the sarin gas attack in the Tokyo subway. One hundred and eighty-nine cult members would eventually be indicted for the attack, with founder Asahara and 12 followers sentenced to death by hanging.

He emerged from his quest having labeled himself a guru. By combining mystical Buddhism and various forms of Hinduism, and then adding a dollop of regimented and vigorous yoga, he began to build the organization known as Aum Shinrikyō.

It was, however, only after he discovered Christianity and its doctrines concerning Armageddon—the final, cataclysmic conflict—that his enterprise began to form into what can only be called a cult. Asahara the con man rose to the surface. He offered products such as electrode caps and astral teleporters. He soon ventured into a pseudoscientific method of transfiguration he called "Magic DNA." All these items and services came with a price, of course, and many people were duped into donating.

In 1984 Asahara had a one-room yoga school, a small number of devotees, and a dream of world domination. By 1994, only ten years later, the group had become known as Aum Shinrikyō, or "Supreme Truth," had 40,000 followers from six different countries, boasted a worldwide network of influence, and had accumulated enough money to buy state-of-the-art lasers, laboratories full of modern equipment, and weapons. Lots of weapons. Varied weapons. Weapons that would soon be employed to massive effect.

He moved his operation to Manhattan and Silicon Valley. Then he established bases from Bonn, Germany, to the Australian outback. He even formed a satellite group in Russia. With the Soviet Union in disarray, his cult followers there found a ready supply of weapons and were even rumored to have somehow obtained a small nuclear bomb.

To increase his following, Asahara began to systematically target Japanese universities, searching for bright, young, vulnerable students enrolled in engineering, chemistry, and physics departments. He recruited medical doctors, who began to perform exotic experiments on humans. He forged relationships with the Japanese crime syndicate known as Yakuza, and he even recruited former members of the KGB.

Why did so many flock to his banner? He promised them relief from their dead-end jobs. He guaranteed enlightenment and supernatural powers. He convinced his followers, largely by an obviously doctored photo, that during intense meditation, he could actually fly. They all wanted similar abilities. He offered something special, and they desperately wanted to believe he could give it to them.

Successful cult leaders attain their status by tapping into social needs and desires that other mainstream leaders miss or ignore. The dispossessed, the lost, the alienated, the discouraged, the overlooked, and the powerless respond to overtures that promise them exciting abilities like telepathy, levitation, political power, and above all, acceptance and meaning.

Somehow in the midst of all this, Asahara managed to escape the radar of both police and media, even though he operated on four continents. Aum Shinrikyō was now one of the richest and most sophisticated organizations of its kind in the world. It might have continued forever were it not for the sarin gas attack it attempted to pull off during rush-hour traffic in the subway system of Tokyo in March 1995.

The whole escapade started with an earthquake. During the Cold War, both the Soviet Union and the United States had attempted to manufacture a so-called death ray. What most of the world didn't know was that Aum Shinrikyō was trying its best to beat both superpowers in the race toward Armageddon.

On January 17, 1995, a sudden earthquake rocked Kobe, Japan, twisting highways, destroying bridges, and sending apartment buildings crumbling to the ground. It claimed more than 5,500 causalities, becoming the worst Japanese disaster since World War II.

Asahara was convinced it was caused by the United States. Aum Shinrikyō's chief scientist, Hideo Mauri, reported that "there is a strong possibility that the Kobe earthquake was activated by electromagnetic power, or some other device that exerts energy into the ground."

When he conveyed his suspicion at a news conference, he was met with derision from the gathered reporters. This infuriated Asahara. He had ardently followed the work of Nikola Tesla (1856–1943). Tesla was a brilliant Serbian scientist who had become a United States citizen. He studied the effects of electric energy over long distances and had predicted that an induced earthquake was possible. Asahara believed it, and he blamed the United States government for the Kobe earthquake.

Tesla had also surmised that it was possible to split the earth in two with electromagnetic forces. It was a claim that probably cost him his job and reputation, but that didn't stop Asahara from believing it. He became con-

The Great Hanshin Earthquake, measuring 6.9 on the moment magnitude scale, struck near the Japanese city of Kobe on January 17, 1995. The quake brought massive destruction to nearby areas and caused the deaths of almost 6,500 people.

vinced that Armageddon was just around the corner and decided to help move things along. Thus, the sarin gas attack.

Asahara and Aum Shinrikyō put together a team of five upper-echelon scientists. One was a doctor. The others were members of the cult's Science and Technology Ministry. Blending in with the morning commuter crowds in Tokyo, they entered the subway system and boarded five different trains, which would converge at Kasumigaseki, a center of commerce and home to 125 million Japanese. The objective was to paralyze the nation and launch the opening salvo in a war for world domination. Asahara suspected that the police were soon going to raid his cult headquarters, and he intended to strike first.

At 7:45 a.m. local time, each team member, having carried aboard with him a container of sarin gas wrapped in newspaper, punctured the package, faded into the crowd, and left the station, fleeing the scene in prearranged getaway cars.

Within a matter of weeks, terrorists in Chile and the Philippines threatened to release their own chemical weapons of mass destruction. Ohio traffic cops in the United States pulled over a suspected white supremacist and found three vials of the bacteria that causes bubonic plague. Two members of a group that called itself the Minnesota Patriots Council were convicted of a plot to use ricin, a biological toxin, to kill federal agents. These last were the first men to be convicted under a 1989 United States law known as the Biological Weapons Anti-Terrorism Act.

Aum Shinrikyō had become perhaps the first nongovernmental group to deliberately produce biochemical weapons of mass destruction. The word spread rapidly. When it came to terrorism, guns were good, but chemicals were better, easier to produce, and much more effective in producing a terrorist's ultimate goal—terror. Anyone with a decent education in biology and access to basic laboratory equipment could manufacture mass death on a budget. All it took was a charismatic psychopath and a dedicated cult of followers.

Are all cults dedicated to bringing about chaos and, possibly, the end of the world? Of course not. But some are, and the fact that many of them stop before they reach that point doesn't mean they wouldn't continue if they had the chance to do so.

Still, that doesn't completely answer our original question. What is a cult, really? Aum Shinrikyō offers a good case study. But it doesn't provide a complete definition of the word. Do all cults have charismatic leaders? Yes. But does every charismatic leader head up a cult? Not necessarily.

Stop in at the local martial arts studio located in a neighborhood strip mall, for instance. You will find a group of attentive young people who follow, without question, the orders of an authoritarian instructor who trains them. The students believe in the leader's rules and methods. He speaks; they respond. They wear designated clothes. They are obedient to a fault. The whole setup seems to be in precise alignment with the definition of a cult with which we began this section. But is it a cult? Probably not. Throughout history there have been cults, such as the Assassins, a Nizari cult associated with Shia Islam, which was based in Persia and Syria in the eleventh through the thirteenth centuries, who incorporated the discipline of martial arts. But they certainly had nothing in common with your child's Saturday morning tae kwon do class.

"Cult" has become a loaded word. Most of us probably have our own definition, usually negative, and it subconsciously kicks in whenever we hear the word. The media has seen to our education in that regard. But if we're going to talk about cults throughout the course of this book, we'd better agree, at least for our purposes, what the word means.

To start with, just because an organization is a cult doesn't mean it has bad intentions. Theologians, for example, often refer to the first years of Christianity as an expression of what they call an early Jesus Cult. So is Christianity, in essence, a cult? There are certainly cults within Christianity. But Christianity as a whole? It's doubtful that it qualifies as such, although some would readily make that accusation.

In the pages that follow, the American cults we are going to examine are, for the most part, pretty evil. So, within these pages, "cult" will have a pretty negative connotation. Just remember, when you close the book and go back into the world, that all cults are not necessarily evil.

A common denominator of almost all the cults we will examine is that they have a recognizable founder or current leader. He—and it is usually a "he"—is a charismatic leader, able to speak in a language that his followers understand. He instinctively knows how to push the proper buttons when it comes to mobilizing people. He will speak to their needs, even if they, themselves, might not be aware what those needs are. Cult leaders are almost always brilliant manipulators. But that shouldn't be surprising. Narcissists and psychopaths are usually manipulative to some degree.

Narcissists generally feel entitled and grandiose. They are at the center not only of their own story but of everyone else's. They usually lack any real empathy, and they display an unmistakable arrogance. They are normally in search of validation, but they might feel at least a small sense of shame when they do wrong, if only because getting caught undermines their self-esteem.

Psychopaths, on the other hand, don't feel any shame. That is why they can generally pass lie-detector tests. They honestly feel they can do no wrong because they are the ones performing the deeds. If they do something, it is obviously justified, because they are the ones doing it.

Going far beyond the laughable vanity of small-*n* narcissism, narcissistic personality disorder is a condition whose sufferers may behave as if they are the center of the universe.

If you have ever associated with someone who manipulates you by saying, "I'm only saying this for your own good!" or "You always act this way," or if your integrity is questioned by means of passive-aggressive domination, you understand the kind of manipulation I'm talking about. Cult leaders do this instinctively. They are master manipulators, and they use their ability to their advantage.

Cults, at least according to our loose definition, usually develop a hierarchy. People who start out at the bottom but demonstrate both talent and allegiance to the leader generally rise to positions of leadership themselves.

Cults tend to separate followers from the world that exists outside the group. They discourage, and often try to cut completely, family ties, previous friendships, and exposure to literature and media that is not sponsored by the cult. Critical thinking is a detriment, not an advantage. Anyone who has had the experience of joining a holiday gathering attended by a family member who has become a "true believer," who reads only the "right" news sources and follows only the "real" media reports, understands this completely. The phrase "do your research" often means "read the correct internet sites." It is a problem that grows with each passing day.

There is one more trait that applies to cults—at least, to the cults we will be examining. It might be the most important of them all. Most of the cults described in the following pages demonstrate two ideologies that figure prominently in their makeup. Together, they entail what I call an obsession with crystal balls and conspiracies. This may be the easiest way to spot a cult, at least given the parameters we have just set forth.

First, cults are almost always fixated on the future. Their leaders claim to have gazed into their own crystal balls, so to speak, and to have foreseen that things are going to change, and probably quickly. There is a better world a-comin', or at least an end to this one. Armageddon is right around the corner, and only the cult's membership will survive the apocalypse. Sometimes the cult leaders become impatient and try to bring it about themselves. Occasionally, they even feel called by God to do so. Often, they relocate to a private piece of real estate where they will be able to survive and, eventually, thrive.

The second ideology is related to the first. Since only the cult (according to the cult) fully understands that things are about to change, it stands to reason that only the cult also knows the secret machinations of the world at large. Cults specialize in conspiracy theory. They, and they alone, know what is really going on behind the scenes. They refuse to be manipulated by the "deep state," the "liberal media," mainstream religious views, or popular opinion as expressed in what they believe are highly questionable polls.

These two traits—a fixation on the future and a tendency toward conspiracy theory—coupled with a charismatic leader are generally the most obvious signs of a cult. They are the ones that flagged the particular examples, out of the thousands of cults that exist in the world, that we will examine.

Members and leadership of the Oath Keepers were arrested following their participation in the infamous attacks on the U.S. Capitol on January 6, 2021.

When Stewart Rhodes, for instance, founder and leader of the extremist group Oath Keepers, was arrested in January 2022 on charges of seditious conspiracy and accused of guiding a months-long effort to unleash politically motivated violence to prevent the swearing-in of President Joseph Biden—an effort that culminated in the January 6, 2021, attack on the U.S. Capitol—he was denied bail. The reason was simple. Not only had he spent thousands of dollars stockpiling a huge arsenal of weapons and ammunition, but he had built a series of escape tunnels and spider holes to hide in if the authorities ever came for him. The court was afraid he might disappear if he were released.

In his own words, in speech after speech, he had predicted that civil war would soon break out and asserted that he and his followers had to be prepared. They were even ready to start such a war, should it take too long to come to pass on its own. This is, by our definition, an undeniable depiction of cult-like activity.

To put things in perspective, then, this list forms a description of the word "cult," which we will use to guide what comes next:

- ◆ Cults don't always have bad intentions, but the ones we are going to study, for the most part, do.

- ◆ Cults begin with a founder who is at least narcissistic and usually psychopathic.

- ◆ Cults develop a top-down hierarchy.

- ◆ Cults tend to separate followers from the world that exists outside the group.

- ◆ The easiest way to spot a cult is to identify an obsession with crystal balls and conspiracies.

With this as place to start, and remembering that our understanding of cults is somewhat arbitrary, given the lack of any precise, universal definition, we can proceed—but with caution. It is easy to get carried away with an emotional response. We will try to avoid that and be as objective as possible, backing up our analysis with public, recorded facts rather than private opinions. One person's cult is another person's religion. It is best to tread lightly. With that caveat, we can begin.

PROLOGUE

WHAT MAKES A CULT POSSIBLE?

Who joins a cult? And why? What personality traits or life situations contribute to identifying with a cult? What is it that influences normal, outwardly well-adjusted individuals to gradually turn over their perspectives, and sometimes even their moral guidelines, to an organization that is, at least on the surface, different from anything they have ever previously espoused? Is there any genetic predisposition that might reveal a future cult member in the making? Is it nature or nurture? What makes a cult possible?

Rachel Bernstein is a marriage and family therapist. Her specialty is dealing with people who want to leave cults and other groups that impose structured control, and she has worked with such people for almost 30 years. She believes that *given the right circumstances, virtually anyone can fall prey to sociopaths and manipulators.* (I emphasize this because it will soon be very important to remember!)

In an interview with *Insider* magazine, Bernstein outlined her findings, based on a lifetime of experience: "A lot of people will say, 'How could you have gotten involved?' It's because you're never given all the information about a group that turns out to be a cult from the beginning. So you only have the information to go on that you've been given, which is very select, and you make your judgment call based on that. No one's able to make a fully educated decision before getting involved in a cult."

From the many articles and books written on the subject, four factors concerning the personalities and life situations of potential cult members rise to the surface again and again. Sometimes this list can stretch out to several more items, depending on the source, but in simplified fashion, here are the primary four:

> **Given the right circumstances, virtually anyone can fall prey to sociopaths and manipulators.**

1. LOOKING FOR LOVE IN ALL THE WRONG PLACES

People join cults because they're looking for love and acceptance. They want answers to the personal problems in their lives. When a person feels lonely and alone, when they feel unloved, or when they feel no one cares about them, they are susceptible to a manipulator who fills the void.

These are all very human needs. Even religious groups capitalize on them. A person who feels "lost" needs a savior. That's how Christianity spreads, for instance. The song "Jesus loves me, this I know, for the Bible tells me so" is a powerful marketing tool. It assures people that a loving savior cares about them and at the same time promotes the group's guiding text, the Bible, in a very short soundbite that comes attached to a singable tune. It's often one of the first songs children from Christian households hear and learn to sing. Many people who long ago gave up Christianity can still sing the song from start to finish. Indeed, once reminded of it, they can't get it out of their heads. That's powerful advertising!

Please understand that parents who teach this song to their children, and churches that teach it to their youngest Sunday school classes, aren't being devious or intentionally manipulative. They really believe that Jesus is the answer to personal problems and that they are doing a good and decent thing by advertising the fact.

Experiences and habits formed during childhood can have a powerful influence on the child's future beliefs and behaviors.

But the same can be said for cult leaders. Most of them, if not just blatantly trying to bilk the public, think they have important answers to life's basic questions. It's a tempting offer. "You have a deeply felt need. Here's a savior who can answer that need." It's as simple as that.

It's a universal marketing technique. I often root for a particular football team, for example, who, a few years ago, lost their all-star quarterback. Who could they recruit to fill their glaring vacancy? When they found a likely candidate, newspaper headlines labeled him a "savior," and the fans bought it. They wanted to believe the new guy would "save" the team from their plight and restore a winning climate to the fan base. It's a common description that, because of its popular appeal, often masks the fact that it can be used by sinister people to prey on needy people.

It's no accident that cult members have sometimes gone willingly to their deaths at the behest of such a "savior." As we shall soon see, the Branch Davidians and the Peoples Temple Full Gospel Church aren't the only examples history has to offer. When people believe strongly enough that their own redemption is tied to the group and its leader, anything is possible.

2. THE QUEST TO BETTER ONESELF

People often join cults because they want to better themselves, whether professionally or personally. The "hook" with which cults catch their membership is usually an appeal that promotes personal growth. Sometimes the promise is one of advancement in a particular field. Sometimes it is couched in terms of spiritual enlightenment or some kind of tantric sex experience. Sometimes they offer a systematic method to encourage the growth of professional skills or self-help techniques. A person with low self-esteem, stuck in a dead-end job, who has just experienced a romantic breakup or suffered the traumatic loss of a loved one, is a vulnerable and susceptible candidate, especially if the offer comes wrapped in a pretty, full-color, glossy brochure pitched by a master manipulator.

3. LONGING FOR COMMUNITY

This leads to the third factor. People join cults to gain a sense of community. Everyone needs human connection. This is exactly what cults specialize in. They offer a ready-made, substitute family of people who claim to have been rescued from exactly the life situation experienced by the new recruit. If a cult leader can create what is essentially a "pack" mentality, his job is almost done. Folks *join* because they sense a connection with people who understand what they have experienced, and then they *stay* because of peer pressure. It's a vicious, and highly effective, loop.

Even language provides an effective tool. It is common for ex-cult members to exclaim, "Those people spoke my language!" Cults develop their own "in-speak"—words used in such a way that only the initiated understand.

This is a technique by no means limited to cults. Anyone who has ever participated in an addiction recovery program like Alcoholics Anonymous is familiar with "in-speak" phrases: "One day at a time"; "Fake it till you make it"; "Are you a friend of Bill?" This kind of identifying language makes people feel they are a part of something that other people don't understand. It promotes "us against them," of course, but that is exactly what a cult member craves.

4. EXTREME VULNERABILITY

People join cults when they are in a state of extreme vulnerability. We're going to develop this point in depth in a moment, but for now it's enough to realize that life is full of ups and downs. Our psychological strength varies accordingly. Ex-cult members often recall that they joined at a time of their life when they felt especially needy. Their faith in a religion, in a job they thought was secure, in the loss of a friendship they thought was meaningful, or their betrayed trust in a respected mentor suddenly shook them to the core. Then, at their deepest point of vulnerability, a new person and a substitute family appeared. Their loss was recognized. A support group was offered. Acceptance felt genuine. How could they *not* respond affirmatively, especially when the new group seemed to be, quite literally, heaven sent?

> **People join cults when they are in a state of extreme vulnerability.**

Once the cult was embraced, any cognitive dissonance between the old life and the new was overwhelmed. Over time, any nagging worries were dealt with by strengthening newfound devotion to the leader and his methods. The more they followed the doctrines of the group, the harder it became to admit to concerns about being manipulated, or even lied to. Their psychological and emotional growth became stunted, but it couldn't be acknowledged because doing so would have been an admission of yet another failure. How could they return to a family they snubbed, and often severely criticized? How could they bear the perceived behind-the-back "I-told-you-so"s of their friends? So, they dug in and tried harder. Another vicious, but very common, circle was now in play.

These four factors constitute traditional dogma when it comes to determining who joins a cult and why: 1) looking for love and acceptance; 2) seeking to better themselves; 3) longing for community; and 4) being vulnerable. They are a psychologist's stock in trade, and they provide a template for providing therapy to cult members who want to get out.

But new ideas that question traditional systems of treatment are beginning to percolate through the field of psychology. Previously I spoke about the work of family therapist Rachel Bernstein. I high-

People are often at their most suggestible when they are going through hard times.

lighted a quotation and said it would soon be very important to remember: "She believes that *given the right circumstances, virtually anyone can fall prey to sociopaths and manipulators.*"

If the four factors just described are the marks of a susceptible future cult member, why would Bernstein insist that "virtually anyone" can fall prey to this kind of manipulation? What about folks who do not fit the normal psychological profile? Are they in danger as well?

In other words, we might ask ourselves, "What about me? Am I at risk? I thought only those who were suffering the personality disorders common to those described with the four factors just outlined were in danger. Am I susceptible to the influences of a cult?"

In a word, yes!

New research indicates that it's not just a matter of "who." It's also a matter of "when."

Doug Shadel, writing in the January 2022 issue of *AARP: The Magazine,* reported on a recent study that attempted to get to the bottom of the epidemic of telephone and internet scams that have generated off-the-chart numbers in the last few years. Both scammers and cult leaders are master manipulators. They share a common modus operandi when it comes to locating and taking advantage of victims. Both kinds of operatives score very low on any scale that measures compassion for their subjects, and both employ the same techniques.

> **Both scammers and cult leaders are master manipulators.**

In an article titled "Revealed! Who Gets Scammed," Shadel begins by sharing the basic premise of why and how people fall prey to master manipulators. His work had begun about 20 years earlier, during his service on a professional research team that had been organized for the purpose of identifying potential victims. The assumption at the time was that the project would be a simple one that wouldn't take long to complete. It was just a matter of identifying what they called "character flaws" that were unique to all those who had been scammed at one time or another. In his words, they "would then share their information with the world, eliminate the scourge of fraud and be done with it."

It didn't work out that way. The more they studied the problem, the more complicated it became. One false theory after another wound up on the cutting room floor.

They had assumed, for instance, that older people were the most susceptible to scams. That turned out to be not the case at all. In January of 2022, for instance, the Federal Trade Commission (FTC) reported a surprising statistic: 65 percent of those who had reported being scammed on social media platforms during the year 2021 were young adults between the ages of 18 and 39. The scammers stole a staggering $770 million from 95,000 people, utilizing both investment and dating platforms. This represents a rather stunning 1,800 percent increase over similar scams reported in 2017. Clearly, those familiar with the internet fell prey to such scammers in greater numbers than those whose age suggested they were less than savvy when it came to modern means of communication.

So Shadel and his team faced a bit of a crisis. They sifted through the biographies of victims, studying such things as college education. That didn't work. Neither did income, savings, psychological characteristics such as introversion and extroversion, and geographical location. After ten years, they seemed to have struck out. They were frustrated and tempted to quit when they had a rather novel idea that, in hindsight, seemed rather simple. Instead of interviewing victims, they began to talk to convicted scammers.

In October 2021 Shadel and his coauthors published *A Moment's Notice: Recognizing the Stressful Life Events, Emotions and Actions That Make Us Susceptible to Scams: An AARP National Fraud Frontiers Report*, a survey conducted in partnership with NORC at the University of Chicago that compiled the results of interviews with hundreds of convicted scammers to determine how they chose their prey. What they discovered was, in Shadel's words, that "it isn't *who* you are that matters, but *how* you are when the pitch gets made." The team called it a "vulnerable moment."

> "It isn't *who* you are that matters, but *how* you are when the pitch gets made."

Scammers, for instance, would scan the obituaries and compile lists of surviving family members. These people proved susceptible to all kinds of approaches. The scammers might claim the deceased owed them money. They might falsely represent themselves as concerned money managers. They knew they were dealing with people who were emotionally vulnerable and ready to be scammed.

In retrospect, this shouldn't have been surprising. Way back in May of 1981, this exact method was used to supply a laugh on the hit TV series *Taxi*. The series depicted the daily life of a group of cab drivers who worked for the fictional Sunshine Cab Company. In season 3, episode 19, the company briefly went out of business, and the cabbies were forced to find other work. One of the main characters was a dispatcher named Louie DePalma, played by Danny DeVito. He was a despicable character whom viewers loved, not for any redeeming traits he might have had but because DeVito's characterization was so entertaining.

This particular episode was called "On the Job," and in it, Louie became a stockbroker. In a memorable moment, he called a widow who, as it turns out, was on her way to her husband's funeral, and he asked if she had given any thought as to how to invest her late husband's insurance settlement. When she brushed him off, he offered to call back after the service. It produced a good laugh from the audience.

The significance is that this episode was familiar to audiences, and they nervously laughed about it, all the way back in 1981! It was obviously a technique people recognized a long time ago but didn't acknowledge as dangerous until the 2021 study. It took 30 years for this scam technique to become fully documented in a formal study.

The interviewed scammers shared other methods as well. They went after those who won the lottery or were about to go to jail. They told them that their computers were about to melt down. Sometimes they claimed that grandchildren had just been arrested for drunk driving or had been kidnapped. In short, they tried anything to make the intended victim feel vulnerable—to knock them out of their right mind for a minute.

To make matters worse, people who had experienced such moments before in their lives were especially vulnerable. "Is this happening again?" they asked themselves.

What this means is that any studies coming to the conclusion that to escape the snares of a scammer, all you have to do is develop certain cognitive skills—to display logic in terms of checking basic background information—are wrong. Logic won't work. It's your emotional state that matters.

The time-honored trope of hearse-chasing hucksters lives on in modern call centers whose operators target the bereaved at their most vulnerable.

Therapist Rachel Bernstein is right: *Given the right circumstances, virtually anyone can fall prey to sociopaths and manipulators.* What works in the scamming game works just as well in the world of the cults. All it takes is a moment of vulnerability and someone to offer a solution to what has you upset, and you, too, can become a victim. It has less to do with logic and intelligence than it does with emotional response. The number-one plea from former cult members is usually a variation on a theme: "How could I have been so stupid?"

The buzzword being used nowadays to describe one method of manipulating is the word "gaslighting." The term goes back to a play from 1938 called *Gas Light*, and it took on added traction when the play was made into the 1944 movie called *Gaslight*, starring Ingrid Bergman and Angela Lansbury. In the movie, a husband tries to convince his wife that she is going mad. He wants to make her lose her sense of reality so he can commit her to a mental institution and steal her inheritance. One of his techniques is to turn the gaslight in their home up and down without her knowledge, and then try to convince her that she is imagining the change.

Gaslighting has come to represent the deeds of anyone who deliberately distorts facts in order to deceive his or her victims, causing them to accept a completely false sense of reality. It entered the American political lexicon early in 2021, when Republican congresspeople described the attack at the U.S. Capitol Building on January 6th. Millions of Americans had seen the violence depicted on their TV screens in live coverage, but within days, some members of the GOP were claiming it was a peaceful demonstration, no different from normal public tours of the facility that are held every day.

It was a patent lie, of course, but, surprisingly, it was believed by millions of people—a vivid demonstration of how gaslighting works even in these days of instant communication and easy fact checking. Gaslighting represents bullying in its most obvious and abusive form, but it has been used by public figures even before George Orwell popularized the technique in his famous novel *Nineteen Eighty-Four*.

> **Every cult leader has gaslighting in their repertoire. Indeed, it's their stock in trade.**

Every cult leader has gaslighting in their repertoire. Indeed, it's their stock in trade. Cults exist because the members of the group embrace an alternate reality. Everything outside the cult's sphere of influence is deemed either false or suspicious. In the case of the fallout from the January 6th riots, even a great number of people who accepted the fact that violence *did* occur laid the blame at the feet of left-wing, liberal conspirators who supposedly infiltrated the rally to deliberately discredit the "peaceful" people who had gathered to protest what they thought was a stolen election.

In the world of gaslighting cultists, up is down, right is left, and nothing in the world is as it appears to be—except, of course, for the word of the cult leader. The technique is dishonest, manipulative, threatening, and extremely effective. Approached correctly, carefully chosen, vulnerable recruits are always waiting in the wings.

The answer to our question, then, is complex. Who joins a cult? The easiest answer is that people who are vulnerable join cults when they are approached and tempted at a low point in their life. It would be nice to think such people are somehow different from the rest of "us," perhaps given to certain psychological or emotional weakness. But the reality, time and again, is that all of us, given the right conditions, seem to be candidates.

In the pages to come, we examine specific examples. By the end of this book, a clearer picture comes into focus. Hopefully, the lessons learned will be there for us in our psyches if we ever need them.

IN THE BEGINNING: WHY IS AMERICA SUCH A FERTILE FIELD FOR CULTS?

According to research studies sponsored by the Library of Congress, there are between 3,000 and 5,000 active groups defined as cults within the borders of the United States. That shouldn't be surprising, considering the fact that modern-day America was molded and shaped by religious movements. Public school history books often begin with a chapter or two about prehistoric and Indigenous cultures, but then they jump right into conquistadors and Puritans. Children are taught that Puritans came to New England because they sought refuge from persecution, and that is, for the most part, true. But what is usually left out is that they weren't persecuted because they were religious. They were persecuted because they were religious fanatics. Their own journals recount their desire to come to America to build, in their words, "a bright city on a hill," where their God could be worshipped in the strict manner their elders taught. They weren't going to be stopped by the people already living in the land where they migrated. Those who dared question Puritan authority were whipped, banished, burned, and often murdered. They saw themselves as the ultimate "in group" who wanted to keep separate from those "others" on the outside. In cult-like fashion, they sought to eliminate private ownership of land and bring about a society in which everyone was equal.

Many modern U.S. Thanksgiving holiday celebrations perpetuate a rosy view of the Puritans who arrived on the *Mayflower,* but a closer look at their history reveals they may have been more like a cult than a religious sect (and that most of them would be horrified by what's become of their shining hill).

Eventually their land reform ideas failed, and some Puritans proved to be "more equal" than others, but initially their movement fit well within the parameters of what today would be called a cult. This would be a good thing to remember next Thanksgiving, when Christians across the width and breadth of America congregate to sing "Come, Ye Thankful People, Come; Raise the Song of Harvest Home" and "We Gather Together to Ask the Lord's Blessing." One of the trademarks of a cult is to "purify" itself by separating from the surrounding social culture, and that is exactly what the Puritans attempted to do.

Ann Lee, founder of a group called the Shakers, went on to famously declare that "there are no sluts in heaven." She preached that the end was coming, and people had best prepare for the return of the Lord. That meant imposing her ideas about sex—that is, that there shouldn't be any—on her followers.

Joseph Smith, founder of the Church of Jesus Christ of Latter-day Saints; Charles Taze Russell, who began the Jehovah's Witnesses; and Ellen G. White, who left the Millerite movement to begin the Seventh-day Adventists, were only a few of the many well-known, self-appointed leaders who founded movements that were, in the beginning, cults but went on to establish themselves as Christian religious denominations.

This shouldn't be surprising, either, for the beginning of Christianity followed much the same pattern. Early Christians were followers of the Jewish prophet Yeshua ben Yosef, Joshua son of Joseph, today known as Jesus. According to Acts 4:32, his followers "were of one heart and soul, and no one said that any of the things that belonged to him was his own, but they had everything in common." According to the Apostle Paul, Jesus had instructed his disciples to "come out of them, and be ye separate ... I will be a Father to you." That's the kind of thing cult leaders say.

The idea of sharing "all things in common" is an aspect of Marxism, of course, and is often decried in American/Christian/capitalist ideology, but it is very common in cultic teaching. Also found in most early cults is the doctrine that the leaders are, in some sense, God incarnate, possessed by God, or indwelt by God. They often insist on celibacy among their followers, and some have been way ahead of their time in accepting women leaders, a circumstance that is still lacking in some major religious movements today.

But perhaps the reason America spawns so many cults compared to other nations is a unique juxtaposition of certain American values. Let's begin with "lip-service religion."

LIP-SERVICE RELIGION

Part of the American mythos involves the expressed belief that somehow it is a "Christian" nation, or at least a religious one. The Founding Fathers, children are often taught, were God-fearing Christians, and they believed religious freedom to be sacrosanct. This idea comes with certain paradoxes, however. On the one hand, the separation of church and state is of paramount importance and guaranteed in the Constitution. Churches don't pay taxes on their property because they are engaged in the business of God, not the business of government. On the other hand, Congress retains a chaplain and opens each session with prayer. "God bless America" is the final statement of almost all political speeches. It's right up there with "Don't mess with Texas!" Finally, there are many who believe America's so-called downfall during the troubling closing decades of the twentieth century and opening years of the twenty-first began when the nation "took prayer out of the schools."

Part of the American mythos involves the expressed belief that somehow it is a "Christian" nation, or at least a religious one.

The fact that none of this is accurate doesn't alter the myth. Prejudices are often more powerful than the truth, especially when they remain unexamined. But when a belief is unsubstantiated by reality, when a myth fails to live up to daily experience, it creates a perfect emotional storm.

Consider this notion: "God is supposed to be there when I need him. I need him now. Where is he? My religion has let me down. Everyone knows faith is supposed to bring about peace and contentment. But I'm messed up and feel abandoned. It must, therefore, be the fault of my religion. It is not living up to the standards I've been taught. The standards are correct. I know that to be true. Therefore, established religion must have abandoned its principles!"

Once such an idea, as faulty as it may be, enters the picture, folks are open to the promise of a religious leader who acknowledges their pain and offers a "better way."

But consider the reality behind the original myth:

America's Founding Fathers, by their own admission, were not primarily Christians, although most attended public church services out of political expediency. George Washington, Thomas Jefferson, Benjamin Franklin, James Madison, and James Monroe were Deists who espoused a philosophical belief in human reason as a reliable means of solving social and political problems. Jefferson edited the Bible, cutting out any passages with which he disagreed. In Franklin's autobiography, he called himself a "thorough deist," rejecting traditional Christian doctrine and instead claiming for himself what he called "moralized" Christianity.

The phrase "separation of church and state" appears nowhere in the Constitution. It came about because the framers wanted to protect the new country from those who might want to establish a state religion. They figured—rightly, as it turns out—that freedom of religion would protect any one faith from establishing the upper hand. Privately, in a letter he wrote in 1802 to the Danbury Baptist Association of Connecticut, Jefferson stated: "I contemplate with sovereign reverence that act of the whole American people which declared that their legislature should 'make no law respecting an establishment of religion, or prohibiting the free exercise thereof,' thus building a wall of separation between Church and State." That's where the phrase originated.

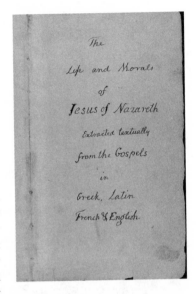

The
Life and Morals
of
Jesus of Nazareth
Extracted textually
from the Gospels
in
Greek, Latin
French & English.

Rejecting all supernatural claims in the Bible, Thomas Jefferson cobbled together passages from several sources to form what he considered the purest account of Jesus's life and morals as derived from his teachings and deeds.

As for not paying taxes, churches are not exempt because they are religious institutions but because Section 501(c)(3) of the United States tax law says they are public charities and thus exempt from federal, state, and local income and property taxes.

Why do both the House and Senate appoint chaplains when government is supposed to be free from religious objectives? The truth is, no one really knows. It is a custom dating back to the Continental Congress of 1774, and it has been debated ever since. Every few years, it seems, someone tries to end the practice. But traditions are tough to change.

And when it comes to prayer in the public schools, thinking back to the day when people my age began every morning by reciting the Lord's Prayer (Catholic version) along with the Pledge of Allegiance, does anyone believe we were really praying?

This recitation of fact, however, will not change the reality. Many people have chosen to accept the myth that religion, especially Christianity, is a firm bedrock of the American story. When the myth fails to deliver the goods, they will look to someone who promises them the reality they are sure should be there for them. That offers fertile ground for cults to flourish.

REBELLIOUSNESS

America was born in rebellion. The years 1776 and 1812 are ones that have gone down in infamy, and the Civil War put the period on the sentence. Rebellion is in our DNA, and cults have long capitalized on that fact.

Take, for instance, the case of Jemima Wilkinson, known to her followers as Publick Universal Friend. She was born into a Quaker family who lived in Cumberland, Rhode Island, in 1752 but often attended church services with a New Light Baptist congregation. Her attendance at those meetings resulted in her being dismissed from the Quaker sect in 1776, when all America became involved in rebellion.

Two months after her expulsion, she fell ill and developed a fever. She recovered from her illness convinced that she had died and been brought back to life by God, who then sent her forth as a new person, this time male, to preach to a "lost and guilty, gossiping, dying World." That was when Wilkinson took on a new name and mission. According to Wilkinson's testimony, Wilkinson was no longer either male or female. Wilkinson's followers used male pronouns to describe him from then on and believed him to be a messiah. The one document historians have that came from his own hand was signed "your friend and brother," and he wore masculine garb for the rest of his life.

> Wilkinson took on a new name and mission. According to Wilkinson's testimony, Wilkinson was no longer either male or female.

Answering now only to the name Publick Universal Friend (or The Friend), he began to preach throughout New England and soon developed a cult following, some of whom were important judges. One of them, Judge William Potter of Rhode Island, was moved to free his slaves, abandon political life, and then build a large mansion to be used by The Friend whenever he was in the neighborhood. Followers became known as Universal Friends and soon drew in congregants from as far away as Philadelphia. All this happened while the fledgling United States was engaged in fighting a war for independence.

In 1784 the Universal Friends published a kind of prayerbook to be used in meetings, called *The Universal Friend's Advice to Those of the Same Religious Society.*

As often happens with religious organizations that break away from established, orthodox denominations, doctrinal disputes eventually broke out. Still, some of Wilkinson's followers openly spoke of him as a messiah, and by 1788 members moved the headquarters to western New York State, near Seneca Lake. By 1790 they had established the Friend's Settlement in what became known as Jerusalem Township, but problems developed over land ownership and rumors circulated about conflicts within the organization over dictatorial rule, harsh punishments for disobeying group rules, sexual misconduct, and what were called "strange rituals." These conflicts led to the final disintegration of the group in 1819, the year The Friend finally "left time," which sounds suspiciously like what other people call death.

JEMIMA WILKISON.

These events happened against the backdrop of the Revolutionary War and the War of 1812. The story offers a classic example of traditional religion's failure to meet the needs of some people during times of conflict and rebellion, and their subsequent turn to cult leaders who offer help and solace during those times, no matter how strange or abnormal those people may seem. In this case, the leader was one with a brazen declaration for the day, changing

The Publick Universal Friend founded a Quaker-like order known as the Society of Universal Friends and preached for more than 40 years in non-gendered attire.

his very gender, along with messianic impulses. But, as is so often the case, such anomalies often offer allure as well as caution.

ENTREPRENEURSHIP

America has a curious attitude regarding entrepreneurs. Legendary rich families, such as the Rockefellers and Carnegies, and billionaires, such as Bill Gates, Steve Jobs, and Warren Buffett, are respected and admired. They give heft to the idea that the American Dream is available to all.

But the facts tell a different story when it comes to the populace. For every young man who dreamed of going from "rags to riches," there were dozens more, especially in the postwar epoch beginning in the late 1940s, whose ideal job was to work for a prestigious company such as General Electric, IBM, Ford, or General Motors, collect some good benefits and a pension, and then retire in comfort. In other words, even as they may have admired the entrepreneurs, most people wanted to play it safe rather than strike out on their own. The unspoken agreement was, "I'll work for you if you'll take care of me."

Such conflicting ideas help establish a perfect breeding ground for cults. Cult leaders want to become entrepreneurial hotshots, and they are assured of many followers who simply want to turn over their lives and possessions to anyone who will promise them safety.

> **Cult leaders want to become entrepreneurial hotshots, and they are assured of many followers who simply want to turn over their lives and possessions to anyone who will promise them safety.**

Filmmaker Will Allen produced a movie that, in 2016, premiered at the Sundance Film Festival. Called *Holy Hell*, the documentary told the story of Allen's 22-year sojourn with the

Buddhafield cult in Southern California. The cult's leader, Michel Rostand, was portrayed as a rather sadistic psychopath who insisted on healthy living. There were strict rules against alcohol, drugs, caffeine, and red meat. Exercise was mandatory, and sex was prohibited.

The cult oversaw every waking minute of the day, and most members accepted the regimen willingly. It offered them structure, something that had been missing from their lives before they joined.

At first, it worked. The group sought to revive the concept of a utopian community, reminiscent of the early Christian Jesus cult, whose members sold all their possessions and lived in unity. But, as usually happens, the combination of an autocratic ruler and a willing congregation proved to be a volatile mix.

Allen was the group's videographer, which gave him both a unique perspective and many rolls of film. The movie proved to be a psychological thriller and was soon picked up by a major TV network. Although outwardly the members seemed to benefit in many ways from the cult's regimen, the sexual, psychological, and emotional abuse that took place behind the scenes revealed the usual salacious secrets of such an organization that surface once members start to rebel and leave.

It takes an entrepreneur to launch a cult. He or she has to have a plan and good organizational ability. That is what the American myth is all about—entrepreneurship. But it takes a willing group of followers, as well, who want someone over them to grant them safety and contentment. Sad to say, that, too, is part of the American experience.

Every four years, for instance, many members of the American electorate attempt to anoint a charismatic leader who offers to escort them to the promised land. But they are just as quick to crucify that person when their lot in life doesn't radically change after his election. When faith in the political establishment fades, the felt need for personal contentment remains, so it is very easy to transfer that need to someone else—a budding entrepreneur with transformative plans for society and an offer of hope.

RELIGIOUS FREEDOM

Religious freedom forms the core of the American myth. Whereas authoritarian states—for better or worse—can ban religious groups deemed to be "dangerous," or at least keep them under close wraps, rights enshrined in the U.S. Constitution and legal system make such restrictions very difficult to impose. Even some democratic countries such as France, for instance, have banned what they call religious "cults" such as Jehovah's Witnesses, Scientologists, and some forms of Pentecostal Protestantism, claiming these groups decrease the opportunity for religious freedom for everyone else. In America, they are considered to be established religions, under the protection of all the laws that protect every other religion.

This raises an important fact about American justice. American political pundits are fond of declaring, in almost sanctimonious tones, "We are a nation of laws!" as if having a law on the books somehow settles everything, once and forever. But laws are designed by people. Laws are enacted by people. Laws are obeyed, or broken, by people. Laws are enforced by people. And people are flawed. No matter how hard we try, it is impossible to legislate morality. Laws intended to protect and ensure safety can, and usually are, manipulated by those who find ways to work within the *letter* of the law while defying its *spirit*.

Anyone, for instance, who has ever worked on tax law knows that ten identical tax returns, prepared by ten different tax experts, can easily produce ten different results, even though each accountant swears they are exactly following the written codes. It is a common doctrine, often quoted by political philosophers, that in America it is better that ten guilty men go free rather than punish one innocent one.

The phrase "laws are meant to be broken" has entered the lexicon of every adult, whether they agree with it or not. So it is that cults, even those that are obviously in violation of its members' freedoms—freedoms that are guaranteed by the Constitution—can find ways to violate the spirit of American law while acting, technically at least, within its limits. When this happens, U.S. policy has usually been to police cult activity rather than banning the cult in question outright.

In an 1864 photo, more than 30 years before Utah would gain statehood, Latter-day Saint bishop Ira Eldredge of Salt Lake City poses with his three wives.

For example, in the 1870s the Territory of Utah had on its books a statute banning polygamy. When this statute was challenged in court by a member of the Church of Jesus Christ of Latter-day Saints, which both permitted and encouraged the marrying of multiple wives, the court ruled that "laws are made for the government of actions, and while they cannot interfere with mere religious belief and opinions, they may with practices."

In other words, the religion *itself* was permitted even as certain *practices* of that religion were condemned. The basic premise of the law continued to be an issue right up to a 1946 ruling by the Supreme Court against what it called a "Fundamentalist cult of the Mormon faith" that was still practicing polygamy, and another ruling in 1978 that enforced the fact that polygamy was illegal, but the religion itself was permitted by law.

The same principle applies to the Jehovah's Witnesses. Members are forbidden by the religion to join the military or participate in pledging allegiance to the flag. When, during times of patriotic fervor such as wartimes, local municipalities passed laws to constrict what were considered challenges to American ideals—such as requiring so-called protestors to register with the city—the Supreme Court tended to strike down such laws. But it did allow restrictions on certain activities. Children under 12, for instance, were not permitted to distribute religious pamphlets in public places. What were called "fighting words" were not permitted by the First Amendment. Religions needed a license to conduct services on public property.

> In essence, then, the Supreme Court ruled that religions were not to be banned, but they needed to adhere to specific laws.

In essence, then, the Supreme Court ruled that religions were not to be banned, but they needed to adhere to specific laws. As we will see when we study the 1978 Jonestown Massacre, however, the issue refuses to go away. The phrase "drink the Kool-Aid" came into use specifically because of the type of cult activity that is called "brainwashing" by some and "religious doctrine" by others. This led directly to the creation of the Cult Awareness Network (CAN) and the practice of "deprogramming," prompted by concerned parents who did not think the laws went far enough in protecting their children. The practice of deprogramming itself was brought to court in New York, Connecticut, Illinois, New York, Ohio, Oregon, Pennsylvania, and Texas, and attempts were made to make it lawful, but all such attempts were struck down.

Currently, membership in religious organizations in the United States is waning. Along with that trend has come a more tolerant view of religions that exist outside the traditional mainstream. Both fear of, and fascination with, cults is still present, but the legal definition of a cult is so broad that laws simply can't cover all groups operating within the United States justice system without infringing on religious freedom.

EVOLVING SOCIAL MEDIA

For people who have never delved deeply into social media or whose online experience hasn't progressed any farther than occasional Facebook posts or a Twitter feed, it's hard to conceive just how consuming the arena can become to those who have fallen under its spell. Social media can easily become a black hole, the depths of which are unfathomable, and the allure of which is habit-forming.

Psychologists have long probed into the effects of big crowds when it comes to turning individuals into automatons, overpowering their personalities and prompting them to do things they never would do by themselves. All you have to do to see this for yourself is attend even a well-meaning, completely aboveboard church service at your local, neighborhood megachurch. As soon as you leave your car in the parking lot, you will encounter smiling ushers and helpful attendants. You will hear carefully selected music designed to put you in a certain mood. You will be surrounded by people who often become ecstatic, waving their arms in the air, closing their eyes, singing, and presumably entering into a closer relationship with Jesus. By the time the speaker, usually a very talented talker, begins to deliver the message of the day, you are ready and willing to receive it with joy.

This is a common tactic and has been employed by charismatic leaders for generations. Adolf Hitler used it with extreme, orchestrated effects. Although hard to resist, it is a common, well-known, and exhaustingly studied technique that has been used for everything from extorting money from the faithful to convincing folks to die for a supposedly good cause.

But what about the phenomenon of seducing a single, vulnerable, usually (but not necessarily) young person who sits alone in a darkened room, enticed by cleverly composed, computer-based pitches designed to, ever so gradually, cajole, compliment, entice, and eventually seduce such a person—perhaps a lonely person who might not have developed the social skills necessary to work efficiently with other people? Perhaps if they had such skills, they wouldn't be spending so much time alone with their computer.

Marketing professionals often knowingly use many of the same techniques employed by cults to build a following.

There is a technique that works with such people. Consider this online pitch for a marketing campaign to boost the sales of a product. This ad is not trying to convert future cult followers any more than most well-meaning churches are. It was produced by a bona fide company with the best of intentions. But notice the language it uses:

> You've researched marketing methods until you're blue in the face. You created a respectable web presence with people who like what you have to offer and have even subscribed to your YouTube channel and are following you on Instagram and Facebook.
>
> So ... now what?
>
> How do you get people to go to your website? How do you engage them enough to keep coming back to see what's new on Facebook? In essence, how do you create that cult following on social media that you keep hearing about?

Notice the carefully selected words: "cult following." Obviously, those who wrote this ad understand that "cults" use certain techniques to create a "following."

The advent of social media has now made it possible, even inevitable, for a well-trained cult leader to attract a following that extends far beyond the traditional practices of face-to-face recruitment and splashy, large group meetings. The alienated, lonely person, at home in the privacy of their own room, who wants to reach out to "someone who understands" is a relatively new phenomenon and is increasingly a target for those who seek just such a person to exploit.

As far back as 1980, E. Mansell Pattison of the Department of Psychiatry and Health Behavior at the Medical College of Georgia, writing in the *Journal of Religion and Health*, was aware of the problem and sought to address it in strong, albeit academic, words:

> The motivation of youth to join esoteric religious cults considered as psychopathology is a limited and reductionistic interpretation. Youthful devotees do demonstrate symptoms of psychic distress, which appear to be significantly ameliorated through participation in religious youth cults. Two major trends in social history re-

veal the sources of youth cults: loss of faith in the rationalistic Western cosmology and loss of the extended family system. The religious youth cult possesses many of the properties of the normal psychosocial system, which is a critical social structure for healthful coping in the world. As a normative social system, the religious youth cult is an alternative healing system for the existential crises of contemporary youth.

These kinds of vulnerable young people have always been a part of society, but before social media it was difficult to reach them. With the advent of computers and smartphones, that is no longer the case. They are available 24 hours a day. You no longer need to entice them with posters that advertise your rally. And you can tailor your approach to each individual as soon as you understand what their individual need is. People from across the country and around the world can now form one cohesive group. They never even have to see each other.

Roger Parloff, writing for *Lawfare*, described the techniques used so effectively by two different organizations on January 6, 2021, to bring people to Washington, DC, in an attempt to disrupt the traditional transfer of power from one administration to the next. Noting the important role played by Parler, a social networking site populated by far-right devotees and conspiracy theorists, he wrote:

> A week before the Jan. 6 Capitol insurrection, Enrique Tarrio, the chairman of the Proud Boys, issued an unusual message to his crew. Originally launched in 2016, the Proud Boys are a violent, far-right group whose members describe themselves as "Western chauvinists who refuse to apologize for creating the modern world."

> In a Dec. 29, 2020, post on Parler, Tarrio called on gang members to "turn out in record numbers" on Jan. 6, but this time "with a twist." He continued: "We will not be wearing our traditional Black and Yellow. We will be incognito and we will be spread across downtown DC in smaller teams."

> That same day, the head of a Florida Proud Boys chapter, Joe Biggs, issued his own Parler post highlighting the importance of "blending in" on Jan. 6th.

"You won't see us," he wrote. "We are going to smell like you, move like you, and look like you. The only thing we'll do that's us is think like us! Jan 6th is gonna be epic."

The right-wing cult protest, identified by most observers as an insurrection, would not have been possible to the extent that it was without the use of a coordinated social media effort.

Another far-right, extremist group, the Oath Keepers, also prepared for that day. On January 4, Stewart Rhodes, founder and leader of the Oath Keepers, posted this message on the group's website:

> It is CRITICAL that all patriots who can be in DC get to DC to stand tall in support of President Trump's fight to defeat the enemies foreign and domestic who are attempting a coup, through the massive vote fraud and related attacks on our Republic.... [W]e will also have well armed and equipped QRF [quick reaction force] teams on standby, outside DC, in the event of a worst case scenario, where the President calls us up as part of the militia to assist him inside DC.

Before the advent of social media, the attack on the Capitol Building, seen live by millions of people on their televisions, would have been extremely difficult to undertake and coordinate.

While very real ground battles rage around the globe, the war for hearts and minds has moved firmly to social media channels.

We simply cannot underestimate this power. Thomas Friedman, writing in the *New York Times* only two days after the Russian invasion of Ukraine, pointed out how times have changed. As Russian tanks crossed the Ukraine borders, mimicking a twentieth-century style of land-grabbing war, Friedman quoted a statistic that had been overlooked by many military experts who had come of age before the days of social media: "The musician and actress Selena Gomez has twice as many followers on Instagram—over 298 million—as Russia has citizens."

True, Gomez can't offer much in the way of air support, but she and others like her can certainly generate a lot of sympathetic followers, and that's not a small thing. In the history of warfare, social media is brand new and untested. Cult leaders were quick to take advantage of this new technology. So far, at least, lawmakers have had a hard time keeping up. Social media platforms claim, correctly, that their efforts can bring people together. They insist that their work brings people closer.

And it does! The rapid success of social media, which in a matter of decades grew to permeate every nook and cranny of society, is a success because good people like it. It's as simple as that.

But bad people like it, too. Where does that leave modern culture? The answer is not yet clear. Once again, as we have already seen, you can't legislate morality.

INFATUATION WITH CONSPIRACY THEORY

In 2021, the persistent belief that somehow a liberal, Democratic-leaning elite was part of a worldwide cabal that was operating a secret, pedophile, and perhaps even cannibalistic cult eventually dissipated. A Democrat who no one believed could even remotely be a part of such a cabal was elected to office, and the world was supposed to return to normalcy. The rumors, promoted by a mysterious, cult-like internet presence called QAnon, were proven unfounded, and the rule of the conspiracy was over. The world was still in the grips of a long pandemic and people were tired, but vaccines were coming, and the end of a terribly upsetting reign of bad news was on the horizon.

Alas, the return to normalcy was not to be. As it turned out, the conspiracies surrounding what was called "fake news" were too well entrenched. By the thousands, and even millions, people turned off the television news that had sufficed during the days of Walter Cronkite and his respected network colleagues. Instead, they turned on their computers. The fact that the news they were gleaning from social media and streaming platforms might have been biased didn't matter. They sought to hear what they wanted to hear, and conspiracies grew even more prevalent.

Cults grow well in fields fertilized by conspiracies.

Social distancing measures early in the COVID-19 pandemic inspired much of the Western world to find new hobbies online, some more positive than others.

Maria Konnikova, writing in a January 2022 edition of *Wired* magazine, reported that "cults have flourished in times of flux, when behavioral norms shift and stability is elusive. If anything has characterized 2021, it has been the sense of constant displacement engendered by a novel disease."

Added to the instability was a rather unexpected phenomenon. To avoid spreading COVID-19, people had to remain isolated. That led to loneliness. They connected through their social platforms as never before. Together, those four experiences—instability, isolation, loneliness, and internet connection—created a perfect storm. It was an ideal breeding ground for the growth of cults. People had time on their hands and grievances to share. Conspiracies multiplied exponentially. It was simply a matter of cause and effect.

In Konnikova's words: "In the early days of [2021], we [saw] people denied social contact because of lockdowns, and some turned instead to the most improbable of alliances, looking for groups that would validate and channel their anger and frustration."

Cults offer a perceived form of safety, stability, and certainty. They feature a group of like-minded individuals who seem to be experiencing the same things. They claim to identify and empathize with the lonely folks at home who are trying to make sense of things.

In short, in times such as this, cults expand into the vacuum created by the collapse of confidence in traditional sources of factual analysis.

This whole phenomenon was captured succinctly by an observation posted on Twitter on December 10, 2019, by a user named Catherine na Nollag:

i still think my favourite thing that's ever happened to me on the internet is the time a guy said "people change their minds when you show them facts" and I said "actually studies show that's not true" and linked TWO sources and he said "yeah well I still think it works"

Such is the power of conspiracies. The response of many people is to say, "My mind is made up. Don't confuse me with facts!"

David Sullivan, who devoted his life to infiltrating cults in order to extricate loved ones from their grip, pointed out that no one ever joins a "cult." They join a community of people who see them.

There is no societal indication yet that this practice will change anytime soon.

LIVING ON "THE EVE OF DESTRUCTION"

Cults thrive when it seems the end is near. They offer protection and security to those whose vision of the future is clouded, at best.

This is nothing new. The early Jesus cult of two thousand years ago believed THE END—that is, the end of this world—was at hand, and followers looked daily for his return. Although waiting for Christ's second coming has had many variants during the last two millennia, it attained cult-like importance in the early 1800s and again in the 1970s.

The War of the Worlds (both the novel by H. G. Wells and the radio broadcast read by Orson Welles), *Star Trek*, and *Star Wars* didn't become blockbusters by accident. This was the world prophesied by the likes of Jules Verne and H. G. Wells. Arthur C. Clarke was its publicist. Carl Sagan and Erich von Däniken, although from two different cultural and academic "denominations," became its theologians.

This age continues right down to the present. The Discovery Channel and the History Channel, among many others, run a lot of programming about alien encounters. The famous actor and narrator Morgan Freeman created a show called *Through the Wormhole* in which quantum physics is called upon to reveal a world much stranger than fiction.

> **End-of-the-world scenarios are the bread and butter of cult dogma.**

The phenomenon of THE END went mainstream in the 1960s. Songwriter (and some say prophet) Bob Dylan wrote in 1964 that the times were "a-changin'," and Barry McGuire enlarged on the theme the very next year in his hit song "Eve of Destruction." The group REM took up the theme in 1987 with their song "It's the End of the World as We Know It (and I Feel Fine)."

This was by no means a new phenomenon. The end of the world has been a big topic for centuries. The Maya, early Christianity, Nostradamus, and—as we discuss in this book—the Millerites, Jim Jones, the Branch Davidians, Heaven's Gate, and various survivalist cults all taught the same thing: the world will soon end, and we can help you get through it.

John of Patmos famously wrote the Book of Revelation, which prophesies a great battle at Armageddon. The word has since become synonymous with the end of the world.

End-of-the-world scenarios are the bread and butter of cult dogma. They offer a way of thinking that appeals to those who are particularly susceptible to cult influence. It goes something like this: *You feel lonely and downtrodden. You feel that no one understands you. You are bitter and angry; you feel isolated. You are the only one who sees the extent of the hopelessness of the world as it is. You want freedom, but you also want vengeance on your enemies—those who have imposed this situation upon you— upon us. We understand. We feel just like you do. But there is hope. There's a new world coming! Your persecutors will be punished, and you will be rewarded. We will survive the coming apocalypse together and come out renewed on the other side. "Vengeance is mine, says the Lord." Stay strong. Come join with us. All will be well!*

It is an appeal as old as the Bible. Consider these words from the New Testament book of Jude, aimed at early Christians who were being persecuted for their faith:

Behold, the Lord cometh with ten thousand of his saints, to execute judgment upon all, and to convince all that are ungodly among them of all their ungodly deeds which they have ungodly committed, and of all their hard speeches which ungodly sinners have spoken against him. These are murmurers, complainers, walking after their own lusts; and their mouth speaketh great swelling words, having men's persons in admiration because of advantage. But, beloved, remember ye the words which were spoken before of the apostles of our Lord Jesus Christ; How that they told you there should be mockers in the last time, who should walk after their own ungodly lusts. These be they who separate themselves, sensual, having not the Spirit. But ye, beloved, building up yourselves on your most holy faith, praying in the Holy Ghost, keep yourselves in the love of God, looking for the mercy of our Lord Jesus Christ unto eternal life.

A popular gospel song written by Christian songwriters Bill and Gloria Gaither has found its way into many a modern Evangelical hymnbook:

The King is coming! The King is coming!

I just heard the trumpets sounding, and now his face I see.

The King is coming! The King is coming!

Praise God, he's coming for me!

Obviously, supposed "inside news" about THE END is a staple of cult psychology, has been with us a long time, and will continue into the foreseeable future.

These, then, are a few of the reasons that the United States of America are a fertile breeding ground for cults:

- Lip-Service Religion

- Rebelliousness

- Entrepreneurship

· Religious Freedom

· Evolving Social Media

· Infatuation with Conspiracy Theory

· Living on "the Eve of Destruction"

There are probably many more. But as we now go on to look more deeply into some specific American cults, beginning with those that began within the fold of traditional religions, this list will help identify how and why such cults came to be.

OFFSHOOTS: BREAKING AWAY FROM TRADITIONAL RELIGIONS

Many cults began as a small but growing gathering of folks within the ranks of traditional religious groups who eventually split off on their own because of the presence of a charismatic or inspirational minister who offered a new slant on old beliefs. Once a group began to form under the tutelage of such a religious entrepreneur, the usual factors revolving around ego-centered power and influence started to shape the organization.

Such was the case with a Shaker named Cyrus Teed.

CYRUS TEED AND THE KORESHAN UNITY

Cyrus Reed Teed was born in Delaware County, New York, in October 1839 and was a member of the Shaker sect, a splinter group of the Quakers, or Society of Friends. The Shaker movement began in England and organized in America during the late eighteenth century. Shakers are most known today for their exquisitely crafted furniture and the musical arrangements (some of them ironically complicated) that are based on their favorite hymn, "'Tis a Gift to Be Simple."

DR. C. R. TEED (KORESH)

Following a vision, Cyrus Teed took the name Koresh and preached an inverted view of cosmology that centered his Koreshan Unity followers as divine.

Teed studied medicine after becoming a doctor in a field that became known as eclectic medicine. This meant that he combined different types of medical treatment depending on whatever he thought his patient might need. Those who adopted this method didn't necessarily feel the need for approval from their peers. They might not have had any solid, scientific evidence for what they did, but they justified their treatment by experimentation and results. If it brought healing or relief to their patients, they did it. There was actually quite a following for this brand of medicine in his day.

In 1869, Teed had what he called an "illumination." The female half of the Deity revealed to him the true nature of the universe. He was commanded to go forth and preach this revelation to the world because he had been anointed a messiah.

Within the year, Teed left his Shaker community, moved to Chicago, and renamed himself Koresh, which was the Hebrew equivalent of Cyrus, a Persian word meaning "throne." His new religion was called Koreshanity, and his followers labeled themselves the Koreshan Unity.

He preached a doctrine that was molded and shaped by Shaker principles: immortality, celibacy (except for purpose of procreation), and a separatist form of collectivism. To this, he added reincarnation and, in keeping with his medical background, alchemy. Two decades later he had a following of more than 4,000 adherents who were established in communities scattered around the country.

During the nineteenth century, many groups of utopian societies flourished in America. The Hopedale Community in Massachusetts is probably the best known, but the Prairie Home Community in Ohio, the Raritarian Bay Union of New Jersey, and the Shalam Colony in New Mexico are additional examples of religious-based cults, most of which embraced either some form of spiritualism or the transcendentalism of essayists Henry David Thoreau and Ralph Waldo Emerson.

What set the Koreshan Unity apart was a unique dogma that formed the basis of Teed's original inspiration. He called it "cellular cosmogony." His 1897 book called *The Cellular Cosmogony; or, The Earth, a Concave Sphere* explained it.

To put it simply, Teed believed the communication he had received from God had taught him that the earth was not round but rather a concave sphere that curved upward at about eight inches per mile. It was, in effect, a dish or bowl-shaped depression. Given the rate of this curve, the world had a diameter of about 8,000 miles and a circumference of 25,000 miles at the upper rim. But it was not just the earth itself that was encompassed by this theory. In effect, "God" held the whole bowl-shaped universe in the palms of his hands. Human beings lived on the inner surface of this bowl, with their heads pointed toward the center. (You may wonder what was outside this concave shell. Apparently Teed did too, but he never explained it.) The whole structure consisted of what Teed called a cellular cosmogony, or "cell."

Within the cell, nested like Russian dolls, were three atmospheric shells. The sun occupied the middle shell. But what we see over our heads is not the real sun. The sun is actually an electromagnetic battery that is invisible to our eyes. The real sun's rays, which we do see, are actually the refracted light that bends, following the curvature of the earth's surface. Teed called this phenomenon "focalization."

> He went on to explain that day and night are not caused by the earth's rotation. The sun is light on one side and dark on the other, and it rotates.

He went on to explain that day and night are not caused by the earth's rotation. The sun is light on one side and dark on the other, and it rotates. The sun's rotation causes the illusion of sunrise and sunset. The curving light rays deceive us into thinking that the sun moves across the sky. But it doesn't. It just rotates in place. The energy that emanates from the dark side of the sun emits pinpoints of light that appear to us as stars. The greatest concentration of these supposed "night" rays appears to us as the moon, but Teed had a much more convoluted way of explaining it. He also went into great detail concerning nebulas and rainbows and the occasional comet.

What about gravity? That's simple. "Gravic rays" emanate from the sun and hold everything down on the ground.

All this required a complete refutation of Copernicus, Newton, atomic theory, chemistry, optics, and surveying techniques, but Teed didn't seem to worry much about such things. Apparently, his followers didn't, either. He simply taught that the whole Copernican system "does not contain a single positive proof of scientific accuracy," and that was enough for them.

All this cosmology overshadowed a deeper dogma. In effect, Teed began to promote himself as a messianic figure. If Copernicus and his whole conception of the universe was faulty, it followed that the God behind the cosmos was utterly incomprehensible to the human mind and intellect, so the reason the universe existed was also a complete mystery. God was, in other words, beyond any dogma or doctrine, beyond even our feeble attempts at worship. But human beings, with the benefit of Teed's illumination, were now within reach of finally obtaining their inheritance, which was nothing less than restoration to the eternal throne and, of course, divinity. We were created in the Eternal and were now on the threshold of returning to our place of origin.

This appealing scenario explains why people responded so enthusiastically to the doctrine of the Koreshan Unity. In the nineteenth century, humankind was beginning to awaken to the reality of the vastness of the universe, and they were terrified by what they saw. Teed offered them something comprehensible—an acceptable cosmos and the chance of attaining divinity. Once again, human beings could be at the center of everything.

Teed's right-hand man, and the one who really generated a lot of the official doctrine of the group, was a journalist by the name Ulysses Grant Morrow. Born in Kentucky in 1864, Morrow was a newspaper editor with a flair for writing riveting copy. Not only did he aid in the composition of Teed's book, he soon became the editor in chief of the group's newspaper, *The Flaming Sword*. Besides his writing skills, he was a talented inventor. Teed and

In 1894, Koreshans converged at a place near Estero, Florida, that the founder claimed was essentially the center of the universe. While setting up a modest community, believers also set about trying to prove the unprovable, designing a series of models and instruments to measure the earth's concavity, like this rectilineator designed by Ulysses Grant Morrow.

Morrow formed a charismatic duo whose skills complemented each other.

In 1894, with a new millennium fast approaching, two Koreshan communities, one from Chicago and one from San Francisco, combined forces to purchase 300 acres of land near Estero, Florida. There they began to build what was to become an ultimate utopian settlement. The acreage was chosen because Teed had come to believe that this particular spot of ground was the "the vitellus of the great cosmogonic egg." In other words, it was near the center of the great bowl that formed the concave earth. He believed this new community would soon become the New Jerusalem, and he predicted that eight million people would soon move in.

His estimate wasn't even close. Even at the very height of its popularity, only 250 people lived there. Nevertheless, the Koreshans went about preparing and building for the influx they thought would soon arrive. They constructed a printing facility for the new newspaper, a great dining hall, a separate post office, a cement factory and sawmill, a bakery and general store, a boat yard, and a small hotel.

The governing body of the community was a council of women called the Seven Sisters. They lived together in a building called the Planetary Court. They even tried to get involved in the local political structure of the nearby town, but their candidates continually lost elections.

Obviously, people outside the organization scoffed at Teed's explanation of what the universe looked like. They continually asked questions that he had difficulty answering. If the earth curved upward from the center of the cosmic cell, for instance, why could they not gaze upward along the curve of the bowl and see faraway places that were higher up on the walls?

Teed knew he needed some confirming science, so he gave Morrow the job of creating the proper instruments to prove his point. Morrow responded by inventing what he called a "rectiline-ator." This was a device made of mahogany and brass, about 12 feet in length, that was supposed to be capable of making observations along straight lines that measured altitude. Using this and another piece of equipment, called a "Koreshan geodetic staff," he produced records that supposedly proved that there was a definite upward curve in the earth extending outward from the complex and even along the surface of the water in the Gulf of Mexico.

Later studies indicated that the rectilineator itself might have suffered from a sag induced by stress on the materials used. Less agreeable evaluators reported that the experiment suffered from expectation bias or even deliberately misadjusted measurements.

By 1902 Teed needed something more to sustain the interest of his followers. In keeping with his rather flamboyant titles, he wrote a book called *The Immortal Manhood: The Laws and Processes of Its Attainment in the Flesh*, which further outlined, in his words, the "theocrasis of Cyrus the Anointed."

He defined "theocrasis" in this way: "the incorruptible dissolution of the physical body by electromagnetic combustion." In other

> **In other words, he believed that upon his death, he would achieve immortality through a process of electromagnetic combustion.**

words, he believed that upon his death, he would achieve immortality through a process of electromagnetic combustion.

After Koresh's death in 1908, his movement dissipated, with the last known follower dying in 1981. What was left of the Koreshan community is now maintained as part of a public state park.

After about a decade in the Florida sun, the Koreshan community began to decay. Ulysses Morrow left four years after the new millennium began as a result of disagreements with the founder. He tried to unite groups in Germany and Argentina whose members believed that the earth was hollow, but he eventually died in 1950, having spent the rest of his life as a type-setter in a publishing house.

Soon after Morrow departed, Teed was injured in a fight that broke out between some of his followers and the residents of Fort Myers. In trying to stop the brawl, the local sheriff beat Teed with the butt of his pistol, and Teed never recovered from the blows. He died in 1908. His followers laid his body out, waiting for the hoped-for resurrection through electromagnetic combustion, but it never happened. After a few days, the local county health officer ordered a burial.

With Teed's passing, the Koreshan Unity began to dissipate, but they still owned the land upon which they had built their community. Even *The Flaming Sword* was published up until 1940, but it never once acknowledged the death of the founder.

By 1961 the community numbered just four members. They decided to deed the property over to the State of Florida. It then became a state park, and today the Koreshan Unity Settlement Historic District can be found listed in the National Register of Historic Places. Eleven structures remain among lawns and nature paths on the property, including the world's last remaining rectilineator.

FATHER DIVINE AND THE PEACE MISSION

Sometimes groups can be labeled as cults and their founders regarded as fakes and charlatans, but if they endure the slander and keep on with their mission, they can thrive and eventually enter the mainstream. This is what happened, for instance, to the Church of Jesus Christ of Latter-day Saints and the Jehovah's Witnesses, as well as earlier groups such as the Quakers and the Shakers. Or, for that matter, such present-day mainstream Protestant denominations as the Methodists and Baptists.

Such is the case with the Peace Mission religious movement and its founder, Father Divine (1877–1965). He called himself the Reverend Major Jealous Divine, and he was worshipped by many of his followers, who called him God, the Dean of the Universe, and even the Harnesser of Atomic Energy, thus attaining cult-like status.

By the time of his death in 1965, he was also recognized as an important advocate of racial equality and self-sufficiency for African Americans and considered to be an important part of the civil rights movement.

Which description best fits this charismatic preacher—cult leader or civil rights advocate? Maybe a little of both.

Accounts vary as to Father Divine's background. Most say his name was George Baker. At least that's what a few people say he was called when he worked as a gardener in Baltimore, Maryland.

Some reports cite his birthplace as Savannah. Others, on a plantation on Hutchinson Island, Georgia. Wherever he was born, it was during the post-Reconstruction period, a difficult time to be Black in America, especially in the South, and even more so in Georgia. Degradation and terror filled the lives of most Black people, and Black messiahs who promised hope and a better day flourished in such an atmosphere. This must have influenced him deeply, because he identified with a religion consisting of primitive mysticism. The Holiness and Pentecostal movements featured manifestations of the anointing and infilling of the Holy Spirit, marked by speaking in tongues and ecstatic utterings, dancing, and being "slain" in the spirit. He was also heavily influenced by Christian Science and a movement called New Thought.

In 1899 he served as an assistant to Father Jehovia, whose birth name was Samuel Morris. Morris was the founder of an independent religious group. By 1907, Baker had established a reputation as a charismatic minister and called himself the Reverend Major Jealous Divine. To his followers he was known as the Messenger.

Records seem to indicate that he left Father Jehovia and emerged several years later as the leader of what would become known as the Peace Mission movement. He married his first wife, Peninnah, a disciple who became known as Mother Divine. But the couple said they had married in 1882, so the time frame is a bit confusing. In 1912, they were apparently living in Brooklyn, New York, and by 1919 they had relocated to Sayville, Long Island.

> **Two days after he was sentenced, the presiding judge died. Father Divine and his followers attributed the death to supernatural intervention. Divine later said, "I hated to do it."**

Troubles began in 1931. His Sayville neighbors complained about the growing attendance at services, which were held in his home. Father Divine was arrested and spent 30 days in jail. Two days after he was sentenced, however, the presiding judge died. Father Divine and his followers attributed the death to supernatural intervention. Divine later said, "I hated to do it." His movement began to commemorate the death by annually publishing accounts of "divine retribution" visited on wrongdoers.

Rumors began to surround the organization, and accusations of cult-like activity arose and spread. Neighbors complained that he was giving lavish banquets for his flock. These constituted a public nuisance.

Female followers of Father Divine were called "angels." One of his male followers, a white convert from California called John the Revelator, was convicted of kidnapping and raping one of them. She was a 17-year-old girl known as the Virgin Mary.

In 1933, Father Divine and his followers left Sayville for Harlem, where he became one of the most well-known and flamboyant religious leaders of the Depression era. In Harlem he founded the first of a series of "Heavens," or hotels, where his teachings became house rules, and his disciples could obtain food, shelter, and job opportunities. Both spiritual and physical healing became the order of the day and the mark of divine approval.

One of Father Divine's "Heavens," a Peace Mission location on New York's East Side in 1941.

During these tumultuous decades of growth, the group surely fit the definition of a cult. It had a charismatic leader and a multi-layered amalgamation of various traditional doctrines and dogmas. Members were secretive, and the group experienced swift and sudden growth. The fact that they were mostly Black made them a target for white society, and Father Divine's success probably grated on mediocre white preachers who were no doubt jealous of him.

They also probably didn't understand his doctrine.

According to Father Divine, heaven is a place where sex either doesn't exist or is experienced only as a spiritual reality—certainly not physically. To symbolize the largess of the hereafter, he threw lavish feasts, which contrasted with the simplicity of the typical Protestant communion service. These feasts were completely integrated, quite unlike the segregation happening in American culture at the time. Father Divine didn't own anything himself because he believed that riches on earth were to be spurned, but by the time his flock reached as many as two million people, he had free access to a fortune and lived a lifestyle comparable to the rich and famous.

His Peace Mission supported Blacks in businesses that became hugely successful, and it provided basic needs to thousands, if not millions, of followers. In practical terms, this translated to the devotion of a host of disciples.

It is no wonder that his work was viewed suspiciously by traditional religious leaders who were not doing nearly as well. During the Depression, the Peace Mission was declared to be a cult. But as the decades rolled on, opinions changed. Today, historians, especially Black historians, hail the movement as an important precursor to the civil rights movement. Key doctrines included snippets of Christianity, Americanism, brotherhood, democracy, Judaism, integration, and the understanding that all religions teach basically the same thing if they are good, honest, and true. It's hard to argue with those kinds of principles.

> **By 1936 these doctrines were codified into a document called the "Righteous Government Platform." It called for an end to segregation, lynching, and capital punishment.**

By 1936 these doctrines were codified into a document called the "Righteous Government Platform." It called for an end to segregation, lynching, and capital punishment. Members of the Peace Mission were cautioned to avoid tobacco, alcohol, narcotics, and vulgar language. They were also instructed to swear vows of celibacy and to "embody virtue, honesty, and truth." The document demanded "a righteous wage in exchange for a full day's work." Members were ordered to avoid debt and were not permitted to possess life insurance.

So far, this seems honorable and certainly not necessarily cult-like in nature. But there was one added clause. Father Divine himself was to be regarded and worshipped as God. That raised a number of red flags, to say the least.

Anyone could join one of the various "Heavens" scattered across the country and in Europe as long as they pledged to abide by the rules of the "Righteous Government Platform," paid 15 cents for meals, and paid a dollar a week for sleeping quarters. During the Depression, that was a pretty good deal.

Through it all, Father Divine affirmed the abundance of God and gave banquets every day, even though he claimed he was living in poverty. Most of his followers were African Americans, but about a quarter of the total were white. The businesses owned by the movement included restaurants, gas stations, grocery and clothing stores, and farms. They provided goods and services at low cost, and they were an important source of jobs for those who swore allegiance.

But the organization was also accused of racketeering. Although the resulting investigations brought verdicts of not guilty, suspicious rumors still circulated.

> **Was Father Divine a cult leader, or was his organization a godsend to poor people, especially Blacks, during the Depression? The law cleared them. The rumors, perhaps inspired by jealousy, persisted.**

Was Father Divine a cult leader, or was his organization a godsend to poor people, especially Blacks, during the Depression? The law cleared them. The rumors, perhaps inspired by jealousy, persisted.

By 1942, it appeared that Father Divine had had enough of New York. He moved to a suburb outside Philadelphia. But even this move raised questions. Many insisted it was to avoid paying a financial judgment in a suit brought by a former movement member.

Shortly after the move, his wife, Peninnah—Mother Divine— died. Four years later he married Edna Rose Ritchings, a white Canadian follower, who became known as Sweet Angel.

In 1946, Father Divine declared that Sweet Angel was a reincarnation of the first Mother Divine. They swore they had a celibate marriage. When Father Divine died in 1965, Mother Divine became the leader of the Peace Mission, but the number of followers declined rapidly—in part, no doubt, because of the vows of celibacy the followers had to profess. At the dawn of the twenty-first century, the total number of followers numbered fewer than 20. They lived with Mother Divine in Father Divine's old estate.

The questions remain. Was Father Divine's Peace Mission a cult that worshipped a man who declared himself to be God? Did they practice secret rituals and hold to esoteric religious ideas? Or was it a bona fide movement toward racial equality and self-sufficiency for African Americans, and thus an important part of the civil rights movement?

The answer, it seems, depends on who is asking the question.

JIM JONES AND THE PEOPLES TEMPLE FULL GOSPEL CHURCH

When Father Divine was at the height of his power and his Peace Mission was firmly established, he met frequently with an aspiring Evangelical minister who agreed with much of what Father Divine preached concerning issues related to integration and civil rights. They had theological disagreements, however, especially about the nature of Armageddon and the end of the world.

The young minister's name was the Reverend James Jones (1931–1978), a Methodist pastor from Somerset, Indiana. He would become infamous throughout the world on November 18, 1978, when Jim Jones, as he was known by then, the founder of the Peoples Temple (sometimes spelled "People's Temple") Full Gospel Church, committed suicide in Jonestown, Guyana, killing himself with a single gunshot to the head. That was the day almost a thousand members of his church, following his final instructions, "drank the Kool-Aid" and joined him in death.

How did this horrible tragedy come about? What were the circumstances that allowed such a thing to happen?

The sad answer is that step by inevitable step, slowly but surely, a well-meaning minister from a respected Protestant denomination walked willingly and surely into pathological nar-

> **Step by inevitable step, slowly but surely, a well-meaning minister from a respected Protestant denomination walked willingly and surely into pathological narcissism.**

cissism. He followed a long and winding road that led to ego destruction and simply never found his way back to sanity.

It all began on April 10, 1949, in Indianapolis, Indiana. That was the day a groundbreaking celebration was held for a small church that was to be called the Laurel Street Tabernacle, on the corner of Laurel and Prospect Streets. It was a project founded by the Assemblies of God denomination. The new church could accommodate only about 200 worshippers, and no one present on that day could possibly have imagined the impact it would have on the whole world.

The Assemblies of God in the United States is a Protestant denomination that traces its roots back to the famous holiness meetings that followed the Azusa Street Revival, a series of meetings that took place between 1906 and 1909 in Los Angeles, California. Led by William J. Seymour, the revival took the country by storm, featuring worshippers speaking in tongues, people being "slain in the Spirit" while fainting dead away into the arms of a waiting deacon, healings, raucous music, dancing in the aisles, and a general feeling that the Holy Spirit of God had descended and was instituting a new work on earth that would precede the second coming of Jesus and the end times. By 1914, the Holiness Movement, as it became known, was sweeping the United States and infiltrating into many mainline Christian denominations. It led to the founding of a new denomination called the Assemblies of God, which followed the doctrine of the Finished Work Pentecostals.

Thirty-five years later, the denomination would begin building the Laurel Street Tabernacle. By 1950, its "Full Gospel and Pentecostal Holiness" revivals would fill it to overflowing. One of the board members who ran the church was a man by the name of Jack Beam. He would later become a pillar of the church in Jim Jones's Peoples Temple.

But 1949, the year the Indianapolis church was dedicated, was a significant year within the denomination. It was undergoing the first of many conflicts common to all Christian denominations. This particular conflict involved a doctrinal dispute called the "five-fold ministry." A significant number of people believed that leadership in the church was to be carried on only by 1) modern-day apostles, 2) prophets, 3) evangelists, 4) pastors, and 5) teachers.

Although these offices are given different names by different denominations, they constitute a fairly standard separation of duties. Conflict arose when the governing board of the Assemblies of God decided that mainstream Christianity had become apostate—that it had abandoned the traditional five-fold ministry. It needed purging, and all church members were told they needed to decide what side of the coming "spiritual war" they were on.

Jim Jones is shown participating in an anti-eviction rally January 16, 1977, in front of the International Hotel, Kearny and Jackson Streets, in San Francisco.

"Choose ye this day whom ye shall serve," a quote from the biblical book of Joshua, became the key declaration. Would members join those who championed the five-fold ministry, purge the denomination from those who were apostate, and declare themselves on the side of God, or would they join the rest of the world in its heathen, polluted religious ways? Jesus was coming soon. The time for decision was now. It was a time of what came to be known as the "Latter Rain," which referred to a prophecy from the book of Joel.

This had ramifications throughout the Christian community around the world. If leaders chose to follow the new doctrine, they would be admitting that their Methodist and Baptist neighbors were apostate and going to hell.

The Assemblies of God convened a meeting held in Seattle, Washington, in the fall of 1949. This convocation decided that the New Order of the Latter Rain was extremist and would lead to a severing of fellowship with like-minded Christians of other, traditional denominations.

They were no doubt justified in their decision. Modern scholars who have studied the Latter Rain movement have unveiled a startling series of coincidences that hint at some rather secular motivations for what was supposed to be a spiritual movement.

Two years earlier, in 1947, a millionaire from Palm Springs, California, named Krikor Arkelian had enlisted the aid of an Iranian faith healer named Avak Hagopian to heal his disabled son. A man by the name of Tatos "Thomas" Kardashian, the great-grandfather of Kim Kardashian, had sponsored Hagopian's United States tour, which created high interest throughout the United States. The tour was also sponsored by Clem Davies, an outspoken anti-Semite and fervent member of the Ku Klux Klan.

Arkelian's son was not cured, so he turned to William Branham, a Pentecostal evangelist from Jeffersonville, Indiana. Branham, who also had strong ties to the Ku Klux Klan and anti-Semitic Christians, had been touring the country while leading healing services of his own. Together with others who promoted a doctrine of British Israelism (a doctrine that claims, among other things, that Britain and certain European nations were descendants of the Lost Tribes of Israel), they ignited the New Order of the Latter Rain movement. It was racially charged, apocalyptic doctrine at its best, and it caught on, eventually splitting the Assemblies of God denomination. Among the groups that followed the movement were the influential Full Gospel Businessmen's Association and a publication known as *Voice of Healing*. By 1950, over one thousand "healing" evangelists were gathering at annual Voice of Healing rallies.

William Branham, right, conducts one of his healing-campaign meetings. The faith-healing evangelist's style and success influenced many high-profile preachers, including Jim Jones.

That rather sprawling history sets the stage for the meetings held at Laurel Street Tabernacle in Indianapolis. Branham, the evangelist, was often a guest of Jim Jones, the Methodist minister who also held nationwide healing revivals and frequented the Tabernacle when not busy at his own church. Jones was friendly to the Latter Rain movement and had followed all the publicity with great interest. At a revival meeting in Columbus, Indiana, he had even been designated a "prophet," placing him within the five-fold ministry establishment.

In 1951, he accepted a large sum of money to hold a series of revivals in Los Angeles, a city that seemed to thrive on such events. Only two years earlier, in 1949, the Reverend Billy Graham (1918–2018) had launched his own career as an evangelist when he was the featured speaker of a Christian group called Christ for Greater Los Angeles. His campaign, originally scheduled for three weeks, had to be extended to eight. This was the famous series of meetings that propelled Graham to fame when William Randolph Hearst, the media mogul, sent a two-word decree to his national network of editors. "Puff Graham," he said. The rest is history.

Jim Jones, when he held his own series of revival meetings, was thus following in the footsteps of the man who would eventually become the confidante of 12 consecutive presidents, beginning with Herbert Hoover.

One of Jones's backers for these meetings was the Reverend Orval Lee Jaggers, an editor for William Branham's books and publications. Jaggers was into a lot of teachings that were peripheral to traditional doctrines. He wrote about the zodiac's influence on Christianity, for instance, and he believed strongly in UFOs. These were both doctrines that became part of the Peoples Temple dogmas.

With all this influence from the Latter Rain folks, Jones changed the name of his still somewhat modest Somerset Methodist Church to "Christian Assembly," thus separating himself from the name "Methodist," and held what he called "Full Gospel Preaching" services. It didn't take long for him to become well known in the Pentecostal community. That led to an invitation for him to preach at the Laurel Street Tabernacle. The Reverend Price, pastor of the church, was about to retire and suggested to his congregation that Jim Jones would be an apt replacement. The Assemblies of God governing board objected. Jones was, after all, still a Methodist, in fact if not in name. That's where his credentials were filed. But the church ignored the board's warnings. Jones became the associate pastor, the name of the church was changed to the "New" Laurel Street Tabernacle, and it began to advertise the fact that thousands of miracles were taking place there. Its slogan became "Deliverance Center for All People," and the church promised "anointed preaching."

When Price finally did retire, the Assemblies of God made a valiant effort to reclaim the church. The Reverend W. L. Thornton, a mainstream Assemblies man, was set to replace Price, leaving Jones on the outside. Because Jones had no degree in theology, he was theoretically ineligible to become a pastor in the denomination, but by then Jones had too big a following to ignore. With the church split ideologically right down the middle, some members changed their name to "Wings of Deliverance" and began having their own meetings. But Jones began to use the name "Peoples Temple Full Gospel" and eventually changed it to simply "Peoples Temple."

He was backed in his endeavor by both the Latter Rain and Voice of Healing communities, and he was offered an honorary certificate of ordination into the Independent Assemblies of God. That gave him the credentials he needed, and he was off to the races. This marked the official beginning of Jim Jones and the Peoples Temple.

Jones was a charismatic preacher, in both the theological and popular senses of the word. For people who have never experienced group meetings filled with "true believers," manipulative music, and powerful, iconic symbolism, it's hard to imagine how people could get so carried away. But it's important to balance what happened in those meetings with what was going on in church circles across America.

> **Jim Jones and Billy Graham came to prominence at about the same time, and they preached to many of the same people. Both conducted well-attended revivals.**

The best way to do that might be to compare what was happening in more mainstream circles. We already mentioned the parallel careers of Jim Jones and Billy Graham. They came to prominence at about the same time, and they preached to many of the same people. Both conducted well-attended revivals. They employed many of the same techniques of music, powerful preaching, and well-organized rallies. Both had a devoted following. There is no doubt that the techniques they employed were well tested. Even Adolf Hitler used them to great success: well-organized prelimi-

nary work, inspirational music, and powerful public speaking. It's a common formula.
Every church and political rally in the
world follows the same pattern.

The difference was not in the techniques or even the message. The difference
was in the heart and personality of the men
at the top. Graham was an extremely humble man who understood both the positive
and negative aspects of fame. He insisted
that he be surrounded by a board of directors
who could put rules in place that would
shield him from the temptations of his
power. He was paid a salary that was set by
the norms of local pastors in the area in
which he was preaching. He never allowed
himself to be in a room alone with a woman
who was not his wife. He avoided even a hint
of scandal. He never appointed "yes men"
who would agree with his every decision.

Jones used his influence to forward
civil rights and other humanitarian
causes. In 1977 he was awarded the
Martin Luther King Jr. Humanitarian Award, presented by Reverend
Cecil Williams.

Jones, on the other hand, loved the power. Probably Billy
Graham did, too. Who wouldn't? But Graham saw the inherent
dangers and insulated himself from them. Jones never did. He believed himself to be above everyone else. He felt himself to be
God's anointed, a common failing of churchmen who attain fame
and power. He really believed he could heal the sick. He thought
he could tell the future.

Like Father Divine, he preached racial integration. At that
time in American history, that position alienated some church
leaders. As in other areas of society, segregation was still very
much a part of the church.

Jones was praised for his work with the homeless. During
the first part of the 1960s, he was even the director of the Indianapolis Human Rights Commission. But in 1965 he moved his entire congregation to California. Why? Because he thought God
had told him a nuclear war was coming. He never fully explained
why he thought California was safer than Indiana, but by 1971 he
was well ensconced in San Francisco.

Shortly after this final move, he began to call himself "the
Prophet." It seems he had fallen under the power of his own leg-

end and became obsessed with the power he wielded. It wasn't long after that when rumors began to spread in earnest. He was accused of diverting the income of church members to his own use. He faced both state and federal investigations.

He obviously began to worry, because in 1977 he decided to move his community again, this time out of North America entirely, to Guyana. There he set up an agricultural commune called Jonestown. He became an absolute dictator over this group of followers, who had sold their homes and given the proceeds to the Peoples Temple. Now in a foreign land, they had nowhere else to go. Jones confiscated their passports. He had sole control over millions of dollars. He threatened, "in the name of the Lord," everything from blackmail to beatings. After all, the Bible talked about "sparing the rod and spoiling the child," and his flock were his "children." He even staged some rather bizarre rehearsals wherein the people practiced how to conduct a mass suicide.

> **He even staged some rather bizarre rehearsals wherein the people practiced how to conduct a mass suicide.**

Reports of family members began to filter up to high places, and in November of 1978, Representative Leo Ryan of California traveled to Guyana to inspect the compound and inquire into the absence of the family members of some of his constituents. He arrived with a group of reporters and relatives of some of the cult members.

His presence alarmed Jones, who was terrified about the story they would tell when they arrived back in the United States. Jones ordered the assassination of the entire entourage, but only Representative Ryan and four others, three of them reporters, were killed. The rest escaped into the surrounding jungle.

Jones knew that news of the attack would filter back to authorities. Cornered and not finding any other way out, he ordered his mass suicide plan. On November 18, 1978, his followers, for reasons known only to them, obeyed. They drank a powdered mix punch (not Kool-Aid, as it happens, but Flavor Aid) to which had been added cyanide poison.

Why did they do it? Could it have been possible that they thought this was just another one of Jones's practice sessions? Did they, like Jones himself, see no other way out? Did they believe they were going to go to sleep, end what had become a nightmare, and wake up in heaven? Did they believe this was really the will of God, who wanted to welcome them home?

No one knows for sure. But the next day, when Guyanese troops entered Jonestown, they reported the deaths of 913 cultists, 304 of whom were children, and Jones himself, who had committed suicide by shooting himself in the head. Together with those who had died in the attack at the airstrip, the total number of dead was placed at 918 people.

How did such a tragedy happen? What had gone wrong? How could so many people have become involved in so horrible a situation?

As we have seen, it all began at a little church in Indiana that seated only 200 people. Step by step, in small increments, religious doctrine had merged with personal egos and manipulative preaching. Slowly, ever so slowly, like a slow-moving train wreck, people had been convinced to follow along, step by step, like lemmings into a sea of despair that ended in tragedy.

Should someone have seen it coming?

Of course! And they did. The directors of the Assemblies of God had warned of the abuses of power and lack of connection to higher bodies that had the power to clamp down on the brakes. But the people in the pews had split away and refused to listen. Family and friends had raised serious objections, but often their attempts at intervention had been spurned. By the time representatives of the government stepped in, it was too late, and even Congressman Ryan lay dead on the tarmac.

Representative Leo Ryan, who was killed among others when he led an investigation into Jonestown in Guyana, sparking the infamous mass murder/suicide.

> **Wherever two or three are gathered together, the possibility of a cult is always present.**

That is the insidious nature of cults. Even a slight variance from orthodoxy can lead to disaster, and religion is all about feelings, not facts.

It probably shouldn't be. Faith is an elusive thing. But faith is also easy to manipulate. Even the purest religious organizations, for the best of reasons, resort to the same kind of techniques practiced by Jim Jones and his ilk. You can go into any small church, of any denomination, on any street corner of America, and identify them—music, inspirational preaching, a welcoming group of believers, an atmosphere that exudes comfort, and symbolic images such as crosses, candles, paintings, and flags. Similar props are the staple of political gatherings as well. They are used in lodge halls and barrooms, for that matter. Wherever two or three are gathered together, the possibility of a cult is always present.

The problem comes when someone like Jim Jones gathers to himself the reins of power and, free from any governing agency, starts his manipulative maneuverings. It was not without reason that the American Founding Fathers built checks and balances into the U.S. Constitution. If someone is allowed, and even encouraged, to resort to autocratic-styled leadership, the end result can be tragic, indeed.

But that, in a nutshell, is too often the story that unfolds within what we call the history of American cults.

JIM BAKKER, *THE PTL CLUB*, AND THE RETURN OF JESUS

In April 1977, Jim Bakker, a minister associated with the Assemblies of God, stood before live television cameras at the dedication ceremony of the PTL Satellite Network and vowed that from that moment on, *The PTL Club* would broadcast Christian programming 24 hours a day until the second coming of Jesus Christ. Presumably, after his return, Jesus would handle his own marketing.

How did an unknown, small-church minister like Bakker rise to such heights? And, having attained them, how did he come to trip up so badly and fall, eventually to wind up serving a five-year term in federal prison?

It's quite a story.

In 1974, Jim and Tammy Faye Bakker had big dreams. They saw the promise of television. Gathering just six or seven friends to help them, they launched a local TV show, which they called *The PTL Club*, from a small former furniture store in Charlotte, North Carolina.

"PTL" originally stood for "Praise the Lord," but eventually Bakker said it also stood for "People That Love." (An elementary school teacher might have pointed out that "Who" would be more appropriate in that construction than "That." But presumably Bakker didn't ask for a teacher's advice.) A few years later, after seeing the amount of money generated by the Bakkers' endeavors, critics would say it stood for "Pass the Loot." Other cynics, referencing Tammy Faye's rather flamboyant style of hair, makeup, and dress, insisted it stood for "Pay the Lady."

Whatever the interpretation, *The PTL Club*, sometimes called the "Jim and Tammy Show," caught on. Within 14 years, the small local TV broadcast grew to an empire, and the couple were the most recognized televangelists in the United States. Their fall would be more rapid than their rise, but for a while, the

> **"PTL" originally stood for "Praise the Lord," but eventually Bakker said it also stood for "People That Love." Critics would say it stood for "Pass the Loot."**

Bakkers were king and queen of a massive enterprise that included their own satellite network, a Christian theme park, and millions of adoring fans.

> **His message was that if you believed hard enough—and sent what he called "seed money" to the PTL ministry—God would bless your offering and cause it to grow exponentially.**

Bakker preached what came to be known as the "prosperity gospel." His message was that if you believed hard enough—and sent what he called "seed money" to the PTL ministry—God would bless your offering and cause it to grow exponentially.

As the Bible says in Ecclesiastes 11, "Cast your bread upon the waters, for you will find it after many days. Give a portion to seven, or even to eight, for you know not what disaster may happen on earth." And in Luke 6, "Give, and it shall be given unto you; good measure, pressed down, and shaken together, and running over, shall men give into your bosom. For with the same measure that ye mete withal it shall be measured to you again."

By 1987, Jim and Tammy had, in the eyes of their fans, epitomized this gospel. They lived what can only be called a life of conspicuous consumption. The had a number of vacation homes and expensive cars, and they traveled first-class with their considerable entourage.

One would think that the fans would resent all this. But just the opposite happened. The Bakkers lived a life completely within the bounds of what they preached. The greater your faith, the more God would bless you. God wanted everyone who had faith to be wealthy. The Bakkers certainly were that. So their lifestyle only confirmed their message.

But there was a deeper problem within all the prosperity and power. There was grit in the machine of the prosperity gospel. The story of the Bakkers' rise and fall reveals the potential and possibilities inherent in fame and fortune, even in the religious

At the peak of Tammy Faye and Jim Bakker's popularity, the fervor of their deep-pocketed believers was matched only by the scorn and disgust of the general public.

establishment. But it also gives a warning about the pitfalls and limits of big religion, no matter how successful it may appear on the outside.

January 2nd is Jim Bakker's birthday. It was the day he usually chose to begin new projects. On that day in 1987, he launched yet another staggeringly ostentatious project. It marked the groundbreaking ceremony for the Crystal Palace ministry center. This was to be a bit more ambitious than the small store-front that began the original TV show. Here was going to be built a glass complex of one-and-a-quarter million square feet that would house a 30,000-seat auditorium and a 5,000-seat television studio. The project would cost $100 million, paid for by loyal fans and followers, and would be the largest such church in the world.

The PTL Club, by any measure, was already a success. The small, local TV program had expanded to a ministry that boasted 2,500 employees, funded by an income of more than $129 million a year. The company owned and operated a 2,300-acre theme park called Heritage USA in South Carolina that drew six million people a year, third only to Disney World in Florida and Disneyland in California. Its satellite network included 1,300 cable stations and reached more than 14 million homes in the United States alone. Forty nations around the world carried its programming, and Bakker was a true international celebrity. Fundraising to feed this growing beast continued nonstop, 24 hours a day.

The site of the planned Crystal Palace, intended to replicate the London exhibition hall of the same name that was destroyed by fire in 1936, was already surrounded by restaurants, a miniature railroad shuttle, a shopping mall, a petting zoo, trails for horseback riding, paddleboats on an artificial lake, tennis courts, miniature golf, a home for unwed mothers, a home for disabled children called Kevin's House, and new housing developments. An 18-hole golf course was surrounded by about a billion dollars' worth of condominiums. There was a nearby village called Old Jerusalem that featured its own hotel, and various campgrounds. Bakker predicted that it would soon become a city of 30,000 residents. Its expanse would be rivaled in Florida only by the Villages, an over-55 retirement community that began in 1982.

Little did Bakker realize that in only two months, the whole thing would come crashing down around him. Back in December of 1980, he had spent an afternoon in a Florida motel room with church secretary Jessica Hahn. After the encounter, he had gone on nationwide television and said, with a straight face and, in retrospect, a hint of a leer, that "to minister to the shepherd is to minister to the flock," and that afternoon he had been "ministered to."

In November of 1987, Jessica Hahn revealed in a 13-page interview in *Playboy* magazine, complete with a full photo spread including topless pictures, that she had indeed been with Bakker on the fateful afternoon, having been told that by doing so she would be "rendering a great service unto God." She was reportedly paid a million dollars for the magazine shoot. She said she had also been paid $279,000 by Roe Messner, one of Bakker's colleagues at *The PTL Club*, to keep quiet about the incident. The funds came from public donations.

Hahn testified that Bakker had forced himself on her even though she was, by her own admission, "a professional who knows all the tricks of the trade."

Once the issue of *Playboy* hit the stands, the rumor mill went into overdrive. Stories appeared in various publications that Bakker was homosexual and had enjoyed many sexual relationships through the years. Others told of his visits to prostitutes, wearing a blond wig as a disguise.

Bakker would later reveal, in 1996, that from the time he was 11 years old and continuing through high school, he had been sexually abused by a man in a position of leadership in his church. The experience left him sexually confused and feeling guilty. Sometimes, he said, the memories were like "ghosts" that "swarmed through my thoughts."

As investigations probed into his alleged misuse of PTL funds, in 1989 Bakker was brought to trial for wire and mail fraud. He had offered time-shares that he called "lifetime partnerships" to apartments at Heritage USA, but he had oversold the available space, and people were turned away after having been guaranteed accommodations. He had also misused money that had been donated specifically for construction.

The trial turned into a media-hyped event under the control of U.S. District Judge Robert Potter, whose nickname was "Maximum Bob." One witness collapsed on the stand from the pressure. Bakker had a psychological breakdown and tried to hide behind his lawyer's couch when federal marshals came for him.

He was eventually convicted and sentenced to 45 years in federal prison, but he was released on probation after only five.

Millions of his former fans and enemies watched, either in horror or glee, depending on whether they felt betrayed or justified. He was a polarizing figure and became a national symbol of the excesses and greed of American televangelists. His opponents claimed he had deliberately defrauded and bilked people out of their money. His proponents say that although that was the final result, he never meant any harm and was just trying to grow his church for the glory of God.

Bakker turned his entire ministry over to Jerry Falwell, the founder and leader of

Jerry Falwell assumed control of Jim Bakker's ministry at the latter's request while the Bakker family dealt with their scandals and fallout.

the so-called Moral Majority and the pastor of the Thomas Rhode Baptist megachurch in Lynchburg, Virginia. It is located on the campus of Liberty University, which was founded by Falwell and was itself later caught in a scandal when Falwell's son and successor, Trey Falwell, was accused of "inappropriate personal behavior and financial self-dealing." Trey was later forced to resign.

Falwell was expected to be simply a caretaker and interim administrator at PTL until the legal mess was straightened out, but his team of accountants soon discovered that *The PTL Club* was more than $65 million in debt and was losing money at the rate of about $2 million a month. Less than seven months later, Falwell's entire staff left the ministry behind, not willing even to be associated with it.

When Falwell took over Bakker's organization, he was quoted as saying it was "one of the major miracle ministries of this century. I doubt there's ever been anything like it in the 2,000-year history of the church." But when he left, he called it a "scab and cancer on the face of Christianity."

> **Was *The PTL Club* a cult? Or was it simply the horrible result of too much power, wealth, and fame being given to someone who simply could not handle it?**

Was *The PTL Club* a cult? Or was it simply the horrible result of too much power, wealth, and fame being given to someone who simply could not handle it?

It depends entirely on your definition of the word "cult." It certainly would not have existed without such a charismatic leader. His fan base adored and almost worshipped him. On the other hand, it all took place in the plain sight of millions of people who blindly sent money without ever setting foot on *The PTL Club*'s campus.

Whatever it was, cult or religion gone horribly wrong, *The PTL Club* certainly demonstrated the power of religion, including its connection with a large segment of American culture. Bakker believed and taught that he was doing what he did because Jesus would soon return. He apparently thought he was preparing the way, standing firmly in the tradition of American revivals that began in small churches, expanded into traveling tent meetings, and graduated to megachurches broadcasting the message from their own television and radio studios.

But Jim Bakker, now divorced from Tammy Faye, ex-con, and for a time the most successful televangelist ever, was gone and seemingly forgotten.

Or was he?

In 2003, Bakker was metaphorically raised from the dead. He began a new TV show called *The Jim Bakker Show* on his old PTL Television Network. He no longer preached about the gospel of prosperity and didn't attain anywhere near his old fame, but he was back at it, and a small but loyal following supports him to this day. His message now is the same as that with which he began. Jesus is coming back soon, and we need to get ready. The apocalypse is right around the corner.

You have to seek him out online and at venues like Roku, DirectTV, and the DISH Network, but he's still going strong. He's married again, to Lori Bakker, a former youth minister who has written several books and hosted her own PTL show called *Life with Lori.*

Tammy is back in the news as well. A movie called *The Eyes of Tammy Faye,* starring Andrew Garfield and Jessica Chastain, was released in 2021. It begins with the time she first met Jim Bakker and continues through their PTL Club years, her divorce, Bakker's prison time, and the imprisonment of her second

> **And with the world in the throes of a pandemic, he started offering a COVID-19 miracle cure he called the Silver Solution. (Just don't drink too much of it, or you could turn irreversibly blue.)**

husband, Roe Messner, who paid the hush money to Jessica Hahn. It also concentrates on her battles with cancer and various addictions. Tammy died of colon cancer in 2007.

Bakker himself, though, seems to be up to his old tricks. Because Armageddon is right around the corner, he is offering TV viewers "food buckets" of freeze-dried packets that contain 154 meals, enough to see you through any coming shortages. They sell for only $135. And with the world in the throes of a pandemic, he started offering a COVID-19 miracle cure he called the Silver Solution—a formula containing colloidal silver meant to be ingested. (Just don't drink too much of it, or your skin could turn irreversibly blue.) Unfortunately for Bakker, credit card companies refused to reimburse sales, so he has been forced to tearfully beg his followers to send checks or cash to keep his ministry alive and help him avoid bankruptcy. And then in June 2021 a Missouri court ordered him to pay $156,000 in restitution to everyone who had bought the fake COVID cure.

Lori and Jim started their show in Branson, Missouri, but moved to "Morningside, USA, nestled high in the Ozarks," after

Jim Bakker was released from prison after serving under five years of what was originally a 45-year sentence. He has since returned to broadcasting from a theme park–like studio set.

receiving a substantial donation of $25 million from Jerry Crawford, one of the original partners of *The PTL Club*. The amenities at Morningside aren't quite what Bakker used to have, but there are condos and a chapel that offers services twice every day. There are also campsites, a general store, a small café, a center for pregnant women, and a 15-foot-tall statue of Jesus.

One of Bakker's guests on the show during 2021 was Mike Lindell, the CEO of MyPillow. He had become famous after trying to rescue his pal Donald Trump following the presidential election of 2020. His message was familiar to all who follow him. He contributed to Bakker's telethon to raise money, revealed that the presidential election of 2020 was stolen from former President Trump, and blamed "cancel culture" for the fact that retailers stopped carrying his MyPillow products.

Jim Bakker is now 81 years old. He suffered a stroke in May of 2020. His followers are few and aging along with him. But he continues doing what he does best—some say better than anyone before him.

Is he a cult leader?

Well, that's a matter of opinion. You be the judge.

THE EVANGELICAL CHURCH, POLITICS, AND THE NRA

Cults are usually associated with a central, unifying figure who claims to be either God or at least godlike and is worshipped by his or her followers. As we have already seen, Father Divine, Jim Jones, and Jim Bakker inspired such a following. They began within an established religious tradition and gradually moved out to form their own fanatic following. But what if the central figure is not a *person* but a *thing*? Can a cult form around a symbol, an inanimate object—one that inspires loyalty and devotion and for which its followers are willing to lay down their life and die if the right to possess the object is threatened?

In other words, is there such a thing as a "cult of the gun"? By asking this question, we now enter the wild and crazy world of the uniquely American devotion to, even idolization of, guns.

Firearms have long been revered in the United States, but in the final decades of the twentieth century, the gun began its meteoric rise to religious-icon status. Ever since the Minute Men gathered in Concord, Massachusetts, to fire "the shot heard 'round the world," rifles and guns have symbolized American freedom. But we have reached the point where the gun can be said to be worshipped. Ownership of guns has, as we shall soon see, reached cult-like status.

Before we go any further, I have a confession to make. I've owned guns all my life. For many years I was a card-carrying member of the National Rifle Association (NRA). Indeed, as a Boy Scout seeking to earn merit badges, I learned to shoot in NRA-sponsored classes. I've hunted my fair share of wild game and have written books about my love of the outdoors and hunting. I still own a few guns, although I gave up hunting more than a decade ago.

> **I am familiar with firearms and support the right of citizens to own them. I also know firsthand about the NRA, of which I am a former member.**

I say all this because when it comes to guns, I know what I'm talking about. I am familiar with firearms and support the right of citizens to own them. I also know firsthand about the NRA, of which I am a former member. I willingly and enthusiastically believe in free elections and democratic principles. And I understand the Evangelical church, having been an Evangelical pastor for many years.

Hence this chapter in a book about American cults called "The Evangelical Church, Politics, and the NRA." My involvement in all three of these movements is well documented in the many books I have written. But this involvement and close association have also led me to believe that, gradually but surely, step by measured step, the ménage à trois between the Evangelical church, politicians, and the NRA is at least bordering on, and maybe has even already crossed over, the line marking cult-like status in the "land of the free and the home of the brave." Religion, politics, and guns have spread out and are now so overlapped that it is sometimes hard to distinguish between them, and the specific rhetoric of each has become the language of them all. How else can we explain the kind of comment often heard at political rallies: "Keep your Bibles open and your guns loaded"?

Indeed, it might not be inappropriate to suggest that religion and politics have finally been brought together by what can only be called "the cult of the gun."

To dig into this strange religio-politico-gun-toting world in an attempt to unravel how it all came about is going to involve some detailed background. Buckle up for a long but fascinating ride!

THE EVANGELICAL CHURCH

First, what exactly is the Evangelical church?

"Evangelical" refers to the Gospel. The word from which it is derived, the Greek word *euangelion*, means "a reward for bringing the good news" or, more commonly, just the "good news" itself.

"Gospel" refers to the Christian teachings about Jesus Christ. The word is derived from the Anglo-Saxon term *god-spell*, meaning "good story."

So, in a sense, Evangelical means "good news" or "good telling." The content of what is being told is found in the four books that are called "Gospels" in the Christian Bible: Matthew, Mark, Luke, and John.

Perhaps the best summary of this "good news" is given by the Apostle Paul in 1 Corinthians 15:

Now brothers, I want to remind you of the gospel I preached to you, which you received and on which you have taken your stand. By this gospel you

A papyrus sheet with passages from 2 Corinthians in ancient Greek is one of the earliest known copies of this letter from the Apostle Paul.

are saved, if you hold firmly to the word I preached to you. Otherwise, you have believed in vain. For what I received I passed on to you as of first importance: that Christ died for our sins according to the Scriptures, that he was buried, that he was raised on the third day according to the Scriptures, and that he appeared to Peter, and then to the twelve. After that he appeared to more than five hundred of the brothers at the same time, most of whom are still living, although some have fallen asleep. Then he appeared to James, then to all the apostles, and last of all he appeared to me also.

This is a synopsis of the Evangelical Christian story. The one who tells it, who brings the "good news," is called an Evangelist. They might be Methodist or Baptist, Episcopalian or Catholic, or any other denomination, but if this is the basis of their belief, they are Evangelical Christians. Some folks consider themselves more "Evangelical" than others, of course, but they are all Evangelical Christians by definition. Over time, "Evangelical" became a noun—something a Christian is if he or she believes the Gospel.

Evangelicalism as a movement arose in the 1950s. Before this, Christians who taught a conservative theology were called Fundamentalists, because they believed in what they called the "five fundamentals" of the faith: the virgin birth, the trinity, the necessity of salvation, the resurrection and second coming of Jesus, and the inerrant inspiration of Scripture. As the twentieth century (and science and education) progressed, however, it seemed the Fundamentalists were losing the war of popular opinion to the Modernists.

Evolution, not creation, was being taught in the public schools. White men returning from World War II were attending colleges financed by the G.I. Bill. (Black soldiers were not eligible.) Having been in contact with different cultures and religions, returning soldiers were not quite so quick to condemn others. Churches were booming, but many of them were moving to the suburbs, where Catholics, Episcopalians, Baptists, and Jews all met in the same bowling league.

The harder Fundamentalists fought against advancement, the more their image became that of the preacher with the clenched fist, unenlightened and unbending.

Although it is difficult to document, a good argument can be put forth that it was the Fundamentalist objection to Billy Graham that finally caused large groups of Christians to distance themselves from the Fundamentalist title.

The Reverend Billy Graham, arguably the most influential Evangelical in America, began as a Fundamentalist, but he was open and inviting to everyone. He often welcomed nonreligious civic leaders to sit on the front dais with him at his revivals. This caused some Fundamentalists to draw back in horror. How can believers associate with unbelievers?

Some Fundamentalists began to picket Graham's famous Crusades. They were called "Separationists." Others were even more extreme. They not only disassociated from Billy Graham; they disassociated from those who associated with him. They became known as "Secondary Separationists."

This was embarrassing to many who agreed with Fundamentalist theology but didn't feel comfortable associating with Fundamentalists. It soon became popular to declare one's theological position by announcing, "I am a Fundamentalist in theology but not in attitude."

> **The term "Evangelical" stuck. It became the name that people of all denominations who followed a fairly conservative brand of Christianity could feel good about.**

It was Harold Ockenga, pastor of Park Street Church in Boston, who coined the term "Evangelical." He preached a conservative form of theology but was greatly respected by the liberal intellectual community. When the popular magazine *Christianity Today* identified with the new label, and when the Billy Graham Evangelistic Association followed suit, the term "Evangelical" stuck. It became the name that people of all denominations who followed a fairly conservative brand of Christianity could feel good about.

These days, Evangelicals can be found in every denomination and every church. It is almost a separate denomination,

Jerry Falwell and his Moral Majority organization helped inspire the rise of today's Christian nationalists.

and it spans the gamut of Christianity. Evangelical members of the United Church of Christ might attend conferences with Evangelical Methodists and Baptists, feeling closer to them in the faith than they do with the more liberal people in their own church. Probably every Protestant church in America has an Evangelical wing in the congregation, even though they may not use the term.

But a problem now exists within the Evangelical community. It all began in 1979 with Jerry Falwell and his Moral Majority, a political organization. Falwell was a Baptist Fundamentalist, but many Evangelicals were drawn to him. Although the Moral Majority was officially disbanded in 1989, in only ten years it reshaped American politics. Its purpose was to advance Evangelical values and link them with politically conservative ideas. This was the beginning of what is now called the "Religious Right."

POLITICS

Now we move from the Evangelical arena into the political fray.

Falwell's Moral Majority was formed as a conservative religious and political organization responding to social and cultural transformations in the 1960s and 1970s that changed the United States. Much of the turmoil was caused by the Vietnam War (both the military action and the protests against it) and the public trials that arose after the 1972 Nixon-inspired break-in at the Watergate hotel. It was a time of rioting from Birmingham, Alabama, in 1963, to the Watts neighborhood of Los Angeles in 1965, and Chicago in 1966. During the entire decade of the 1970s, *All in the Family*, featuring weekly disputes between Archie Bunker and "Meathead," his son-in-law, echoed what was going on in many American homes. The *Smothers Brothers Comedy Hour*, one of the most controversial shows in television history, was broadcast on CBS between 1967 and 1969. It had, most definitely, a pro-liberal bias.

Christian Fundamentalists were threatened by developments portrayed on these popular shows. In their view, traditional American moral values were being undermined. The civil rights movement, the women's movement, the draft, the gay rights movement, the seemingly permissive sexual morality being embraced by a younger generation, and even the teaching of evolution were all seen as upsetting the status quo. The U.S. Supreme Court rulings that banned adult-led group prayer and Bible readings in public schools were especially distasteful to them. Abortion was adopted as a value concern to oppose, and the 1973 ruling *Roe v. Wade*, which affirmed the Constitutional right to abortion, was portrayed as a ruling inspired by the devil.

In opposition to all this, Falwell founded the Moral Majority. It was, according to his description, a pro-family, pro-American movement that advanced conservative social values and specifically opposed abortion, pornography, the Equal Rights Amendment (ERA), and gay rights. It also supported increased military defense spending, a strong anti-communist foreign policy, and continued American support for Israel.

To accomplish his aims, of course, Falwell needed to wed his brand of religion to government policy. Thus arose what became known as the Religious Right. Although it theoretically included all religions and was especially embraced by the Evangelical movement, many of its proponents opposed the inclusion of Catholics, Mormons, and Jews. Despite this, the movement quickly grew to several million members, who soon began to work hard at voter registration, lobbying, and fundraising. Jerry

Falwell was quoted as saying, "We need to get these people saved, baptized, and registered to vote!"

The movement's impact on American politics was almost immediate, and it took interesting turns, especially when it deserted Democrat Jimmy Carter, an Evangelical Baptist Sunday school teacher, in favor of Republican Ronald Reagan in the presidential election in 1980. Clearly, by rejecting one of its own—a Southern, conservative Democrat—in favor of an actor from liberal Hollywood, religion took a back seat to politics.

The Moral Majority remained a political force to be reckoned with through the 1980s. But as time went on, it began to face problems it had not considered. Financial support began to dwindle. In 1987, Falwell resigned as the organization's president, creating a power vacuum. Several prominent televangelists and pastors became embroiled in scandal. (With the public exposure of Jim Bakker, Jimmy Swaggart, and Jim Jones, I must confess it was an uncomfortable time to be an Evangelical preacher named Jim!) Falwell backed George H.W. Bush rather than Pat Robertson, a fellow Evangelical televangelist, in the 1988 presidential campaign. Fundraising slumped.

By 1989, the Moral Majority was finished. It was recognized as neither "moral" nor a "majority." Falwell declared publicly that the organization had accomplished its mission, but he admitted that a number of problems persisted. Abortion was only one of them.

But in ten tumultuous years, the Moral Majority had left its stamp on America. It established the Religious Right as an influential force in the field of politics. Conservative Evangelicals had, in effect, joined the Republican Party. In 2016, conservative white Evangelicals were the primary group that voted Republican candidate Donald J. Trump into office.

THE NRA

One of the main tenets of faith within the Evangelical movement is the insistence that the Second Amendment to the Constitution guarantees the personal right to own and use firearms. That moves us into the arena of the NRA and guns in church.

In the June 2021 issue of *Religion Unplugged*, Paul Glader and Michael Ray Smith wrote a fascinating article called "God and Guns: Why American Churchgoers Are Packing Heat." They write:

> Before COVID-19 quarantines and protests over racial injustices, people of faith who attend church, synagogue, mosque and other places of worship have been increasingly thinking about security measures. After 19 fatal shootings at houses of worship since 2000, more Christians across the U.S. from Texas to Maine are toting guns to church. LifeWay Research, an arm of the Southern Baptist Convention, conducted a telephone survey of 1,000 Protestant pastors in 2019 and found 45 percent said their security measures involve armed church members. In the same survey, 62 percent said they have some plan for an active shooter and 80 percent said they have a security measure in place during worship. This all makes for an odd moment in church history and brings tension with theology that emphasizes non-violence.

From the outside, the near-religious obsession many show in promoting an unrestricted view of the Second Amendment may not make sense without understanding where, for many, that message is learned.

The article goes on to quote informal studies conducted by various organizations that outline the trend of parishioners, especially those belonging to primarily Evangelical churches, arming themselves in church for the supposed purpose of protecting themselves against violence. The authors quote the Reverend Mike Sowers of First Baptist Church in Buies Creek, North Carolina: "We are striking a balance between the Great Commission and security."

These days, weekly Bible studies and choir rehearsals are sometimes replaced by sessions at the shooting range. Sometimes, Evangelicals say, this is a practice that pays off. On December 29, 2019, there was a shootout at West Freeway Church of Christ, in Texas. A man pulled out a gun during communion and shot two church members. He was subsequently killed by one of the church deacons in a gun battle that was recorded and then broadcast via YouTube. For many people, this validated the position held by the National Rifle Association that guns deter and detain crime.

Evangelical theologians were quick to take sides, quoting seemingly contradictory Bible verses to support their positions.

Where once churches had "worship teams" and people who were "called" to certain ministries within the church, the security movement has written its own lexicon. Parishioners express a "call" to protect. They might be part of a "gatekeeping team" that labels themselves "watchmen" or "sheepdogs."

Glader and Smith report in their article that they "spoke with more than two dozen church security team members in Colorado, South Dakota, Nebraska and other states, most of them men, and many of them special operations soldiers, retired military officers and avid hunters. The men say they see protection of fellow churchgoers as part of their personal ministry. They enjoy the camaraderie of training with each other, discussing all aspects of security tactics and being on the alert at strategic vantage points during a church service." Some even say they might not attend church as often if they didn't feel the need to be there for possible police action. It gives them an excuse to tear themselves away from their coffee and the Sunday paper.

Furthermore, according to the article, "'The church security movement says that if you come into our house of worship aiming to do harm, you will leave in a pine box,' said the leader of one church security team, a former special forces soldier. 'I would be surprised if any church in North America doesn't have armed security.'"

In the 1985 movie *Pale Rider*, Clint Eastwood plays a mysterious preacher who arrives in a small mining town when a woman prays, quoting Psalm 23 as she seeks protection from thugs. Eastwood's character, called only "the preacher," saves the town from the bad guys and finally says, "Well, the Lord certainly

> But I always had the idea that the person who was packing heat would be, dare I say it, almost thrilled if he had a chance to shoot someone who was bent on stealing from the offering plate.

does work in mysterious ways." The title of the film comes from the biblical book of Revelation: "And I looked, and behold a pale horse: and his name that sat on him was Death, and Hell followed with him." If the movie is at all historically accurate, it would seem that guns and the work of the Lord have a long history.

As a former pastor myself, I have had a chance to question those who feel the need to carry guns with them into church. I tried to remain neutral, despite a natural tendency to side with those who feel there needs to be a place that is free of weapons, and church should be one of them. Back in those days, men wore jackets and ties to church, and the weapons were always concealed. I rarely knew at the time if someone was carrying unless they told me afterward. It never became an issue, so I didn't make it into one. But I always had the idea that the person who was packing heat would be, dare I say it, almost thrilled if he had a chance to shoot someone who was bent on stealing from the offering plate. Such action would affirm their purpose.

Those days are long gone. I am no longer the pastor of a church. I am quite happy those years are behind me. It's a different day. But some of the same issues I faced as a pastor are now experienced by those who walk the halls of state and federal Capitol buildings. Members of both houses of Congress in Washington, D.C., report that some of their colleagues not only carry guns to work but are open about displaying them.

I am quite amazed when I contemplate the current situation in American religion and politics. Conservative politics and conservative religion were separated in the America in which I grew up. Now they have become not just close but intertwined. It frankly baffles me that what brought them together, in large part, was the combination of the NRA and the Cult of the Gun.

JOSHUA, JESUS, MUHAMMAD, AND THE IMPLICATIONS OF JIHAD

Strictly speaking, the three main monotheistic religions known to the world today as Judaism, Christianity, and Islam began as cults. The same can be said of Buddhism, Confucianism, and Daoism. They all began with a charismatic leader who gathered to himself a group of followers and introduced a new vision of how to live a spiritual life in a materialistic world. Each movement grew and, over time, organized itself into a religious system.

Because these are all accepted, traditional religions today, it sounds odd to call them cults, even though they tick all the right boxes. But at the beginning, that's what they were. In the case of monotheism, a message about violence at the end of the world was a central component of the founder's vision.

Here a few selected texts from their revered books.

JUDAISM

And there shall come forth a rod out of the stem of Jesse, and a Branch shall grow out of his roots: And the spirit of the Lord shall rest upon him, the spirit of wisdom and understanding, the spirit of counsel and might, the spirit of knowledge and of the fear of the Lord; And shall make him of quick understanding in the fear of the Lord: and he shall not judge after the sight of his eyes, neither reprove after the hearing of his ears: But with righteousness shall he judge the poor, and reprove with equity for the meek of the earth: and he shall smite the earth: with the rod of his mouth, and with the breath of his lips shall he slay the wicked. And righteousness shall be the girdle of his loins, and faithfulness the girdle of his reins. The wolf also shall dwell with the lamb, and the leopard shall lie down with the kid; and the calf and the young lion and the fatling together; and a little child shall lead them. And the cow and the bear shall feed; their young ones shall lie down together: and the lion shall eat straw like the ox. And the sucking child shall play on the hole of the asp, and the weaned child shall put his hand on the cockatrice' den. They shall not hurt nor destroy in all my holy mountain: for the earth shall be full of the knowledge of the Lord, as the waters cover the sea. And in that day there shall be a root of Jesse, which shall stand for an ensign of the people; to it shall the Gentiles seek: and his rest shall be glorious. And it shall come to pass in that day, that the Lord shall set his hand again the second time to recover the remnant of his people, which shall be left, from Assyria, and from Egypt, and from Pathros, and from Cush, and from Elam, and from Shinar, and from Hamath, and from the islands of the sea. (Isaiah 11)

CHRISTIANITY

And I saw a new heaven and a new earth: for the first heaven and the first earth were passed away; and there was no more sea. And I John saw the holy city, new Jerusalem, coming down from God out of heaven, prepared as a bride adorned for her husband. And I heard a great voice out of heaven saying, Behold, the tabernacle of God is with men, and he will dwell with them, and they shall be his people, and God himself shall be with them, and be their God. And God shall wipe away all tears from their eyes; and there shall be no more death, neither sorrow, nor crying, neither shall there be any more pain: for the former things are passed away. And he that sat upon the throne said, Behold, I make all things new. And he said unto me, Write: for these words are true and faithful. And he said unto me, It is done. I am Alpha and Omega, the beginning and the end. I will give unto him that is athirst of the fountain of the water of life freely. He that overcometh shall inherit all things; and I will be his God, and he shall be my son. But the fearful, and unbelieving, and the abominable, and murderers, and whoremongers, and sorcerers, and idolaters, and all liars, shall have their part in the lake which burneth with fire and brimstone: which is the second death. (Revelation 21)

ISLAM

Because Muslims recognize the sacred texts of the Qur'an only in their original language, we cannot duplicate them here

As told in the Book of Revelation, an angel brings John a vision of the new earth and new heaven.

for English-speaking people. But according to Islam, the end of the world is referred to as the Hour. At that time, Isa (Jesus) will return to Damascus to put an end to al-Dajjāl, an antichrist figure who has ruled over the peoples of the earth. When al-Dajjāl is destroyed, a time of perfect unity and harmony will follow. Isa will later die a natural death. This will then bring about a time of destruction, and after that will come the Hour.

Here are some English approximations from the Qur'an:

"They see the Hour far off, but we see it quite near."

"The hour of judgment is near, and the moon is split."

"Verily the hour is coming. God's design is to keep it hidden, so that every soul be rewarded by the measure of its endeavor."

"Closer and closer to people is their reckoning, while they in neglect turn away."

MONOTHEISM AND STRUGGLE

If monotheism was born out of cult-like activities designed to spread a message of love to a world destined for destruction, that would be one thing. But the facts of history tell quite a different story. Both early Judaism and Islam were bent on conquest early on. Christianity didn't start out as a conquering force, but there is no question that it eventually took the same path.

Listen, for instance, to this passage from the Hebrew Scriptures, the Christian Old Testament. In it, Joshua has taken over leadership after Moses, the original cult leader, had died before leading his followers over the borders of the Promised Land: "But thou shalt utterly destroy them; namely, the Hittites, and the Amorites, the Canaanites, and the Perizzites, the Hivites, and the Jebusites; as the LORD thy God hath commanded thee" (Deuteronomy 20:17).

That sounds like a rather drastic order from on high, considering it was given only a few decades after the Ten Commandments, in which God said, very clearly, "Thou shalt not kill."

As for Islam, the world has never seen such a rapid spread of a new religion. In 635 CE, Damascus had come under Muslim control. Persia followed by 636, Jerusalem in 638, and Egypt by 640. Regions we now identify as Spain, North Africa, the Middle East, India, Pakistan, and parts of China quickly followed. If it had not been for Charles Martel's victory at the Battle of Tours, Europe would have probably been conquered as well.

Early Christianity did not start out with mighty armies, but its adherents made up for it once it became the state-supported religion of Rome in the fourth century.

Christianity and Islam had, as their stated purpose, a missionary component that eventually became militarized. Although Judaism did not grow by conversion, it, too, stated its intentions clearly in the passage from Deuteronomy quoted above. Joshua meant to conquer by means of the sword, as did Muhammad.

This brings us to the Islamic concept of *jihad*, which is not limited to Muslims. Many cults have, without using the word, adapted it to suit their own ideologies.

Jihad is an Arabic word that means "to struggle" or "to strive." The term appears in the Qur'an in various contexts. Sometimes it is used to describe forms of nonviolent struggles—a struggle to become a better person, for instance. This falls under the category of "jihad of the self," which is an important subject in Islamic texts.

There is also a concept of a jihad against invisible enemies— the world's various lusts and temptations. That is something everyone with moral principles must face at some time or another.

It also means warfare against visible enemies. This was the understanding that led the Islamic desert riders on their quest to take over the world of their day. When an enemy was defeated, the opportunity to convert was offered. "People of the Book," meaning people who followed the Bible—that is, Jews and Christians—were shown special treatment, but the end result was the same.

Civilians were generally granted immunity from actual warfare. But there are loopholes to this clause. Osama bin Ladin, who, in the 1980s, founded the destructive cult al-Qaeda, argued that American civilians could be targeted in his jihadist attacks

The poster child for jihad over the last three decades, Osama bin Laden argued in favor of targeting civilians, despite the opposing viewpoint of most Muslims.

because, in his view, American forces had previously targeted Muslim civilians. This followed the "eye for an eye" rule that is found in the Qur'an.

Many Muslim scholars, however, disagree with this argument, so we have to be careful when it comes to identifying jihad only with Islamic terrorism. Often, jihad is more an excuse for battle than a call to it.

The point of all this is that when cults form, they may find it tempting, after establishing an "us against them" mentality, to take the next step and arm themselves for the final war that is surely coming. Such action can have long-lasting consequences.

> **When cults form, they may find it tempting, after establishing an "us against them" mentality, to take the next step and arm themselves for the final war that is surely coming.**

Take, for instance, the case of Kerry Noble, a leader of a cult called the Covenant, Sword, and the Arm of the Lord (CSA). He planned on starting a revolution because he and his group hated homosexuals, Blacks, and Jews. That's why in 1984—a year that, thanks to the novel of that name by George Orwell, was significant to a lot of cults across the United States—Noble entered a Kansas City church that supported gay men carrying a briefcase full of C-4, which is a highly explosive material. There were about 60 people present, and Noble planned on murdering them all. His plan was to set a timer, walk out the front door, and wait 10 or 15 minutes for the explosion.

The CSA, founded by James Ellison in 1970, grew out of a small survivalist Christian church called Zarephath-Horeb.

Noble had joined in 1977. Ellison believed the end was coming soon, when God would mete out justice to those who opposed him. As it turned out, "those who opposed him" consisted mostly of gays, Blacks, and Jews, according to the cult. The group gradually appropriated the philosophy of Christian Identity, an ideology that followed a convoluted white supremacist theology based on a racist interpretation of the Bible. To prepare for the coming apocalypse, the group began to raise its own food and collect weapons. In 1978 it raised $52,000 to buy weapons of various kinds, and members engaged in paramilitary training on their 224-acre compound in northern Arkansas.

As training intensified, the group changed its name from Zarephath-Horeb to the Covenant, Sword, and the Arm of the Lord, and it attracted the attention of other white extremist groups, such as the Aryan Nations and The Order, who began to train with them. A later federal investigation revealed that CSA members sold weapons and engaged in criminal activity while routinely distributing hate literature. Their plans grew in the process.

One of their members, Gordon Kahl, a North Dakota white supremacist, killed two United States marshals in a February gun battle that took place in 1983. He died during a federal raid a few months later.

In the eyes of his fellow CSA members, that made him a martyr. In retaliation, they planned to assassinate the government officials who had prosecuted Kahl before his death. These included a judge, an attorney, and an FBI agent. The assassinations were never carried out, but members of the group went on a 1983 crime spree in which they set fire to an Arkansas church that hosted a largely gay congregation and to a Jewish center. They also attempted to bomb a natural-gas pipeline.

In short, they began to engage in their own version of jihad, and they used biblical references to justify it. They were convinced that God was on their side just as surely as he was on the side of the Israelites when they entered the Promised Land.

Basically, they became guerrilla fighters. Not good guerrilla fighters—they

A stable plastic explosive that must be detonated by a blast, C-4 packs a lot of punch into a small package.

inflicted only minor damage to the buildings they bombed—but Christian guerrilla fighters just the same.

The day after the attempted pipeline attack, Richard Wayne Snell, one of their number, killed the owner of a pawnshop. Snell believed the man to be Jewish. In 1984, he went on to murder a Black Arkansas state trooper. This led to his capture and prompted Noble's bombing excursion at the gay-affirming church.

But Noble never set off the timer to detonate the C-4 on that fateful day. Something rather miraculous took place instead. As he sat among his supposed enemies, they became real people to him. After a time, he realized he couldn't simply walk away and kill them. He started to think about the consequences of his actions. This would have been, had he carried it out, the largest single terrorist attack of this kind that the United States had yet experienced. The people who he had hated somehow seemed to be, in his words, "no different than anyone else."

He didn't suddenly change his ideas, but he began to think about them.

> **As he sat among his supposed enemies, they became real people to him.**

He had to keep his slowly evolving philosophy to himself, however, because the CSA kept up its activities while exhibiting more and more anger, which was now tinged with frustration at its meager results.

On April 19, 1985, more than 300 federal agents and local police surrounded the CSA compound. They believed that David Tate, a member of The Order, a group closely affiliated with the CSA in both philosophy and practice, was heading there to hide after having shot and killed a state trooper from Missouri.

This marked the first time United States federal authorities had ever confronted a well-armed militia group. The standoff lasted for four days and finally came to an end through negotiation rather than violence.

James Ellison was among those who surrendered. So was Kerry Noble. David Tate, the man who had prompted the whole affair, wasn't among them. He was later arrested in Missouri.

Noble spent the next two years in a federal prison and then six more trying to overcome the effects of mind-control the group had held over him. Eventually, he felt free enough to begin to work with others who had experienced similar cult leanings.

These examples demonstrate how jihad-inspired cult activity from as long as 3,500 years ago were carried out, written down, and eventually codified by religious tradition into what were called "sacred" texts, which were then used by twisted logic to justify the activities of extremists who considered themselves soldiers in the same cause. Tales from Jewish history, for instance, in which God supposedly told the Hebrew people to "utterly destroy [Gentiles] ... as the LORD thy God hath commanded thee" were turned against the descendants of the very people who wrote down and canonized the texts in the first place. Christian "white supremacists," such as James Ellison and Kerry Noble, sought to murder other Christians "in the name of the Lord." Muslim terrorists such as Osama bin Laden sought loopholes in their own Scriptures to justify killing their supposed enemies.

It would seem that extremist cult activity, in its perverted form, has a long, involved history, recorded in the very Scriptures folks hope will bring about peace on earth. It also appears it has a long, long shelf life, as ancient evil deeds inspire modern forms of jihad.

DAVID BERG AND THE FAMILY INTERNATIONAL: FROM TEENS FOR CHRIST TO GROWN-UP CULT

In the final years of the 1960s, a man named David Berg decided to begin a Christian ministry aimed at those who were then called "hippies," who had begun to congregate in Huntington Beach, California. The resultant group, part of the Jesus People movement that was then sweeping through the U.S. hippie communities, became known as Children of God (COG). Various other names would be employed over the years, such as Teens for Christ, the Family of Love, and The Family. But their common denominator was Berg himself.

In 1969 the group left California because Berg was convinced the Lord had revealed to him that there would soon be an earthquake. At that time, they were called the Children of God. Berg's "children" believed that Berg was God's messenger for the end times. He changed his name to Moses David and by 1970 was delivering a series of apocalyptic messages claiming the end was near. Members of the group dressed in sackcloth and conducted demonstrations across the country, declaring that America had abandoned God.

Berg taught his followers that, based on his interpretation of the Bible, they were to carry out a worldwide ministry aimed at redeeming the sin of the world. Full-time missionaries, soon scattered across many countries, were united through correspondence with the head of The Family. These messages were called Mo Letters. They were later published as a periodical called *The New Good News*.

Rumors soon began to circulate about secret activities of the group. What was to become the very first anticult organization in the United States was formed. Calling themselves the Parents' Committee to Free Our Children from the Children of God, also

known as FREECOG, members alleged that the cult was guilty of child abuse and the use of sex in recruiting members to its ranks. This accusation stemmed from an evangelistic technique Berg taught that he called "flirty fishing": he encouraged female members of his following to use sex to entice lonely men into the fold.

Berg soon started feeling pressure from the outside, mostly caused by relatives of his followers who wanted to know what was going on. He ordered a reconfiguration of his organization and changed its name to The Family. At the same time, he encouraged sexual "sharing" among the adults in his group, urging them to cast off worldly taboos against various sexual practices.

River Phoenix is one of a number of noteworthy people who were raised within The Family but later left.

Predictable problems soon arose. During the 1980s, herpes ran rampant among Family members. Even worse, the sexual freedom he preached drew a number of pedophiles to the group, who preyed upon members' children.

> **This accusation stemmed from an evangelistic technique Berg taught that he called "flirty fishing": he encouraged female members of his following to use sex to entice lonely men into the fold.**

By 1983, Berg was forced to rescind his orders. Child protection rules were instituted. In 1987, flirty fishing was discontinued, but the sharing of adult partners within the group continued unabated. During the 1990s, this remained one of The Family's most distinctive and controversial practices, which resulted in a series of raids on the homes of Family members in several countries. Government agencies had become concerned about child welfare. A series of investigations, however, discovered no cases of abuse. The Family had apparently reacted in time to rid itself of this objectionable activity.

In 1994, Berg died, and his wife, Maria, succeeded him as leader of the cult. A year later, she instituted what she called the Love Charter, a constitution that carefully spelled out the rights and responsibilities of all Family members. In 2004, the group again changed its name, this time to the Family International. It now claims it has more than 10,000 members in its ranks and boasts chapters in at least 90 countries. If these figures are correct, it is the largest and most successful communal group to emerge from the 1960s counterculture, hippie, Jesus People movement.

THE WATCHTOWER SOCIETY AND JEHOVAH'S WITNESSES

Are Jehovah's Witnesses a cult? That depends entirely on who you ask. They say they are not, and that even though individuals need proper guidance from God, everyone should do their own thinking.

In 1992, however, the Methodist minister J. Gordon Melton, founding director of the Institute for the Study of American Religion and a distinguished professor of American religious history with the Institute for Studies of Religion at Baylor University in Waco, Texas, placed the Jehovah's Witnesses denomination on his list of established cults.

Jehovah's Witnesses don't stand for the national anthem or salute the American flag—or any flag, for that matter. They don't vote in elections or serve in the military. They believe their allegiance belongs only to God and that their actual government is in heaven.

This sounds suspicious to many fundamentalist or even mainstream Christian folks, who tend to think anyone with Christian beliefs that differ from their own must be a member of a cult. Besides that, they are suspicious of anyone who goes door to door to promote a religion, unless it is *their* religion.

Practically synonymous with door-to-door evangelism, Jehovah's Witnesses have been hitting the streets with pamphlets since their earliest days in the late 1800s.

So, who are these people who claim to be doing the work of the Lord? We probably should start with most obvious connection most folks have with the Jehovah's Witnesses.

The Fuller Brush man doesn't travel door to door anymore, and vacuum cleaners are sold in stores these days. But door by door, one visit at a time, Jehovah's Witnesses quietly go about the business of what is probably the most audacious grassroots marketing campaign in history. In short, they are trying to reach, one at a time, more than seven billion people with their message.

In June 2002 the Supreme Court of the United States ruled that, irrespective of local bylaws, the Jehovah's Witnesses have the right to ring every doorbell in the country. Their organizational structure is superb, their dedication inspiring. Two by two, well-dressed, polite laypeople who believe in their cause are out to speak personally with every soul in the world.

> **In June 2002 the Supreme Court of the United States ruled that, irrespective of local bylaws, the Jehovah's Witnesses have the right to ring every doorbell in the country.**

There are over eight million Witnesses in the world right now, although their numbers are declining by about 70,000, or roughly 1 percent of the total, every year. They spend an average of 189 hours per person per year getting the word out. During the COVID-19 pandemic they switched their methods more to mailing or passing out literature at populated places, such as shopping plazas. Each member fills out a form documenting every house visited, with standard notations such as NH for "Not Home."

These numbers tell a story. Through all kinds of weather, enduring vicious dogs, verbal abuse, and friendly, if evasive, chit-chat, they believe they have a story to tell and go about the business of telling it. They convert some people and irritate others. They are the brunt of jokes and slander, but they keep at their business.

Their title comes from a biblical name for God, specifically from the Hebrew Scriptures, which Christians call the Old Testament. When you approach the Witnesses to find out what they are about, they will attempt to channel you into a home Bible study, where you can be introduced to God.

God has a name, just like anyone else. And if you want to get to know God, you ought to first know his name, they will tell you. It's in the Bible, and it is spelled YHVH. That's a little hard to enunciate. No one now living knows how it was pronounced, so we have to go with our best guess.

Historically, the vowels used to make the name pronounceable are "a," "o," and "e." That makes it *Yahoveh*. But the Hebrew letter that corresponds to the English "Y" becomes "J," and somewhere along the line the original "a" morphed into the English "e." The final "e" began to be spelled with an "a."

So, meet Jehovah. Whenever the words "THE LORD" appear in English-language Bibles, it's a translation of YHVH. Christian academics coined the spelling "Jehovah" long ago.

In the ninth chapter of the Gospel according to Luke, Jesus sent the disciples out into every town to preach the Gospel and be witnesses to the power of God. The order was never rescinded, so Jehovah's Witnesses believe they are simply doing what Jesus asked of his followers. They are "Witnesses" of "Jehovah." "Ye are my witnesses, saith Jehovah." Hence the name.

> **"Ye are my witnesses, saith Jehovah."**
> **Hence the name.**

But they have been called by many other names since their movement began shortly before 1872, when their founder, Charles Russell, began meeting with a small group of Christian believers to examine the Scriptures "relative to the coming of Christ and kingdom." They have been known as Millennial Dawnists, International Bible Students, members of the Watchtower Bible and Tract Society, Russellites, and sometimes Rutherfordites.

It all began when Russell, a Congregationalist by religion and haberdasher by trade, "stumbled across," in his words, an Adventist preacher who sparked his wavering faith. In 1879, Russell published his first book, *Food for Thinking Christians: Why Evil Was Permitted and Kindred Topics*. By 1884, his adherents had formed a movement called the Zion's Watchtower Society. The name came from the third chapter of the book of Ezekiel. God warned the prophet that he was to be "as on a watchtower." If the enemy came and the watcher didn't warn the people, their blood would be on the hands of the watcher. But if the people were warned and didn't listen, the fault would be on their own heads.

Russell traveled incessantly, and he published a constant stream of pamphlets to help his followers. Like so many before him, he tried to figure out dates for the return of Christ. The year he decided on was 1914. That was when "the full establishment of the Kingdom of God would be established."

The year came and went without the coming of Christ. But upon reexamining Scripture, Russell concluded that the date was right; it was only the interpretation of how the kingdom would come that was wrong. The year 1914 was when Christ returned "in Spirit," a prelude to the physical return. Armageddon would still take place, but not before those who responded to the call of the Spirit witnessed to the truth. They became the "watchers" on the wall, warning the people of what was to come.

Charles Russell, founder of the Jehovah's Witnesses movement, instructed his believers to consider themselves personally responsible for saving the souls of the unenlightened, with a biblical foundation for the Witnesses' unique brand of prosetylization.

Some religious scholars and secular historians have noted that 1914, the year World War I began, was indeed a year that changed the world. Jesus warned of "wars and rumors of wars" in Matthew 18. They would come "before the time of the end." So Russell died believing he had got it right, but not before he gathered a host of scandals around him. They involved divorce and the attempted sale of what he called "miracle wheat."

Russell died in 1917, and after a severe struggle among the 15,000 adherents, Joseph Franklin Rutherford, a judge in Missouri, assumed command. Under the popular slogan "Millions now living will never die," the society rebounded from the rumors of Russell's scandals. It was Rutherford who, in 1931, coined the term Jehovah's Witnesses and provided the witnesses with phonographs so they could play records of the judge's comments when they made their house calls. By 1942, when the judge died, a board of directors was appointed to lead the organization. The cult of personality disappeared, along with the phonographs. Now the Witnesses entered into their greatest period of growth and, with no single visible leader, began to shake the reputation of being a cult.

The original message was very definitely aimed at those who were considered to be "culturally deprived." Satan's power, they said, is wielded through "the religious, commercial and political combine." These are forces that oppress the righteous. One power structure does the bidding of the other in an evil conspiracy to defeat the righteous. Churches and religious organizations are "tools of Satan." Some ministers, they say, are probably well meaning, but duped. Others, backed by entrenched political forces, are out to steal the cash of their innocent congregations.

Jehovah's Witnesses have become famous for a few of the doctrines they espouse. Genesis 9:3 warns people not to "eat meat that has life blood in it," so many of them are vegetarians. And Leviticus 17:14 says "the life of any creature is in the blood," so they refuse blood transfusions as well. They are forbidden to take part in ecumenical dialogues or events, so they are often criticized for believing their religion is the only correct one. Of course, many other Christian believers follow along the same lines. They believe Jesus Christ is God's son, the "first created" of all things, and so inferior to God. But he will return to Earth to rule.

So the Witnesses are issuing the warning. Some people are hearing the message, and the Witnesses believe it won't be long until Christ returns and the world will be restored. A total of 144,000 of them (the number comes from Revelation 14) will someday go to heaven, but the vast majority of the faithful, "a great multitude," will remain on earth to live life the way it's supposed to be lived. "The wolf will lie down with the lamb ... they shall not hurt nor destroy" in all the earth (Isaiah 11).

Until then, Jehovah has his witnesses. They are passing out their magazine, *The Watchtower*. They offer books and lessons free of charge. They are dedicated, polite, and motivated. But are they a cult?

Some Christians insist that they are, but it's hard to defend that position based on the definition of "cult" that we are following in this study. Yes, their teachings stress strict separation from secular government. But they are law-abiding people who believe that governments are established by God to maintain peace and order. They don't celebrate birthdays, but the older I get, the less I celebrate them, too. They, however, differ from me in that they believe that such celebrations displease God. They don't celebrate Christmas or Easter, because they believe that these festivals are contaminated by pagan customs and religions. But Jews don't celebrate those particular holidays either. And the truth is that the Witnesses are correct in recognizing the pagan customs in Christian holidays.

So the fact that some people refer to the Watchtower Society and Jehovah's Witnesses as a cult probably reflects more of a bias toward the accuser than the Witnesses themselves. As is the case with many major religions, they may have started out that way. But time has a tendency to mellow us all.

WESTBORO BAPTIST CHURCH

What's going on at the Westboro Baptist Church (WBC) in Topeka, Kansas?

Most churches have signs out front that welcome visitors. Westboro's is apt to remind passersby that "God hates fags and proud sinners."

Most churches advertise their denominational standing. WBC is a Baptist church that is not affiliated with any Baptist denomination, having been denounced by the Baptist World Alliance, the Southern Baptist Convention, and other mainstream Baptist denominations.

Most churches honor military veterans with religious ceremonies. In 2005, WBC members traveled around the country to picket the funerals of U.S. soldiers killed in Iraq and Afghanistan while carrying signs that proclaimed "God Hates the U.S." and "Thank God for Dead Soldiers." Things have gotten so bad that the church has been labeled a hate group and is monitored by the Anti-Defamation League and Southern Poverty Law Center.

Many churches sponsor vigils to reflect on national tragedies. The WBC condoned the terrorist attacks of September 11, 2001, and celebrated the mass shooting at an elementary school in Newtown, Connecticut, in 2012, calling it "God's retribution for sin."

So, we return to the question: What's going on at the Westboro Baptist Church in Topeka, Kansas?

Members of the Westboro Baptist Church demonstrate at the Virginia Holocaust Museum on March 2, 2010. The church is known for its hatred of Jews, Muslims, LGBTQ people, and military veterans, among others.

The church was founded in 1955 by Fred Waldron Phelps (1929–2014). It was an offshoot of the East Side Baptist Church of Topeka, which began in 1931 and selected Phelps as its associate pastor in 1954. He was then put in charge of the new extension, Westboro Baptist Church, and served as its pastor until his death in March of 2014.

Once on his own in the new church across town, Phelps immediately broke off from the East Side Church and began his practice of hate-filled sermons and outlandish, offensive public displays. Most of the original congregation got fed up and left to join other Topeka churches.

WBC was never a large church. Most of its membership of less than a hundred people consisted of Phelps's extended family, including some of his 13 children. Because of its terrible reputation in Christian circles, young members rarely dated outside of the church. If they wanted to have any kind of a social life, they usually left. But its impact on the American religious scene was disproportionate to its size. Some former members accused the church of being a cult and brainwashing its members.

Phelps certainly engaged in practices most pastors shy away from. Besides the public hate speech, in 1964 Phelps started a law firm, which went on to sue communities that were targets of Westboro's protests. That's not typically something most Christian pastors engage in.

> **WBC was never a large church. Most of its membership of less than a hundred people consisted of Phelps's extended family, including some of his 13 children.**

Phelps described his church, in his words, as an "Old School Primitive Baptist Church." Primitive Baptist churches are independent. They are unaffiliated with any organized denomination, so they have no liturgical body to keep them within prescribed theological or social parameters. From the beginning, it claimed to follow a strict interpretation of the Calvinist principles that are held by many mainline churches. These include salvation by grace alone, predestination, the sufficiency of the Bible for Christian instruction, and principles common to most traditional churches, such as Presbyterians and Congregationalists, in the Protestant Reformed tradition.

What made WBC unique was the unhealthy dose of obnoxious, public hate that, however offensive it became, was upheld in 2011 by the U.S. Supreme Court as free speech on "matters of public concern." Even so, however, a few state legislatures responded to WBC members' picketing by establishing funeral buffer zones that prohibited protest activity inside a certain area. Canada and the United Kingdom went even further. They barred members of the church from entering their countries.

How did this happen? When did the hate begin?

We will never get inside the head of Fred Waldron Phelps, but we know that everything came out into the open in 1989.

That was the year WBC began protesting homosexuality in a very public way. According to sources familiar with the church, Phelps and his church discovered what they called a "tearoom." It was a public lavatory they believed was being used for homosexual liaisons.

By 1991, not satisfied with the support they were receiving for broadcasting this news, they began to picket in a place called Gage Park, a few blocks from the church. They believed Gage Park to be "a den of anonymous homosexual activity." The protests spread across the city. Within a matter of only three years, the church took its show on the road and began to stage public demonstrations across the country. When protests against the protests grew, Phelps declared that all the negative press coverage was proof of his righteousness. This led him to escalate his endeavors. He began to hold public, press-covered protests against Jews, Mormons, and Catholics, in addition to continuing the protests at military funerals and celebrity events. Often WBS members went out of their way to offend by incorporating deliberately inflammatory statements on their signs and flying the American flag upside down.

On August 20, 1995, a pipe bomb exploded outside the home of Shirley Phelps-Roper, Fred Phelps's daughter. Although

Westboro Baptist Church in Topeka, Kansas

no one was injured, the blast damaged an SUV, a fence, and part of the house. A year later two men were arrested for the bombing, and both admitted to causing the blast. During the trial, they admitted that they had believed Phelps-Roper's house was that of the pastor. They wanted to retaliate against Westboro's anti-gay protests at Washburn University. One of the bombers was fined $1,751 and sentenced to 16 days in prison plus 100 hours of community service. Phelps was outraged at the leniency he believed had been shown the bombers, and he vowed to escalate his endeavors.

In 1998 his cause went viral. The church picketed the funeral of Matthew Shepard, a gay college student from Wyoming, whose beating, torture, and murder were widely condemned as a hate crime.

Fred Phelps died in March of 2014. Many believed the church would fall apart after that since his presence seemed to be the glue that held the whole thing together. But it didn't happen. Although not nearly as active in the public eye, WBC continues on. Only after his death did it become public knowledge that Phelps had been voted out of his leadership position and that there was no defined pastor of the church. Shirley, his daughter, simply said that a public funeral would not be held "because Westboro does not worship the dead."

After Phelps's death, with no clearly designated leader, the church began to fade from public view, or at least public concern. A cult usually needs a designated person at the top, and WBC no longer had one.

Was it a cult during its heyday? Ex-members called it that. They raised complaints such as brainwashing and coercion. There was a clearly defined leader who was vocal and public, to say nothing of offensive and deliberately hateful, under the guise of religion. Members believed the end of the world was coming and sought to emphasize their belief system while there was still time. They kept a lot of secrets.

Once again, we are left with an American phenomenon that rose to prominence, had its day in the sun, and then, in the manner of many cults, largely faded into the mists of time.

JANE WHALEY, THE WORD OF FAITH FELLOWSHIP, AND THE GOSPEL OF PROSPERITY

On any given Sunday morning, if you decide to worship at the Word of Faith Fellowship church in Rutherford County, North Carolina, you will experience a typical charismatic church service. There will be loud and boisterous music. People will speak in tongues, dance, and hop around, under the influence of the Holy Spirit. The pastor, 83-year-old Jane Whaley, declares that "God has freed us to be loud."

Whaley has been the pastor of the church since its beginning, in 1979, when she and her husband, Sam, bought a steakhouse and converted it to a chapel. She was a math teacher at the time. The church grew to more than 750 members and then exploded when it began ministries in Brazil, Ghana, Scotland, Sweden, and a few other countries. Soon the membership listed more than 2,000 members.

Being a teacher married to a car dealer, Whaley had no formal training as a minister. But she certainly had gifts as a speaker and leader. The church now occupies a complex of some 35 acres. It boasts tight security, thanks to all the publicity it accrued.

The Word of Faith Fellowship will introduce new members to their long list of new no-nos.

If you decide to join the church after attending one of its services, you will be made aware of a few rules. Here are your instructions. You will have to give up:

◆ Alcohol, including beer, wine, and liquor, along with root beer and ginger ale. This includes alcohol used in cooking. It also means not dining in restaurants that serve alcohol.

◆ Cigarettes.

◆ The wearing of cargo pants, anything that has a Nike logo, and black tennis shoes.

Besides these, there are a few more general rules:

◆ You will be told not to decorate your house unless Jane or her helper can advise you, and not to buy or sell a car or truck without first checking with Sam.

◆ If you are a male of African descent, you will not be allowed to shave your head. Likewise, men, don't grow a beard or mustache.

◆ Don't start a relationship or, heaven forbid, decide to get married without checking it out with the pastor. Along those same lines, don't have a conversation with someone with whom you might form a relationship without someone listening who can "guard the conversation."

◆ Both men and women who go swimming must wear a T-shirt.

How did Jane get her start as a pastor? Well, that's quite a story.

Jane Whaley was born Jane Brock in 1939. She grew up nurtured by a Baptist church in North Carolina. In high school, she competed on the swim team and played soccer. Eventually, she graduated from Appalachian State University and got a job teaching high school math. She then met Sam Whaley, got married, and had a daughter named Robin.

So far, she seemed to have lived a fairly normal life. But then things changed.

By the 1980s, Sam was a staff preacher at the Rhema Bible Training College in Tulsa, Oklahoma. In the course of his job, Sam had the opportunity to travel around the world, preaching the same "prosperity gospel" that was to lead to such excesses at *The PTL Club* under Jim and Tammy Bakker and is still a main component in the ministries of megachurch celebrities such as Kenneth Copeland, Benny Hinn, and Joel Osteen. The message is simple. If you pray long and loud enough and give some "seed money" to your pastors, God, who wants you to be rich, will answer your prayers. All you have to do is, as the preachers say, "name it and claim it."

With Sam gone much of the time, Jane kept the home fires burning while leading church services and holding rallies of "deliverance" that were not sanctioned by the Rhema ministries. Kenneth Hagin, a Pentecostal preacher who had by that time developed quite a following as the founder and leader of the Word of Faith movement, a worldwide Christian movement teaching that Christians can access the power of faith through speech, was associated with Rhema ministries and did not approve of what Jane was doing. He ordered Sam to leave the church, so Sam and Jane moved back to North Carolina.

Now that she was no longer under the umbrella of Hagin's ministries, Jane felt free to preach her own version of the prosperity gospel. At this time, Sam felt God spoke to him saying, "Jane is the pastor," so she moved into the forefront. Sam had already developed the reputation of being a likable guy, friendly and always ready to laugh. He was, after all, a used car salesman. So he was ready and willing to move into the back seat and let Jane drive. This she was ready to do, since she felt Sam read his Bible too much. She didn't want to operate under that kind of restriction.

Through visits to Brazilian churches, Jane met a Baptist missionary named John Martin. He had started Ministerio Verbo Vivo (Live Word), near Belo Horizonte. Apparently, Jane and Sam visited Martin's church in 1986. Two years later, the small but growing group joined with Solange Granieri and Juarez De Souza Oliveira and began the Ministerio Evangelico Comunidade Rhema (Rhema Community Evangelical Ministry) in Franco da Rocha. They now had an authentic, international influence.

> **Some members were forced to sit in what was called a "prayer chair" while members circled them and shouted out prayers to remove demons.**

Meanwhile, back at home, troubles began. Many of them are outlined in a book called *Broken Faith: Inside the Word of Faith Fellowship, One of America's Most Dangerous Cults* by Pulitzer Prize winner Mitch Weiss and Holbrook Mohr. They spent a lot of time interviewing hundreds of people who have had connections to the church over the years and provided secret recordings, videos, and documents that outlined many behind-the-scenes events that would not have been apparent to people who simply attended the church services.

According to them, the church was investigated for child abuse in the 1990s. More than 40 former members had notified the Forest City *Daily Courier* and other news outlets about what they believed had happened. No charges were filed.

In 1995, several former members alleged to the TV show *Inside Edition* that beatings to remove a "destructive spirit" had occurred on numerous occasions. Some members were forced to sit in what was called a "prayer chair" while members circled them and shouted out prayers to remove demons. Both Jane and Sam denied the accusations.

In 2000, a woman testifying in a child custody case said her one-year-old son was subjected to such "blasting" for hours. She also reported that her son had been beaten enough to cause bruises. When asked about the charges, Jane Whaley testified that God had ordained that children should be beaten. It was what the Bible meant, she claimed, by "spare the rod and spoil the child."

More charges followed, some alleging other instances of abuses from fraud to human trafficking.

In 2011, Michael Lowry claimed to have been beaten and held prisoner by the church in an attempt to drive out his "gay demons." He testified before a grand jury, but in 2013 he rejoined the church and recanted his statement. Later Lowry again left the church and now says he stands by his earlier testimony.

Five people charged with assaulting a former member of the church told stories of a member being beaten to expel "demons of homosexuality" in 2013. Again, no convictions.

A number of church critics and former members have testified that Jane Whaley is

The Word of Faith Fellowship's reputation has long been tarnished by allegations of widespread abuse against members of all ages.

the leader of a cult, but so far, she has only once been convicted of wrongdoing. She was found guilty of a misdemeanor assault in 2004 as a result of an incident that had happened two years earlier. Former member Lacy Wien described "blasting" by a group of members, followed by an assault by Whaley. Wien sued the church for $2.5 million, but after five years of appeals, the conviction was overturned.

Perhaps the harshest treatment of anyone by the church is alleged to have been meted out to former member Jamey Anderson. He claims to have been sent frequently to a storage area called the green room as a child. There, he was, in the words of another former member, "brutally paddled." His accusers were other children, who were encouraged to report such incidents.

According to Anderson, when his grandfather died, he was not allowed to attend the funeral. He also left out of the obituary. He was forced to work, and in 2002 he was punished along with four other boys by being put in a room during school hours and forced to watch videos of Jane Whaley. Outside of school he was restricted to his home.

After finally leaving the church, his family members who remained were denied any contact with him. Whaley's attorney, of course, denied the allegations.

> She had everybody inform on each other.
> And ... she would have them tell her their
> deepest, darkest secrets. And then she kept
> a file of those secrets.

Anderson's mother and grandmother have stated Jamey was not abused and that "they have always deeply loved Jamey," even though he is "spreading lies to paint a horrible picture about his loving family."

NPR reporter Rachel Martin conducted an interview with Mitch Weiss and Holbrook Mohr after the publication of their book, in which Mohr described how a so-called "normal" church could seemingly go so far off the rails. After accusing a sheriff, a district attorney, and a lot of other people of "looking the other way" and "just not doing their job," Mohr expressed surprise that such things could happen. He also detailed the treacherous slippery slope that has caused the ruin of so many cult leaders:

> I think that in the beginning, when people would go to the church, they were shown a lot of love. You know, the members of this church, they live in nice homes. They drive nice cars. The children are well-mannered. They have a Christian school. So I think when a lot of families first go there, everything seems great. But over time, Jane Whaley and her other ministers, they take more and more control of your lives. In fact, a lot of times they'll remove children from their family's home and place them with ministers to be raised. And what that does is over time, sometimes those kids care more about the ministers than their own parents. So it makes it difficult for families to leave. So it's not a quick thing where you just walk in the door and they say, hey, come on in. You can come in and you can never leave. We're gonna take your television, magazines, radio, all that away from you and institute all these rules. It's a slow, progressive thing.

Weiss contributed his own interpretation on how the system progresses:

> You have to realize they believe that Jane Whaley was a prophet, that God spoke to her and everything she said was the gospel. And one of the techniques that she used was that she had everybody inform on each other. And ... she would have them tell her their deepest, darkest secrets. And then she kept a file of those secrets. And if they threatened to leave or did something wrong, she had all the evidence she needed there to keep them in line....
>
> It was something that really got worse over time. And you have to understand what her philosophy is. The doctrine is really pretty simple—devils are real. And if you're a drug addict, it's because you have this drug devil. If, you know, you're an alcoholic—the same. If you're having an affair, it's the same thing. There are

lustful devils. And so what she would do is it was called Devils in Deliverance, where they would have people surround you and scream at you to get the devils out. Get out, devil. And it would go on and on and on. Perfect example is with a baby. If babies cried, it wasn't because they were hungry or they had a dirty diaper. It was because there was a devil inside them that was making them cry. So you would have groups of people surrounding an infant and screaming until that baby would just get tired and finally, you know, go to sleep....

> **If babies cried, it wasn't because they were hungry or they had a dirty diaper. It was because there was a devil inside them that was making them cry.**

And that's how she started at the beginning with her congregants. Over time, it became more and more violent. It wasn't enough just to scream, to scare the devils out of people. Now you had to punch people. You had to hold them down and restrain them. You had to choke them. You had to do everything possible to get rid of that devil. And that's when it became extremely violent. That's where the people who've recounted their stories would break down to us. They would tell us about their injuries. And they couldn't go to doctors. They couldn't be treated because they knew what would happen. So they had to keep it secret. But it's those beatings that [are] really still seared into their brains now. They can't get rid of those images, those nightmares.

In April of 2020, in the midst of a worldwide pandemic, an attorney for the church confirmed three members had died of COVID-19 and that it was not known how many had the virus. The church claimed to be "100-percent compliant" in terms of following federal guidelines. But because the county in which the church was located had a high number of cases with respect to the population, some local people blamed the church. Subsequently, the church claimed they had begun to receive threats of violence.

The Associated Press began its own investigation after reports of abuse began to reach a national audience. Reporters conducted interviews with 43 former members and reported stories of physical abuse, injuries that were not treated, families that were separated, and some male members of the church being held prisoner in a storage building for as long as a year.

It was quite common for members to testify that they were afraid to leave the church or even to oppose Whaley because they feared public reprimand, or worse. Children at the church's school were allegedly beaten for minor offenses, sometimes by other children.

According to reports, the church considered all afflictions to be caused by the devil, giving members the commandment to participate in the cure by increasingly violent means.

The investigation included documentation and recordings of Whaley that were made without her knowledge. She denied all claims and defended some of her actions, either by quoting the Bible or the First Amendment of the Constitution. She refused to be interviewed for the Associated Press investigation and claimed that the former members were lying.

And so it goes. The Word of Faith Fellowship still thrives, although a number of critics and former members have described the church as a cult and accused the church of abuse. All accusations are disputed by current members and church officials, and nothing has stuck in a court of law. Current members claim that through prayer, fellowship, Biblical teaching, and an encouraging community, lives are still being changed.

And maybe they are. But the question remains, in what way?

DAVID KORESH AND THE BRANCH DAVIDIANS

In this section we've been studying cults that were offshoots of traditional Christian denominations. Branch Davidians are actually the offshoot of an offshoot.

The story begins in the nineteenth century with Ellen White (1827–1915) and the beginnings of Seventh-day Adventism. White, along with her husband, James, and Joseph Bates, were the founders of the church. Her introduction into spirituality began when she suffered a disfiguring accident at the age of nine. This set her apart, and when she was 17, she began to experience a series of some 2,000 recorded dreams and visions that lasted for the rest of her life. She believed they came from God. Some were very brief, lasting only a minute or so. Others stayed with her for four hours or more. She began to write down what she had experienced and, in the process, became one of the most prolific women writers America has ever seen. Her topics ranged from religion to nutrition.

A small group of followers who accepted her revelations grew up around the three founders, and the group soon emerged as the Seventh-day Adventist Church. The church was very similar to most Protestant churches in terms of doctrine. There were only four areas that separated them.

The first was their respect for White's writings. They are accepted as divinely inspired, but not on the same level as the Bible. They are not a substitute for Scripture but an addition.

A second difference lies in the Adventists' understanding of what is called the Heavenly Sanctuary. The New Testament book

of Hebrews describes a heavenly sanctuary in which Jesus reigns as high priest. Most Christian theologians interpret that as a metaphor. Adventists believe it represents an actual tabernacle or sanctuary that exists in heaven as a reality that will one day be brought to earth. It is a real place in which Jesus, as high priest, provides cleansing for human sins by the sacrificial shedding of his blood.

The third Adventist belief leads us to one of the names by which Adventists became known—that of the "seventh day." Adventists believe that God's commandment to the Jews to keep the seventh day, the Sabbath day, holy was never rescinded.

Ellen White's writings would come to distinguish Seventh-day Adventists from adjacent denominations.

For them, Saturday, not Sunday, remains the Sabbath day ordered from heaven.

The final theological difference is the one that will eventually lead to the Branch Davidians, and it is also found in the name Seventh-day Adventist. "Adventist" refers to the imminent return of Jesus Christ—his advent, or second coming to earth.

Thus was born the Seventh-day Adventist Church, which is still very active today.

In 1918, the Bulgarian Victor T. Houteff (1885–1955) removed himself from the Bulgarian Orthodox Church and adopted Adventism. He became a teacher in Sabbath classes in his Los Angeles church and began publishing a series of tracts called *The Shepherd's Rod*. He enthusiastically embraced Adventist teaching, but when he attended the church's annual meeting in 1929, he criticized what he called worldly tendencies that he thought were growing in the denomination. Like all Adventists, he looked forward to the return of Jesus Christ. This is, after all, one of the central beliefs of the movement. But Houteff believed that the messiah prophesied in the book of Isaiah was not embodied in the historical Jesus. He believed that personage was yet to come. He believed 144,000 followers on earth would form a truly reformed and cleansed church. The number comes from the book of Revelation. Jesus would not return, Houteff taught, until this group had formed and had done the requisite preparations.

His message was rejected by the gathered Adventists at the 1929 convention, so Houteff left the meeting, and in 1935 he established his own group of 37 members at a site located about two miles away from Waco, Texas. They called it Mount Carmel.

By 1940, despite the Great Depression, the group was flourishing. They had established a quasi commune in which everyone worked, farmed, and built together. But because there was not enough income for the whole group, some traveled to nearby Waco to secure employment. At this time the organization consisted of 64 residents and 10 buildings on 375 acres. They had constructed water and sewage systems and installed electricity and telephone services.

Houteff was now recognized as a prophet, and he exercised full authority over the community. His followers believed that he, and he alone, could unravel the biblical texts that predicted the second coming of Jesus. In 1942, he renamed the group the General Association of Davidian Seventh-day Adventists. "Davidian" indicated his belief that the group was returning to the Davidic Kingdom of Israel that had to be established before Jesus would return.

They worshipped on Saturday, practiced vegetarianism, and observed strict rules of conduct, which meant no tobacco, no dancing, and no movies. Women used no cosmetics and wore distinctive long dresses. The group even built its own printing press to publish Houteff's books and Bible tracts. Through this process, scattered pockets of Adventists throughout the United States were able to identify with them.

Finally, in order to achieve conscientious-objector status for his followers, Houteff changed the name of the group once more to Davidian Seventh-day Adventists. This tied them, in name if not in fact, to the already recognized Seventh-day Adventist Church, who were regularly given conscientious-objector status.

Houteff died in 1955, but his wife, Florence, continued in leadership. The city of Waco, however, had grown too much for them and was closing in on Mount Carmel, offering its big-city brand of temptations. So in 1957 the group sold its property and bought a 941-acre farm nine miles east of Waco, which they called New Mount Carmel.

Believing fervently that the kingdom of God was drawing nigh, they sent out invitations to gather at New Mount Carmel before April 22, 1959, which was Passover. Some 900 people from California, Wyoming, Canada, and other places far and wide sold their businesses, farms, and houses, moved to New Mount Carmel, and waited for a sign from heaven that the end was near. The meetings began on April 18, and by April 22, hope reached a fever pitch.

But nothing happened. God's kingdom didn't come down to earth. The Davidians began to swallow their disappointment and

> **But nothing happened. God's kingdom didn't come down to earth.**

disperse back to their former lives. They sold all but a 77-acre parcel of land from the New Mount Carmel acreage. Some congregants, defying the commandments of the Bible not to sue other Christians, even took the Davidians to court.

This was when a young Davidian named Vernon Howell (1959–1993), who was to become famous as David Koresh, took over. He believed he was the promised messiah that Houteff had predicted would come to earth.

Being a messiah had its perks. His new group, now called Branch Davidians, were ordered to practice celibacy. But not Koresh. He was the only one permitted to procreate. And he went forth and multiplied. At one point he had at least 20 wives. The word was that he "knew" them all, and often.

But the work of a messiah is never done. While the rest of the group labored, Koresh studied. His focus of concentration was on the complicated passage from Revelation, the last book of the Bible, that speaks of the mysterious seven seals being broken before the return of Jesus. The seals are said to bind up a scroll that was seen by John of Patmos in a vision. When the seals are opened, the document will be released, and Jesus will return in a blaze of glory, known as the Apocalypse.

Because Koresh was the messiah, he believed he held the key to opening the scroll and releasing fire, blood, and thunder upon the earth. God told him, he assured his followers, that the end was near, and they were doing the work of heaven.

In 1993, it all came to a head. The Bureau of Alcohol, Tobacco, and Firearms (ATF) had evidence that the group was stockpiling illegal weapons in its compound. Arrest warrants were issued for Koresh as well as a select few of the group's members. But when the ATF attempted to serve the warrants, a gunfight broke out, resulting in the deaths of four government agents and six Branch Davidians. The Federal Bureau of Investigation (FBI) surrounded the compound and initiated what was to become a siege that lasted for 51 days.

This mug shot of Vernon Howell, who later became famous as David Koresh, was taken in 1987.

During the standoff, Koresh tried to negotiate with both the FBI and the ATF. He told them he was working on a manuscript that interpreted the now-infamous biblical passage about the opening of the seven seals. When he was finished, he said, the Branch Davidians would surrender.

> **The FBI surrounded the compound and initiated what was to become a siege that lasted for 51 days.**

The FBI, however, would have none of that. Agents employed siege tactics involving closing off all supply lines while blasting loud rock music toward the compound all day and all night to prevent those inside from sleeping, thereby reducing their resistance through fatigue. They shone huge spotlights all night long. What they didn't realize was that they were duplicating exactly the kind of condition Koresh had warned marked the coming of the end, as described in Revelation:

When he opened the seventh seal, there was silence in heaven for about half an hour. And I saw the seven angels who stand before God, and seven trumpets were given to them. Another angel, who had a golden censer, came and stood at the altar. He was given much incense to offer, with the prayers of all God's people, on the golden altar in front of the throne. The smoke of the incense, together with the prayers of God's people, went up before God from the angel's hand. Then the angel took the censer, filled it with fire from the altar, and hurled it on the earth; and there came peals of thunder, rumblings, flashes of lightning and an earthquake.

Then the seven angels who had the seven trumpets prepared to sound them. The first angel sounded his trumpet, and there came hail and fire mixed with blood, and it was hurled down on the earth. A third of the earth was burned up, a third of the trees were burned up, and all the green grass was burned up. The second angel sounded his trumpet, and something like a huge mountain, all ablaze, was thrown into the sea. A third of the sea turned into blood, a third of the living creatures in the sea died, and a third of the ships were destroyed. The third angel sounded his trumpet, and a great star, blazing like a torch, fell from the sky on a third of the rivers and on the springs of water—the name of the star is Wormwood. A third of the waters turned bitter, and many people died from the waters that had become bitter. The fourth angel sounded his trumpet, and a third of the sun was struck, a third of the moon, and a third of the stars, so that a third of them turned dark. A third of the day was without light, and also a third of the night.

As I watched, I heard an eagle that was flying in midair call out in a loud voice: "Woe! Woe! Woe to the inhabitants of the earth, because of the trumpet blasts about to be sounded by the other three angels!" (Rev. 8:1–13)

Koresh had warned of the tumultuous signs of the end times. Now they were coming to pass, duplicated through the inept methods of law enforcement people who knew nothing about these scriptural texts.

Before Koresh could finish his work, authorities raided the house. Ruth Riddle, one of the Branch Davidians, managed to escape with a copy of the manuscript's first installments. *Newsweek* magazine later acquired a copy and revealed that Koresh had reinforced his belief that he was the Lamb of God and had been born to usher in the Apocalypse.

The FBI considered Koresh extremely unstable, but *Newsweek* reported that "two religious scholars, who won Koresh's trust during the standoff, analyzed the manuscript, and determined that far from the ravings of a madman, it is a serious exegesis, carefully organized and reasoned."

Eventually, on April 19, 1993, the FBI launched an assault and initiated a tear gas attack to force the Branch Davidians out of the compound. New Mount Carmel Center became fully engulfed in flames. Seventy-six Branch Davidians, including 25 children and two pregnant women, died in the conflagration, as did David Koresh.

A propane tank explodes at Mount Carmel, the Branch Davidian compound in Waco, Texas, on April 19, 1993, ending the FBI's siege of the compound.

The event was called "the Waco Siege" by some, "the Waco Massacre" by others. It was carried out by the United States government, not local authorities, and remains a disputed act to this very day, with strong opinions by historians on both sides of the issue.

One particular sticking point revolves around what started the fire. In 2000, an internal Justice Department investigation concluded that incendiary tear gas canisters were used by the FBI but that sect members had started the fire. A panel of arson investigators concluded that the Davidians were responsible for igniting it simultaneously in at least three different areas of the compound. But others disputed the report, claiming it was biased.

Unfortunately, Waco wasn't the only such incident like this. A law enforcement siege at Ruby Ridge in August 1992, less than a year before the Waco incident, has been cited by commentators as a catalyst for the Oklahoma City bombing on April 19, 1995, by Timothy McVeigh and Terry Nichols, as well as the modern-day American militia movement and a rise in opposition to firearm regulation.

Once again, we have to face the fact that history never comes wrapped in a neat package. There are no easy answers, despite the views of armchair commentators who read a few news reports and draw an opinion before they head off to a quiet and secure dinner.

Religion moves people to experience deep emotions. Sometimes people are genuinely motivated by spiritual feelings, even if they are misguided. Sometimes power-hungry leaders seek to bilk their followers out of their possessions and their freedoms. Sometimes they come to really believe their own message. Sometimes even *they* know they are fraudulent.

We cannot lump what we believe to be cults together and issue a blanket opinion. We have to judge cults one at a time. And they aren't always led by religious nutcases. Sometimes cults can hide in plain sight. They may not be religious in nature at all but simply employ the same control techniques developed by unscrupulous, or even well-meaning, enthusiasts. Who knows? You may even be surprised to discover a cult right in your own backyard.

SCIENCE, POLITICS, ECONOMICS, AND METAPHYSICS: A TRICKY LINK

When most of us think of the word "cult," we almost automatically associate the term with religion. The words "religious cult" seem to go together. But are there other sorts of cults? Can the word be applied to other areas of experience?

Remember the description we began with back in the introduction:

- ◆ Cults don't always have bad intentions, but the ones we are going to study, for the most part, do.

- ◆ Cults begin with a founder who is at least narcissistic and usually psychopathic.

- ◆ Cults develop a top-down hierarchy.

- ◆ Cults tend to separate followers from the world that exists outside the group.

- ◆ The easiest way to spot a cult is to identify an obsession with crystal balls and conspiracies.

That description seems to eliminate at least some of the arenas of science, politics, and economics that we are about to consider, but others remain in a sort of gray area. So why bring them up at all?

The answer is that *we* are not bringing them up, but commentators in the media are. Celebrated experts speak and write about the "cult of scientism," for example, or the "cult of Trumpism." The internet abounds with videos either promoting Multi-Level Marketing (MLM) schemes or warning us against them. Because these topics show up so often in our newsfeeds, we have to at least ask whether the word "cult" is being popularly misused or indeed applies to the cultural arena.

Remember, however, what else we said about cults in the introduction: "Successful cult leaders attain their status by tapping into social needs and desires that other mainstream leaders miss or ignore. The dispossessed, the lost, the alienated, the discouraged, the overlooked, and the powerless respond to overtures that promise them exciting abilities ... and above all, acceptance and meaning."

> **Perhaps certain belief systems have replaced religions in our secular society, and perhaps cults exist that embrace these belief systems.**

Given this broader definition, perhaps the idea of cults that might be found in areas other than religion are fair game to consider. Or—and this is important—perhaps certain belief systems have replaced religions in our secular society, and perhaps cults exist that embrace these belief systems. In other words, perhaps since traditional religions are on the decline throughout contemporary society, people have chosen to transfer what has usually been associated with their "religious" faith to something else. Instead of "believing in God," they choose to believe in something else as a substitute.

Take the response to the COVID-19 pandemic, for instance. How should society face it squarely? Well, one way is to follow the guidelines put forth by the World Health Organization (WHO), the U.S. Centers for Disease Control and Prevention

(CDC), or the National Institutes of Health (NIH). It has become common to hear experts advise us to "believe in the science" that purportedly guides them. But what does it mean to "believe in" science?

We can accept scientific findings. We can decide whether or not scientific facts stand up to scrutiny. We can examine evidence and draw conclusions. But what does it mean to *believe in* science? "Belief" is a word usually associated with things that cannot be proven—with faith, not facts. In the face of incontrovertible evidence, we can *decide* whether or not something is true. But does that mean we *believe* in it?

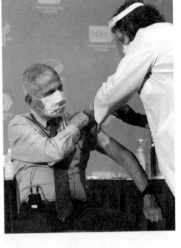

Official U.S. responses to the COVID-19 outbreak created a spark point for heated discussions about the need for rigorous scientific inquiry versus faith in science versus pure distrust of governments and corporations. Public institutions like the WHO, CDC, and NIH (with Dr. Anthony Fauci, above left, as its public face) were caught in the crossfire of many fiery debates.

The same thing can be said about our political dialogue. We watch news reporters interview people at rallies who say they no longer "believe in" government policies. Notice the extra word they often use—the word "in." It's not just that they don't believe what a particular official or candidate says. No, they say they don't believe "in" him or her. Instead, they believe "in" someone else. We somehow seem to have evolved away from listening to speeches and then deciding who to vote for based on what they promise. We have come to the point where we need to believe "in" the candidate as a person, rather than simply believing what they say.

That has far-reaching implications that smack of religious belief "in" a god or guru, not an informed political debate. If we "believe in" someone, and if we are willing to follow them based on that belief, do we give them an opportunity to establish what can only be called a cult following?

I once wrote an entire book devoted to an exegesis of one simple Greek word, πιστις. In English it's spelled "pistis."

Six letters, but they are loaded with meaning for the ancients who invented the word. Basically, it means "faith." You can have faith that the sun will come up in the morning. You can have faith in the god of your own particular religious tradition. But it goes deeper than that. It implies that faith leads to "trust," or action. Your implicit *faith* that the sun will come up tomorrow leads you to perform an act of *trust* based on that faith. You set your alarm clock. But there is another meaning associated with the word—that of "belief."

Let me explain with a concrete example. Imagine that your beloved tells you she will meet you at a particular time and place to share a romantic dinner for two. You have such *faith* in her promise that you book a table for two in a quiet corner of a restaurant and expect her to show up. That's more than faith. That's faith in action. You *did* something, based on *trust*.

But when you arrive early, perhaps because you're eager, it is obvious to the other diners who are surreptitiously watching you out of the corner of their eye that you are doing more than just hoping she will arrive. You exude confidence. You don't just hope, or think, or suspect that you will have company for dinner. You *believe* it in the very marrow of your bones.

And then comes the moment of truth. She walks through the door, spies you in the corner, walks to the table, and sits down.

Let the good times roll! You had *faith*, which inspired *trust*, which caused you to *believe*. That's what the Greeks call *pistis*. It's faith, trust, and belief all wrapped up in one package. One leads to the next, and the whole is greater than the sum of the parts. It is the wedding of thought and action, trust and activity, leading to a life of expectation and fulfillment.

Without *pistis*, we are miserable creatures indeed. The poet would never put pen to paper if she thought her muse would remain aloof. The composer would never retire to his studio if he thought the music of the spheres would mute its perpetual melody. The great novel would remain a mystery. The prophet would never have said, "I have a dream."

The triumph of the human race is the story of those whose faith made them trust enough to believe individuals could make a difference. The tragedy of the human race is the story of those who lost hope and gave in to despair.

So we repeat the original question. Can we "believe in" science, politics, and economics?

Let's take them one at a time.

THE CULT OF SCIENTISM

It might help to first explain the word "science."

Here's the definition used by the National Academy of Sciences: "Science is the use of evidence to construct testable explanation and prediction of natural phenomena, as well as the knowledge generated through this process."

In other words, science is a process, not a singular "thing." It is a method for exploring the way things work—a *scientific* method. To "believe in" science is to trust in a continually growing body of knowledge that is ever advancing and never finally arriving.

For that reason, scientists are often accused of changing their minds and offering conflicting views. Of course they do! That's the way science works. When new knowledge supersedes old findings, the understanding grows and expands. That's the nature of the scientific method. It's not trying to deceive anyone. Quite the opposite, in fact. It's trying to continually shine the light of discovery into the dark room of the unknown.

But, like all fields of endeavors, there are scientists—and then there are scientists. Some of their number have, in the past, become wedded to a certain set of beliefs and refused to alter those beliefs when new evidence shows up. Sometimes the new evidence is dismissed or not even considered.

Other scientists have felt pressure from people who don't know as much about a particular field of knowledge as they do and have reacted by disparaging the ones they consider to be less than knowledgeable, or even inferior. The amount of back-biting and vicious attacks by those in the scientific community against each other, let alone outsiders, is legendary.

While Aristotle is considered the father of the scientific method, Ibn al-Haytham later developed the model we're familiar with from all those experiments in science class.

When a scientist has spent an entire career learning the specifics of a particular subject, the tendency can become overwhelming to simply dismiss those who argue as not being worthy of their time and effort. This, too, is a relatively common occurrence. Many are the well-recorded debates that have degenerated to sarcasm instead of penetrating argument. It is an all-too-familiar story.

So what happens when a well-studied scientist meets an equally well-informed and educated philosopher or theologian? Or worse, what happens when a scientist comes up against someone who is not very educated at all and presents arguments against science that are just not credible? The scientist can't very well educate his or her opponent in just a few minutes of interaction.

This is what happened to the scientists who were studying the rapidly developing COVID-19 pandemic in early 2020. They found themselves on stage with a president, for instance, who demonstrated little knowledge about biology and suggested everything from drinking bleach to flooding the inside of the human body with light. They were preposterous suggestions, but the forum simply didn't permit a meaningful dialogue to evaluate them. To counter such ideas and protect the listening public while keeping the commentary brief, news analysts began to say, simply, "Trust the science," or even, "Believe in the science."

That is the situation that formed the basis for a Pew Research Center poll taken in February 2022. This is its finding:

Americans' confidence in groups and institutions has turned downward compared with just a year ago. Trust in scientists and medical scientists, once seemingly buoyed by their central role in addressing the coronavirus outbreak, is now below pre-pandemic levels.

Overall, 29% of U.S. adults say they have a great deal of confidence in medical scientists to act in the best interests of the public, down from 40% who said this in November 2020. Similarly, the share with a great deal of confidence in scientists to act in the public's best interests is down by 10 percentage points (from 39% to 29%), according to a new Pew Research Center survey.

In reaction, those who *do* "trust in science" sometimes react in frustration and oversimplify their argument. This leads to elevating certain individuals who are seen as folks who can do no wrong. Trust is thus transferred to a person, rather than a process, and a new cult is formed—one that believes a particular spokesman or spokeswoman can be trusted without necessarily questioning the sometimes-confusing facts that particular person presents. "If so-and-so said it, I believe it, and that settles it!"

What we have created is a belief in science per se, rather that the facts science has discovered. This is the process that has created what some people are now calling the "cult" of *scientism*.

Scientism is the view that science and the scientific method are the *only* means by which people can determine normative, or epistemological, values, or that the natural sciences constitute the most authoritative worldview. You can see where the average theologian, metaphysician, supernaturalist, or paranormalist might object.

> **What we have just presented is a step-by-step process whereby a healthy respect for science can slowly become a belief that science is the only way of perceiving truth.**

What we have just presented is a step-by-step process whereby a healthy respect for science can slowly become a belief that science is the only way of perceiving truth. Many scientists themselves do not follow this route, but some do, along with a lot of laypeople. Often, it becomes a rejection of religion. It is a journey that ends with the elevation of "science" to a status it never claimed for itself—that of an objective "thing" rather than a continuing "method." It is no wonder that some bona fide scientists who have a gift for public speaking can easily be elevated to the status of cult-like figures. It also becomes very tempting for them to step outside their area of expertise and begin to offer advice in response to questions that they are not at all qualified to give.

Well-known scientists who are also outspoken atheists, such as Richard Dawkins and Christopher Hitchens, for instance, have strongly advocated for scientism over religion, and they have gained an almost cult-like following because of it. Instead of sticking to their chosen field of training, they have reveled in debating religionists about matters concerning meaning, purpose, and significance, all areas of study that science has traditionally shied away from. Sarcasm sometimes gets out of hand at these debates, and scientism tends to deeply deprecate any knowledge that stems from moral, aesthetic, philosophical, or religious experience, thus attacking character rather than ideas. But how can the scientific method possible analyze, dissect, or put in a test tube such things as metaphysics, ethics, and aesthetics, let alone meaning and purpose-oriented issues relating to ultimate reality, goodness, or beauty?

As scientism began to proliferate, two definitions rose up to describe the phenomenon.

The first is *strong scientism*—that science is the *only* path to knowledge.

This belief, in its simplest form, asserts that the material, physical universe is the only reality. It was first stated by Carl Sagan, who established quite a cult following after his TV series, *Cosmos*, became such a popular sensation. In it, he asserted: "The cosmos is all that is, or ever was, or ever will be." This has since been disputed by other scientists, who have adopted a much more complex view of reality by speculating about a multiverse, or a many-worlds hypothesis that extends reality beyond this present universe.

Carl Sagan famously argued for rigorous critical thinking, with one of his most enduring quotes, "Extraordinary claims require extraordinary evidence," becoming known as the Sagan Standard.

Still, most of them insist that reality is only material or physical in nature. That raises another problem. How do we know that science is the only way of verifying truth claims about reality? Can we prove such a thing objectively? This approach renders things like morality, aesthetics, and religious knowledge superfluous.

Weak scientism is the notion that science is the *best* path to knowledge.

This approach backs off a bit. It acknowledges that religion, philosophy, and other areas of study are helpful when it comes to studying ultimate existence. They have a place at the table, but science is still the best way to get the job done.

So when science becomes a "thing" that stands on its own—in other words, when we hear phrases such as "believe in *the* science" or "trust *the* scientists"—we make science into a cult with popular proponents and talking heads, thereby reducing a method of study to a list of seemingly sacred dogmas called scientism. Thus, the specter of a cult comes forth from the shadows into the light of day.

THE DOGMA OF POLITICS

It is not only science that can find itself drawn into the world of cults. The word has recently been applied to quite a different realm.

In 2021, Steven Hassan wrote a book called *The Cult of Trump*, thus bringing another specter into the light—the world of politics. The book is one of the first serious attempts to put forth the argument that what Hassan calls "Trumpism" is a cult.

It was probably inevitable that Hassan was the one to write this book, because he is a former "Moonie," the member of a cult led by Sun Myung Moon that originated in the Unification Church of the United States and rose to prominence during the 1970s, and he has published widely on cults and mind control. But Hassan is not alone in his characterization of Trumpism. Former Republican strategist John Weaver agrees with Hassan's conclusions, as do veteran news anchor Dan Rather and Anthony Scaramucci, the former White House communications director.

Hassan's argument is that many followers of former U.S. president Donald Trump form a unified group that fits the definition of "cult." They band together at rallies and wear a sort of uniform consisting of red MAGA (Make America Great Again) hats and T-shirts. They carry and even wear American flags as a unifying symbol, call themselves "patriots," and seem to accept the words of their leader without question, even in the face of seemingly contradictory statements. The former president, in Hassan's words, "employs many of the same techniques as prominent cult leaders and displays many of the same personality traits."

The former president, in Hassan's words, "employs many of the same techniques as prominent cult leaders and displays many of the same personality traits."

Whether Hassan makes a good argument is debatable, of course, but he is at the forefront of a growing number of political thinkers who seem to agree with him. Moreover, many members of the Republican Party, such as South Carolina senator Lindsey Graham, are on record as saying that Trump controls the future of the GOP. On December 30, 2021, in an interview with Fox News host Pete Hegseth, Graham said, "The next presidential election is former president Donald Trump's to lose, and he will have the Republican nomination if he wants it."

When Graham goes on to say he will not consider voting for any Republican leader who does not have a good working relationship with Donald Trump, it speaks volumes, to say the least. In the year 2020, there wasn't even a Republican platform offered for candidates to run on. The committee just said it would agree with whatever Trump said, and that was it. It was a first in modern American politics. To paraphrase a famous bumper sticker, "If Trump says it, I believe it. That settles it!"

It's not just the political right that has drawn cult-like comparisons. In January 2022, President Joe Biden suggested that extreme news from reporters who have a cult-like following are operating from both sides of the political spectrum, and

While campaigning in 2016, Donald Trump said, "I could stand in the middle of 5th Avenue and shoot somebody and I wouldn't lose voters." Through scandal after scandal—including a church-front photo op in 2020 that involved a massive show of unnecessary force against protesting citizens—his followers have continued to demonstrate steadfast loyalty.

he noted similarities between Fox News, on the right, and MSNBC, on the left. On the other hand, commentators from *US News and World Report*, the *Washington Post*, the *New York Times*, and other varied sources refute this opinion and quote polls that suggest Fox viewers are more apt to elevate their favorite reporters to cult status than the more liberal side that tends toward MSNBC.

Notably, a charismatic leader is usually necessary for the attainment of cult status. Politicians and news commentators alike may secure loyal fan bases all along the political spectrum, but only one U.S. leader in modern times has commanded a following to such an extent that a mob of 2,000 adherents would, for example, invade a national political chamber, attacking and even killing police officers in the process, in an attempt to halt a national election. Influence and obedience to the point of insurrection is certainly a strong indication of cultish behavior.

Many of those who were arrested and charged after their actions on January 6, 2021, accused of breaking into the U.S. Capitol Building, attacking Capitol police, threatening lawmakers, and attempting insurrection, claimed they felt justified in doing so because they believed they were following the orders of their leader, President Donald Trump. Does this defense fall under the rubric of patriotism or of cult control exerted by a powerful leader? The conclusion is very much up for grabs, with strong opinions held by those on both sides of the political divide.

MULTI-LEVEL MARKETING CULTS (MLMS): PYRAMIDS, PONZIS, AND PROFITS

First, some definitions:

A *pyramid scheme* is an illegal business model that promises returns on investments based on recruitment membership fees rather than investment gains. Because it depends on a continually growing market base, it is ultimately unsustainable.

A *Ponzi scheme* is an illegal investing scam that generates returns for early investors by taking money from later investors. Like a pyramid scheme, it depends on a continually growing market base and is therefore unsustainable.

MLMs, or multi-level marketing companies, recruit and maintain participants using tactics such as recruitment pitches, financial manipulation, and the promise of large profits. They usually, either overtly or subliminally, employ methods such as thought control, magical thinking, isolation, and self-blame.

In the January 14, 2022, issue of *Psychology Today*, Dr. Steven Hassan, the author of books such as *Combatting Cult Mind Control*, *Freedom of Mind*, and *The Cult of Trump*, labels MLM companies as cults. An author, educator, and mental health counselor specializing in destructive cults, Hassan has been described in various publications as "one of the world's foremost experts on mind control, cults and similar destructive organizations." Social scientists are, of course, divided about his work, but he raises some interesting points through his research when it comes to identifying cults by the practices they employ to recruit and maintain membership.

Hassan, himself a former cult member, has come to believe that just as religious and political cults manipulate and control members by using tried and true influences such as deception and coercion, the same is true for MLMs.

First of all, what companies are we talking about?

In 2020 the title lending company TitleMax compiled a list of the top 25 MLMs operating around the world, along with their annual income. Here are just a few of the most well-known American-based ones:

- ◆ Amway: $8.8 billion
- ◆ Avon: $5.7 billion
- ◆ Herbalife: $4.5 billion
- ◆ Mary Kay: $3.5 billion
- ◆ Tupperware: $2.21 billion
- ◆ Young Living: $1 billion

They all follow a similar pattern of recruitment that relies on one person recruiting others, who then recruit others, and so on, funneling income from those new recruits up the chain of command.

Let's follow a typical step-by-step pattern that is probably familiar to anyone who has been approached by either a friend or family member about an MLM investment opportunity.

You bump into someone who informs you she has just come across a great business opportunity wherein you can make a lot of money, set your own working hours, and be your own boss. Maybe you are given a snazzy brochure. You are, of course, suspicious, but you agree to read the brochure. Perhaps you google the company and peruse its website. It looks intriguing, and you can always drop out if you are not interested. Why not take a chance?

You are then invited to a home meeting of some kind. A small group of like-minded people arrive and listen to the pitch.

Positivity is the name of the game. If you believe in yourself, the sky's the limit. You become a little more interested.

You are then invited to a seminar that will be held in a nearby hotel conference room, airport meeting room, or similar venue. When you arrive, the atmosphere is electric. There are lots of positive people, some wearing the familiar uniform of similarly colored T-shirts with company logos. Everyone is upbeat. Everyone is excited. Infectious music plays over the din. A talented motivational speaker brings the crowd to a fever pitch. All you have to do is buy a starter kit and you are ready to be a success. The kit doesn't cost very much, usually between 50 and 100 bucks. But you have to spend money to make money, you are told, so you decide to gamble a little.

The speaker convinces you that you have to be positive. You can't surround yourself with negative people, absorb their energy, and expect to produce positive results. If that means separating yourself from family members and friends who don't seem to understand what you're doing, so be it. You don't need them. You've got a new family, and you're going to be a success.

Then you go home, the weeks pass by, you're not making a lot of money, and your dreams seem a little dim. No problem, though; there's a new seminar coming. The speakers know what you're going through. They look successful. They drive nice cars and wear good clothes. Mary Kay top sellers famously drive pink Cadillacs. They exude positivity. The problem must be you. You haven't really committed to the program. So you buy a next-level kit and head out once more, ready to take on the world.

I could continue, but you get the idea. So far, the pitch and method have been exactly the same as those used by a cult-like church that wants to recruit you for Jesus. The music has the same beat. The speakers sound the same. The infectious crowd is the same. Only the product has been changed. You have slowly been acclimated into not thinking critically about what you are doing. Rather, you've adopted the group-think of the organization. You have been enticed away from your friends and family. You have begun to doubt yourself.

You have been brainwashed. Guilt now fills your very being—guilt over not succeeding, guilt over trying this at all, guilt over second-guessing yourself—but since guilt is negative, you

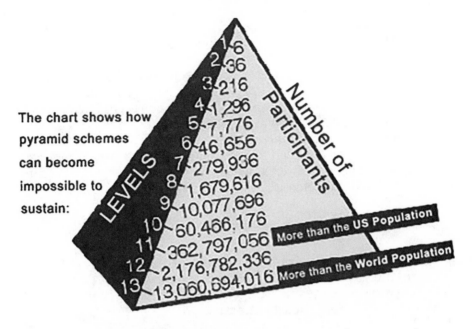

The chart shows how pyramid schemes can become impossible to sustain:

LEVELS	Number of Participants
1	6
2	36
3	216
4	1,296
5	7,776
6	46,656
7	279,936
8	1,679,616
9	10,077,696
10	60,466,176
11	362,797,056 — More than the US Population
12	2,176,782,336
13	13,060,694,016 — More than the World Population

This diagram from a U.S. Security and Exchange Commission report demonstrates the unsustainable geometric progression of a classic pyramid scheme.

can't think about it. You have become dependent on your new "family" and are now a member of a cult. The pitch was money and success. The method was the typical cult method of operations. You have been hooked.

There is money to be had in these groups, to be sure. But it is made only by those at the top. And they didn't get it by selling a product. They got it by recruiting you—and thousands like you. Your entrance money was channeled to the person who recruited you, and upward to the person who recruited them, et cetera.

The problem is this. There is not an unlimited supply of new recruits. Eventually the company reaches a saturation point and begins to decline. According to research by the Federal Trade Commission, 99 percent of recruited sellers lose money in an MLM venture. That means just 1 percent actually turn a profit. According to an article posted on MagnifyMoney.com, in a recent survey that interviewed more than one thousand marketing scheme participants from a variety of MLMs, the average recruit in the United States makes less than 70 cents an hour, and that's before deducting business costs. Sixty percent of participants reported that they had made less than $500 in the previous five years.

Recruiters have learned the techniques that are most efficient when it comes to convincing unwary candidates. They might withhold or distort vital information to ensnare you if you have not learned about cult mind-control techniques. Once you attend your first gathering, their job is done. The experts take over from there. They tell inspiring rags-to-riches stories and make you believe their experience can be yours. It is mesmerizing, scripted, and relentlessly effective.

> **They tell inspiring rags-to-riches stories and make you believe their experience can be yours. It is mesmerizing, scripted, and relentlessly effective.**

But suppose something doesn't feel right to you. You begin to raise questions. You will probably then be subjected to subtle emotional manipulation and pressured to stay in the group. Social media even comes into play. Distributors spend a great deal of time, effort, and money to establish their presence on internet sites. The social media "community" offers support. Giving up can become frightening. If your recruiter was a close friend when she recruited you or became one afterward, or if she was a family member, you will no doubt suffer from shame and guilt when your relationship falls apart. There is even a legitimate fear of retaliation from the organization itself.

Multi-level marketing has been around for a long time, but the recent COVID-19 pandemic restricted in-person shopping and caused a lot of people to lose their jobs, including five million American women. MLMs have historically been female-dominated. The Direct Selling Association, a trade organization of MLMs, estimates that 74 percent of the 16 million Americans involved in direct selling are women. This has prompted some detractors to start calling participants "huns," taken from what is called the "sorority sister speak" that representatives encourage their recruits to emulate.

When you look seriously, with a level head, at MLMs, you can't help but notice the cult-like aura that surrounds them:

- MLMs offer the promise of a utopian existence—cash flow, working from home, doing what you love, and joining an exciting family of new friends.

- There are usually godlike figureheads stationed up the pyramid from you who are metaphorically, if not literally, worshipped.

- There are usually mysterious and certainly unscientific secrets to success. One of them is almost always a variation on what is called the Law of Attraction. If you are unsuccessful, you'll be told that you have a negative mindset or that you're just not working hard enough. It's never the fault of the model. The guilt is placed on you.

- MLMs encourage alienation from negative, dissenting voices, even from family and friends trying to reason with you. If someone tries to question what you are doing, you will be told they are either negative or otherwise jealous of your chance for success.

- They employ shame-and-fear terms such as "wage slave" to describe those on the outside. They also use fear as a control method and authoritarianism to keep their representatives in line. If you dare question anything, you're shamed for not "believing" or "trusting."

- They often support charities to cover their image, establishing a high moral ground.

- If you carefully study folks who have been involved for some time, you can often spot subtle personality changes.

- MLMs demand unquestioning devotion. Income statements are usually hidden from all except the very top people and rarely shared with anyone else.

These kinds of complaints make it seem as if MLMs are cults, or at least employ cult-like techniques, even if they are not religious organizations. Perhaps the definition of "cult" thus needs to be expanded to include the collection of techniques rather than just a type of organization. If scientific, political, and economic systems make use of similar techniques, the problem may be intrinsic to the human species. Perhaps we might also ask: Can it also extend to an arena outside space and time?

THE WORLD OF METAPHYSICS: "IT SEEMS TO ME ..."

Most of the cults we've surveyed so far have at least one thing in common. Whether they are religious or political, they usually at least pay lip service to a set of texts. Religious cults based in Christianity usually begin with the Bible. They may add their own writings or veer off the beaten path with some unusual interpretations, but at least they start from an accepted point that is some variation on the theme "Thus saith the Lord!"

The cult of scientism is based on established precedent. They may argue about gurus ranging from Newton to Einstein, but they all agree that their interpretation of truth is based on what has come before, and they quote some pretty strong examples to prove it. Even in the field of psychology, language is revealing. A psychologist might claim to be a "Freudian," a "Rogerian," or a "Jungian." This certainly smacks of cult-like veneration of a particular person rather than a history of evolving ideas.

Political cults have their own texts, too. In America, at least, they usually at least claim to honor the Constitution, the U.S. law and court rulings, and the collected works of the Founding Fathers. Again, interpretations may vary, sometimes to a great degree, but at least they make the claim to historical precedent. Thus, we find there are "Jeffersonian" Democrats or Republicans who belong to "the party of Lincoln."

Even MLMs have a set of texts. They work within the financial system.

But now we move to a different area entirely. From "Thus saith the Lord!" we enter the world of "It seems to me ..." In other words, the next group of cults doesn't start from a body of texts or compiled wisdom. It begins in the far-out world of metaphysics.

The Greek phrase μετα τα φμσικα ("meta ta physika"), literally translated, means "after (or about) the things of nature." In the times in which we live, metaphysics questions or speculates about ideas, doctrines, or realities outside our perception realm—things that cannot be seen or understood through objective studies of the material reality that surrounds us. It is a field that deals more with potentialities than actualities.

Generally speaking, philosophers divide metaphysics into three categories:

- ◆ General metaphysics, sometimes called "ontological" metaphysics, is about the study of "being" or "existence." It doesn't ask how we physically got here as much as why we are here in the first place.

- ◆ Religious metaphysics, sometimes called "psychical" metaphysics, deals primarily with questions about God, eternity, freedom, and immortality. It asks questions about the nature of human existence rather than material existence itself.

- ◆ Physical metaphysics discusses the real nature of time, space, laws of nature, and matter. In other words, it asks whether something exists outside, above, or even beyond what we call reality.

Of course, no one can know anything for sure about any of this. One guess is as good as another. That is why science shies away from the field of metaphysics. If you can't see it, smell it, taste it, feel it, or hear it, what good is it? It is beyond our ability to measure.

But the committed metaphysician says the fault of that logic lies in science, not reality. If we do not even consider a world beyond our senses that either brought about or caused us to have consciousness in the first place, to question existence, or to question a reality that scientists deny simply because they can't perceive or measure it, then that reality will never be found. Not that it doesn't exist. It's just that we never looked for it.

Metaphysics is a bona fide system of study beloved by philosophers. You might ask one of them, "Why is there something rather than nothing?" That's like holding red meat in front of a hungry wolf. But it is a subject that is easily abused. Without a secure starting point, such as an accepted text, and some solid, agreed-upon guidelines, literally anyone can go off in any direction they want, and a cult will form if they can attract enough of a following to make it profitable.

Here are some examples of cult leaders who did exactly that.

SUN MYUNG MOON AND THE UNIFICATION CHURCH

On September 2, 2012, the *New York Times* published an excellent article written by Daniel J. Wakin announcing: "Rev. Sun Myung Moon, Self-Proclaimed Messiah Who Built Religious Movement, Dies at 92."

Not a bad epitaph for a man who came from a small village in North Korea and managed to build what amounts to a worldwide empire that earned millions of dollars a year. Especially since he had to take some time out to serve time in a U.S. prison for tax evasion.

Sun Myung Moon's official biography says he was born in January of 1920, joined the Presbyterian Church when he was ten years old, received a vision from God sometime around Easter of 1935, and came to believe he had been anointed by Jesus Christ to establish the kingdom of heaven on earth. "Thy kingdom come ... on earth as it is in heaven." From that vision, the Unification Church was born.

Moon walked quite a twisting, turning road between his vision in 1935 and his death in 2012. Life wasn't always easy. As many others before him have learned, for a self-proclaimed messiah, it never is. Along the way, besides serving time in prison both in the United States and in North Korea, where he was allegedly tortured by

Sun Myung Moon and his wife, Hak Ja Han.

communists, he managed to survive a helicopter crash in 2008 and experienced the deaths of two sons, one from a car crash and the other from suicide.

The wife of his eldest son wrote a book in which she accused her husband, Moon's son, of being a womanizer and a cocaine addict who watched pornographic movies and often beat her, once when she was seven months pregnant. Moon also fought "deprogrammers" who, financed by friends and family members of some of his followers, kidnapped a number of them to "save" them from supposed brainwashing. Add to that the vicious print campaign against his movement and accusations of all sorts of illegal activities allegedly going on behind closed doors in what was seen as a cult led by a power-hungry, authoritarian, narcissistic, heretical madman, and he experienced a life filled with conflict.

But it wasn't all negative. Along the way he managed to hobnob with famous and important figures such as U.S. housing and urban development secretary Jack Kemp, actor Bill Cosby, Soviet leader Mikhail Gorbachev, and U.S. presidents George H.W. Bush and Gerald R. Ford. Most of them later claimed they had no idea he had a connection to the organizations that had invited them to participate in these various events.

He even managed to have himself crowned "humanity's savior" in front of astonished members of Congress at a Capitol Hill luncheon.

On March 23, 2004, what was billed as a "peace awards" banquet took place at the Dirksen Senate Office Building in Washington, D.C. Members of Congress were among the invited guests. During the banquet, Representative Danny Davis, a Democrat from Illinois, wearing white gloves, carried in two gold crowns on a pillow. They were placed on the heads of Moon and his wife.

Members of Congress could only sit and stare. Most said afterward that they had no idea that Moon was even going to be at the affair. But that just means they hadn't done their homework. The banquet was hosted by the Interreligious and International Federation for World Peace, a foundation affiliated with the Unification Church.

As a result of that "crowning," Moon was later able to boast that "kings and presidents had declared to all heaven and earth that Reverend Sun Myung Moon is none other than humanity's savior, Messiah, returning lord, and true parent." Still later, he claimed that the founders of the world's great religions and philosophies, along with notorious (and deceased) governmental leaders such as Vladimir Lenin, Adolf Hitler, and Joseph Stalin, had "found strength in my teachings, mended their ways, and been reborn as new persons."

> As a result of that "crowning," Moon was able to boast that "kings and presidents had declared to all heaven and earth that Reverend Sun Myung Moon is none other than humanity's savior, Messiah, returning lord, and true parent."

How did one man manage to experience all of this? The answer lies in a fascinating story of megalomania, business acumen, and spiritual zeal.

Perhaps the best place to start is in 1941. A 21-year-old Sun Myung Moon began his formal education by studying electrical engineering at Waseda University in Japan. In 1943, he returned to Korea, where he married a woman named Sun Kil Choi. The two had a son together, but in 1946 he left his young family behind and moved to Pyongyang, which is now the capital of North Korea. There he became the founder of the Kwang-Ya Church, the predecessor of the Unification Church. But by doing so, he came under the scrutiny of the Communist Party, who put him in prison.

His official biography claims that United Nations forces freed him in 1950 and that he then walked all the way to Pusan, on the southern tip of the Korean Peninsula, a distance of some 320 miles. There he is said to have built a church building out of U.S. Army ration boxes while living in a shack on a nearby mountain. Two years later he divorced, moved to Seoul, and founded the Unification Church. Over the course of the next year, some 30 new outreach ministries had grown from his original church.

A church requires a theology, and Moon articulated his in a book he wrote over the next few years. At least, he says he wrote it.

> He is said to have built a church building out of U.S. Army ration boxes while living in a shack on a nearby mountain.

His daughter-in-law later claimed it was written by one of his followers. But when it was published, it was called *Divine Principle*.

To call it a compressive theological statement is an understatement. Perhaps the best way to describe it is to say that it is extremely dense. Moon never uses a simple phrase when a complex one will do. It covers subjects that scholars refer to as cosmology, theodicy, Christology, soteriology, and, most important to what came later, eschatology—the study of the end times, with an emphasis on the coming messiah and the future of the world.

At the risk of simplifying what is a convoluted piece of writing, this is Moon's interpretation of the Bible story, liberally dosed with his take on what's going on outside our perception realm, behind the scenes of human history.

Moon believed that Adam and Eve were created by God so that they could enter into a loving relationship with God. God's plan was that the two humans would first reach a stage Moon called "responsibility." Then they would progress to a second stage he called "perfection." During this second stage they would marry, and their children would populate the world. Only then would they achieve what Moon called the "Third Blessing." Summarized, it looks like this:

- Stage 1: Individuals learn how to "perfect" themselves.

- Stage 2: The ideal, or "God-centered," family becomes the basic unit of what Moon called a "true" society.

- Stage 3: Humanity's dominion of love over the whole of creation is the realization of God's "Third Blessing" to man.

Unfortunately, things did not go according to plan. God had given the archangel Lucifer the job of watching out for Adam and

Eve until they fulfilled Stage 1 and obtained sufficient maturity to marry. But in a classic case of "dad always liked you best," Lucifer was jealous of Adam and Eve. So he sexually seduced Eve, who then coerced Adam into premarital sex. This meant their marriage was not "God-centered." Their children, their grandchildren, and so on were all born under the curse of this "original sin" and therefore inherited a "fallen nature."

Following the logic of this sequence of events, the "Fall" of humankind is seen as the misuse of the most powerful force in the cosmos—love. History then becomes the story of how certain key persons and nations fought to restore the kingdom of heaven on earth and to reestablish the ideal, God-centered family. Only this would end the suffering that God has been experiencing since the Fall.

Is it any wonder that mass weddings—or blessing ceremonies, as they are called—became the most well-known activities of the Unification Church? They are what the public most identified with. At one event in Seoul in 2009, ten thousand couples exchanged or renewed vows, with Rev. Moon presiding. The church saw these weddings as the culmination of the biblical command "Go forth and multiply ... fill the earth, and subdue it."

Mass weddings, called blessing ceremonies, are perhaps the most well-known activities of the Unification Church.

According to *Divine Principle*, Jesus was the perfect man, who was meant to marry and establish a God-centered family. He was supposed to have been officially pronounced as such at the occasion of his baptism. But John the Baptist fudged a bit and didn't unambiguously proclaim him to be the messiah. Therefore, Jesus was murdered on the cross before he could get married. A substitute was needed.

Moon worked out a series of parallels between Abraham and Jesus that involved mathematical calculations based on numerology, cosmology, and other factors, indicating that the "Lord of the Second Advent" was scheduled to be born in Korea between 1917 and 1930.

Surprise, surprise! As luck would have it, Moon was born in 1920, at the precise time and in the exact place the calculations predicted.

> **The "Lord of the Second Advent" was scheduled to be born in Korea between 1917 and 1930. As luck would have it, Moon was born in 1920.**

For this reason, although Moon didn't have to claim it for himself, his followers made the connection and pronounced him the promised messiah. He put off the official announcement until 1992, at which point he proclaimed to the world that he and his wife, Hak Ja Han, whom he had married in 1960, were the "True Parents." Together, the two produced 13 children.

Divine Principle does not introduce all of Moon's teachings. The work has been transcribed and modified over the years. There is even a version that quotes from the Qur'an as well as the Bible, aimed at an Islamic audience. Since Moon is the messiah, his commands and proclamations cannot be limited to one time or one iteration. Revelation, after all, is a continuing process.

Take, for instance, the Holy Wine Ceremony, a ritual that takes place before the marriage blessing. This ceremony ensures that the new generation of "blessed children" will, just like Adam and Eve, be born without original sin. In short, it cleanses people of sin.

It began in the 1990s, and the custom of blessing marriages in this way has been extended to millions of non-church members, who, if the truth were known, are not always aware of the implications. It has further been extended to some who have died and watch the ritual from the realm of the spirit. Saints such as Confucius, Jesus, and Muhammad, as well as sinners such as Hitler, Stalin, and Kim Il Sung, are no doubt appreciative.

What this blessing implies is that Moon controls both the world of matter and the world of spirit. He is both a cosmological and a spiritual presence.

Besides *Divine Principle*, more than 230 volumes of Moon's speeches have been published. They are available online (https://www.unification.net/teachings.html), and most have

In 1974, at the height of the Watergate crisis, Sun Myung Moon arranged for his followers to publicly pray and fast on President Nixon's behalf. Nixon welcomed their support and met officially with Moon at the White House.

been published in the 15-volume work *Hoon Dok Hae* ("Gathering for Reading and Learning"). Unification Church members are encouraged to study them for an hour every day.

With the church launched and its theological underpinnings established, Moon began to send out missionaries and build up his business empire. During the 1960s and early 1970s, he set out on some world tours, and in 1972 he decided the United States was the new promised land when it came to church growth. "I came to America primarily to declare the New Age and new truth," he said. And that's exactly what he did. But not without controversy.

One of his early endeavors involved Richard Nixon. Moon was convinced the president should be forgiven for his role in the Watergate break-in. Church leaders held rallies in support of Nixon that drew thousands of people to Yankee Stadium, Madison Square Garden, and the National Mall.

In 1982 Moon expanded his interests into the Hollywood movie business. A company linked to the church put up $42 million to bankroll the movie *Inchon*, a Korean War epic. Unfortunately, the gift of prophecy was not among the gifts God had awarded to Rev. Moon. Even though the movie starred the formidable Laurence Olivier as General Douglas MacArthur, it was notable only for the negative reviews it garnered.

> **Over the years Moon acquired interests in commercial fishing, jewelry, fur products, construction, and real estate.**

Over the years Moon acquired interests in commercial fishing, jewelry, fur products, construction, and real estate. He bought many properties in the New York area, including the New Yorker Hotel in Midtown Manhattan and the Manhattan Center nearby.

He held controlling interests in newspapers such as *Noticias del Mundo* and the *New York City Tribune*. He owned or controlled four different publications in South Korea as well as a Japanese newspaper called *Sekai Nippo*, the *Middle East Times* in Greece, *Tiempos del Mundo* in Argentina, and *Últimas Noticias* in Uruguay. In 2000, a church affiliate bought the news agency United Press International. The *Washington Times* was founded in 1982, and Moon contributed more than $1 billion in subsidies to sustain it.

He even received an honorary degree from the University of Bridgeport in Connecticut. The school had been saved from bankruptcy thanks to donations from a group tied to the Unification Church.

Despite its successes, the church began to have some real problems in the late 1970s. It had come to the attention of various federal agencies that behind-the-scenes activities should be investigated. There were allegations that Moon was involved in efforts by the South Korean government to bribe members of Congress to win support for President Park Chung-hee. A Congressional subcommittee claimed it had evidence of ties between Moon and Korean intelligence officers and that the church had raised money in the United States and then smuggled it across international borders. This practice was in violation of immigration and local charity laws.

It only got worse. In October of 1981, Moon was named in a 12-count federal indictment, accused of failing to report $150,000 in income from the years 1973 to 1975. The prosecution claimed he owed interest on $1.6 million that had been deposited in New York bank accounts under his own name.

Moon was defiant and claimed he was the victim of racism. "I would not be standing here today if my skin were white and my religion were Presbyterian," he said. "I am here today only because my skin is yellow and my religion is Unification Church." He claimed that the case was a government conspiracy brought against him to force him to leave the country. Regardless, he was convicted of tax fraud and conspiracy to obstruct justice and was sentenced to 18 months in prison.

With the decline of his church in the United States, Moon seemed to have a change of heart toward his adopted country. Where once he had seen America as the world's salvation, he now began to call it "a repository of immorality—Satan's harvest." He changed his marketing appeal away from a Messianic religion to a crusade for moral values. By 1997, he was preaching that America had persecuted him, and he started verbally attacking homosexuals and immoral American women.

Back in 1977, he had said, "I don't blame those people who call us heretics. We are indeed heretics in their eyes, because the concept of our way of life is revolutionary. We are going to liberate God."

Twenty years later, he wasn't quite so charitable.

> **Megachurches were flourishing, and cults seemed to be everywhere. In this kind of environment, all kinds of strange things can happen. And they did.**

The era during which Moon's Unification Church had risen to power was a wild one for religions and cults in the United States. Hare Krishna and transcendental meditation were all the rage. Televangelists were inspiring some people and completely disillusioning others. Money flowed freely and, as we have seen time and again, often unwisely.

Megachurches were flourishing, and cults seemed to be everywhere. In this kind of environment, all kinds of strange things can happen. And they did. Sun Myung Moon was only one of those who considered himself to be a savior, a messiah.

During those decades, words attributed to Jesus in Matthew 24 were often quoted from pulpits across America:

As Jesus was sitting on the Mount of Olives, the disciples came to him privately. "Tell us ... what will be the sign of your coming and of the end of the age?"

Jesus answered: "Watch out that no one deceives you. For many will come in my name, claiming, 'I am the Messiah,' and will deceive many. You will hear of wars and rumors of wars, but see to it that you are not alarmed. Such things must happen, but the end is still to come. Nation will rise against nation, and kingdom against kingdom. There will be famines and earthquakes in various places. All these are the beginning of birth pains.

Then you will be handed over to be persecuted and put to death, and you will be hated by all nations because of me. At that time many will turn away from the faith and will betray and hate each other, and many false prophets will appear and deceive many people. Because of the increase of wickedness, the love of most will grow cold, but the one who stands firm to the end will be saved. And this gospel of the kingdom will be preached in the whole world as a testimony to all nations, and then the end will come."

It is no wonder that the clean-cut, polite young people who sold flowers and trinkets at airports and on street corners, who left their families and friends to disappear into a different world and got married in mass weddings, were looked on with suspicion. They became known as "Moonies."

Among the many properties owned by the Unification Church is the New Yorker Hotel, an iconic Art Deco landmark. Now operated by Wyndham Hotels, it is also said to serve as the Unification Church's U.S. headquarters.

It didn't help his image that Moon ostentatiously lived the life of a cult leader. He owned an 18-acre compound in Irvington, New York. It boasted a ballroom, two dining rooms (one of which contained a pond and waterfall), a kitchen with six pizza ovens, and a bowling alley.

If you couldn't find him there, Moon might be on an estate called Belvedere, near Tarrytown. Or perhaps he might be visiting his church-owned home on the Hudson River, near the Unification Theological Seminary in Barrytown, otherwise known as the Unification Church Interfaith Seminary.

Or perhaps he might be overseas in South Korea, checking on his construction companies that built hospitals, schools, and ski resorts. He was into newspapers, auto parts, pharmaceuticals, and beverages.

He even owned a professional soccer team and controlled commercial interests in Japan, where right-wing nationalist donors were said to be one source of his financing.

All this was funded ostensibly by the kids who sold flowers at the airport. It is no wonder he seemed to have almost invited investigating agencies to check him out. Another source of money was funneled up the line by church members, each of whom (according to Douglas E. Cowan and David G. Bromley in their book *Cults and New Religions: A Brief History*), as a condition of membership, "agrees to contribute to the payment of personal indemnity for human sinfulness, and looks forward to receiving the marital Blessing and building a restored world of sinless families."

It's hard to imagine a bigger, more well-funded cult. It seems to tick all the boxes that describe what a cult is. Yet members, who are still, to this very day, active around the world, insist it is merely a church.

Indeed, on September 12, 2021, Hak Ja Han Moon, the founder's widow, organized a New York conference called the Rally of Hope. It was sponsored by the church and held to commemorate the twentieth anniversary of the September 11, 2001, terrorist attacks on the Twin Towers and the Pentagon. The keynote speaker at the event was the former U.S. president Donald Trump.

Maybe the Unification Church will yet, as so many other cults have done, outlive its critics and attain respectability. Only time will tell.

ECKANKAR: DISCOVERING GOD

Since before recorded time, Sugmad, neither male nor female, has existed. Sugmad is God. From the heart of Sugmad flows the ECK current, connecting with every person and to all levels of existence, and then returning to Sugmad. ECK manifests itself (according to Eckankar.org) as an "Inner Sound." It is the "Voice of God, calling us home." You might hear it in nature, or perhaps in music. It is also perceived as an "Inner Light," which is a beacon

Practitioners generally chant or sing a mantra for half an hour each day. "Hu" is a common mantra, similar to the Buddhist "Om." It is thought to be an ancient name for God and is considered a love song to God.

Worship services might consist of readings, chanting "Hu" in unison, silent meditation, and open discussion about various topics concerning spiritual growth.

An individual's progress is marked by what are called initiations. Each signifies a new stage of development. At the Second Initiation, for instance, the chela makes a personal commitment to the process, marked by a partial or even full fast every Friday. At the Fifth Initiation, he or she is pronounced a *mahdis*, or high initiate. This marks the achievement of a rank similar to what is called clergy in Protestant denominations.

There are rules along the way, of course. Abortion, divorce, sexual orientation, and suicide are personal matters, but the use of tobacco, alcohol, and drugs are frowned upon. Community service is recommended.

There are, however, seven spiritual laws of life that are unchangeable:

1. The Law of Pure Potentiality

2. The Law of Giving

3. The Law of "Karma" or Cause and Effect

4. The Law of Least Effort

5. The Law of Intention and Desire

6. The Law of Detachment

7. The Law of "Dharma" or Purpose in Life

Without going into detail about each of the seven spiritual laws, the third, Karma, is of particular interest. It is very similar to what is taught in many forms of Hinduism.

Human beings suffer from temptation due to what are called The Five Passions:

1. Anger

2. Greed

3. Lust

4. Undue attachment to the physical world

5. Vanity

Through attachment to one or all of these passions, we accumulate bad Karma. To undo its effects, we need to be reincarnated to pay off, in the next life, the debt we have accumulated in this one. The ultimate goal of Eckankar is to pay off all this accumulated debt. When that happens, we achieve "self-realization" in our present life.

After this goal is met, we no longer need to return to Earth in the body. We are freed from the endless cycles of reincarnation. In Hinduism, a similar belief says that we are able to step off the Wheel of Samsara.

Is Eckankar a cult? Some religious scholars call it that.

Yes, it involves a revered leader. But so does Catholicism.

Yes, it requires spiritual discipline. But so do most traditional religions.

Followers consider their religion to be the *best*, but not the *only*, path to God realization. Many fundamentalist denominations can't make that claim. They believe Jesus is the Way, and those who don't accept him as savior are going to hell.

Eckankar does not require its followers to leave their current religion. Even Christianity is recognized as an alternate path that can aid a follower to achieve a degree of enlightenment.

Its members do not attempt to evangelize the world by aggressively converting others to their way of practicing spirituality.

Finally, Eckankar is legally a nonprofit religious group with members in over 100 countries.

Nevertheless, the accusations continue. Perhaps the most vocal exponent has been Joe Sykes in his book *Victims and Sur-*

vivors: Escapees from the Eckankar Cult. Sykes paints quite a different picture of the group.

In his view, Eckankar is a top-down, full blown, authoritative cult. Or at least it was when it began. His story is that Paul Twitchell was a man who got indicted for assault, spent six months or more in a mental institution, moved away from his ashram in California, and began a reign of authoritarian autocracy and bullying that his successor Darwin Gross, while still remaining a disciplinarian, cleaned up. According to Sykes, the only reason Twitchell started the group in the first place was that he succumbed to nagging from his wife, who wanted an income.

If you turn to the internet, things aren't much clearer. The Quora website (at https://www.quora.com/How-dangerous-is-the-Eckankar-cult) asked for personal testimonies from people who have been involved in one way or another, and Jen Blodgett, a former member, related her story in 2020:

> Basically, my whole family was involved in this cult in the 70's and 80's. It started with my grandma. Then my mother and all of her siblings joined the cult. They brought my cousins, and my brother and me to the meetings and conventions. I thought it was cool back then, until my mother met a sinister man at one of the meetings. He was much older than her. He moved in with us. Within weeks, he started molesting me. He molested me for three years. He was one of their so called "Masters." I was nine years old when it started. He destroyed the relationship I had with my mother. She and I have never been the same. Many of the people were beautiful people, hippies, but many of them were just weirdos. Beware of the Eckankar CULT!! If you feel the need to try something new like this, leave your children out of it!!

Jen Blodgett credits Eckankar for causing and enabling the abuse she suffered at the hands of an Eckankar Master.

By contrast, a contributor calling themselves Anonymous stated in 2016:

> No, it's not a cult, nor is it dangerous. Eckankar is the most pure teaching

I've discovered. And no worries, you're in perfectly wonderful company among Eckists. The basic beliefs of Eckankar are that that all souls exist because of God's love. Rather than blind faith, Eckankar offers real tools that when practiced, can help you to see more of God's love in all of life. You can learn about singing the word "HU." "HU", when sung in a long drawn-out breath for 10-20 minutes a day will open your heart to God's love. All people, regardless of their belief (Hindu, Christian, etc.) are welcome at ECK functions, and many people from many different faiths attend Eck functions and sing HU. The foundation of the teaching is about God's love after all. Who couldn't use more of that in their life? Rather than convince you, why not ask to have your own spiritual experience about truth and see what it brings you. Maybe to church, maybe in nature, or maybe to Eckankar. It is a most beautiful teaching.

So, we are left with opposing views, as is so often the case when we ask, What is a cult? One's person's cult seems to be another person's religion, just as one person's religion might be another person's cult.

Short of joining up and experiencing the group's dynamics on a personal level, there just doesn't seem to be a clean and clear answer.

THE UNIVERSE AND BEYOND: ANSWERS FROM THE FINAL FRONTIER

What causes human beings to look for help from a higher source when they feel threatened?

Sometimes our extinct is to pray. In 1988, Dan Quayle was the running mate to George H.W. Bush in a bid for the presidency of the United States. He was asked by a reporter, "What would you do if you became the president?" His answer was mocked from coast to coast, which was a strange reaction in a country that takes pride in believing it is a "nation under God." He famously said, "First, I'd pray." He never lived it down.

Some believe the answer is found in Freudian psychology. In this system of thought, we never outgrow our emotional dependence on our parents. Hence the urge to pray to a "Heavenly Father" or "Mother Mary."

Whatever the reason, the feeling of wanting help "from above" is real. Historically, that feeling has been placed within a religious context. President Ronald Reagan's favorite painting was that of General George Washington, soon to become the nation's first president, kneeling in the snow at Valley Forge when the American cause seemed hopeless. That image, Reagan said, "personified a people who knew it was not enough to depend on their own courage and goodness. They must also seek help from God, their Father and their Preserver."

Many cults have doubled down on religious faith, hoping that God will intervene before THE END comes even as they claim divine knowledge about how and when that will occur.

> **What happens when religion declines among the population, and yet the psychological feeling of needing help "from above" remains or grows even stronger? Enter the aliens.**

But what happens when religion declines among the population, and yet the psychological feeling of needing help "from above" remains or grows even stronger?

One answer is to substitute something else for God.

Enter the aliens.

In 1953 Arthur C. Clarke wrote a book called *Childhood's End*. In it, aliens come to Earth to put a stop to humanity's self-destruction. Because of their intervention, wars cease. There is no more poverty, famine, disease, or crime. All around the world, there is found only utopian bliss. At least for a while.

In the 1970s, an idea called the zoo hypothesis came into vogue. It proposed that we are being watched over by aliens. Perhaps they are even protecting us, as we humans protect animal specimens kept in a zoo. There, we provide the right environment to ensure the animal's safety, and we step in from time to time when needed to stop fights and otherwise make them feel comfortable.

In other words, the theory suggests that planet Earth might be a kind of cosmic zoo, kept as a source of either entertainment or enlightenment by aliens. With more than four thousand planets charted in the Milky Way galaxy alone, it seems plausible to think that at least one of them might be home to an intelligent species such as ourselves, only much more advanced. Maybe they are watching us and will intervene if we mess things up too much.

Arthur C. Clarke, a sci-fi writer who has been called the "Prophet of the Space Age," framed a number of stories around encounters between humankind and extraterrestrials.

Genetic science seems to have settled the fact that every living human being on earth is descended from a single woman called the Mitochondrial Eve who lived about 200,000 years ago. Something mysterious happened at that time. A single change in a single gene was somehow made, and every person born since then has received the benefits. Was that "something" due to gene manipulation cause by alien intervention? And have they been watching us ever since to observe their handiwork? If so, can we expect that they will step in to save us from ourselves now that our technology has created powers that we don't seem to be able to handle?

One can only hope. And many do. Some have even turned that hope into a movement. And some of those movements have been classified as cults.

Enrico Fermi (1901–1954) was an Italian physicist who created the world's first nuclear reactor, thus earning himself the distinctive title "architect of the Nuclear Age." In 1950, Fermi was having lunch with a group of physicists who found themselves engaged in a discussion about alien life in the galaxy. The conversation moved on to other things, but Fermi was lost in thought. Suddenly he blurted out, "Where is everybody?"

At that moment, the famous Fermi paradox was born.

In a nutshell, the problem is this. If alien life is statistically highly probable, why haven't they contacted us? Why is there only a great silence? Have they just not discovered us yet? Or, for whatever reason, are they just observing us without intervening, following the kind of "prime directive" made popular in TV's *Star Trek* universe, prohibiting the explorers from interfering with the worlds they found?

Various cults have arisen around leaders who claim to know the truth in these matters, both religious and secular. Here are a few of them.

THE CHRISTIAN RAPTURE, CARL JUNG, AND FLYING SAUCERS

John Nelson Darby was a nineteenth-century Irish evangelist. His study of the Christian New Testament convinced him that the Bible presented an outline of human history divided into eras, which he called dispensations. According to Darby's interpretation, there are a total of seven of them, five of which have already passed, a sixth that we currently occupy, and a seventh yet to come.

Our age is called the Church Age. It began with the birth of the Christian Church at Pentecost, described in the first chapters of the New Testament book called the Acts of the Apostles, which is a continuation of the Gospel according to Luke. The age began when the Holy Spirit entered into the assembled believers with a sound "like a mighty wind." This age will end just before the seventh dispensation, which he called the Millennium. The name comes from the anticipated thousand-year reign of Christ on earth.

Just as the Holy Spirit, the third person of the trinity, descended at the beginning of the Church Age, he will be recalled

Some Christians believe that when the end times comes, true believers will be flown bodily to heaven, leaving the heathens behind to suffer the Apocalypse.

at its end. But since the Holy Spirit now resides in human beings, when he returns to heaven, those people will go with him. This event is called the Rapture. After that, Jesus will return, and he will reign over all the people who are left on planet Earth. Because he will return *before* the Millennium, the seventh dispensation, this doctrine came to be known as *premillennialism.*

According to Darby, Jesus's return will take place in two stages, marked by two separate events. The first event is called the Rapture, from the Latin word *raptura.* It means to "snatch up." Those believers still living on earth will be "snatched up," or "raptured," before Jesus returns to earth in the same body he had after his resurrection. He will be, in effect, a benevolent monarch, reigning from Jerusalem.

There are, of course, variations on this theme. Darby taught that the sixth age will end with a seven-year period called the Tribulation, during which an antichrist, or Christ look-alike, will strive to take over and rule in place of Jesus. Some Christians came to believe the rapture will take place before this last gasp of evil. They are called *pre*-tribulationalists. Others look for it to occur in the middle of the seven-year period. They are called *mid*-tribulationalists. Still others look for the return only after the time of troubles has come to an end. They are, of course, called *post*-tribulationalists.

> ## Darby's work took the Christian world by storm.

Darby's work took the Christian world by storm. Fundamentalists began advertising their churches as "pre-trib, pre-millennial, and Bible-believing." In 1940, William Eugene Blackstone wrote his groundbreaking book *Jesus Is Coming.* It soon sold more than one million copies.

Evangelical Christians soon fell under the sway of this doctrine, especially after Hal Lindsey wrote his own blockbuster book, *The Late Great Planet Earth.* It popularized the Rapture as no book before or since has been able to do. Released by the Zondervan Publishing Company in 1970, it shot to the top of the *New York Times* nonfiction bestseller list and stayed there for the next ten years. If Rapture theory can be considered an interdenominational cult, Hal Lindsey is its leader.

Young people read it and, because they expected Jesus to return any day soon, dropped out of high school and became self-appointed missionaries. Families were broken up. In one personal case (full disclosure here), a young man who fit my clothes very well even quit his job as a public-school music teacher and went off to seminary, totally unprepared for what he was getting into.

It is hard to overemphasize the effect all this had on the Evangelical community. Erin A. Smith, writing for the National Endowment for the Humanities in 2017, quoted an online reviewer at Amazon:

Every 3 years Hal Lindsay [sic] writes a new book denoting how the world will end in 5 years. Each subsequent book explains how he WASN'T wrong in the previous book and the world will really end in 5 years.... He has followed this pattern for 3 decades and is now acknowledged as "the foremost authority on Biblical prophecy in the world today." ... I'm an electrician. If I had been doing my job POORLY and WRONG for 30 years, I doubt I would be "the foremost authority." In fact, I dare say I would have ceased to make a living in my chosen profession in the first 10 years.

In 1977, *Publishers Weekly* had this to say:

Hal Lindsey ... is an Advent-and-Apocalypse evangelist who sports a Porsche racing jacket and tools around Los Angeles in a Mercedes 450 SI. And even though his best-selling books of Bible prophecy warn that the end is near, Lindsey maintains a suite of offices in a posh Santa Monica high-rise for the personal management firm that sinks his royalties into long-term real estate investments.

Bantam books, having secured paperback rights to Lindsey's book, issued the text with a new cover that was deliberately modeled after Erich von Däniken's *Chariots of the Gods?*, a popular story about how ancient aliens visited the earth long ago. As a result, book stores placed the Bantam version on science fiction shelves along with books about transcendental meditation and UFOs.

The Jesus People, a popular movement that attracted many young people in the 1970s, particularly responded to the message. Centered on the West Coast, they concentrated on street ministries, communes, and coffeehouses that ministered primarily to drug addicts and runaways,

Meanwhile, Lindsey, a graduate of Dallas Seminary, began a Bible school called the Jesus Christ Light and Power Company near the University of California, Los Angeles, and appealed primarily to college kids and athletes.

The main effect of *LGPE*, as the book came to be called by those in the know, was to transfer the main message of Christianity away from the traditional church and toward the individual believer. In public speaking engagements, Lindsey talked about "apostate churches" (that is, false or wrong ones) from all denominations and urged readers to embrace true belief, however "anti-church" or "narrow-minded" or "dogmatic" that true belief might be labeled by others.

Between the environmental movement, which had been gathering momentum ever since Rachel Carson's book *Silent Spring* was published in 1962, and the Cold War, which had climaxed with the 1962 Cuban Missile Crisis, people were afraid. If Lindsey believed the Soviet Union was about to take on the United States; that the Trilateral Commission, another of Lindsey's targets, was bent on taking over the world; and that the European Common Market was going to expand to ten nations (as was prophesied in Revelation) and become the home of the antichrist, people believed him.

Meanwhile, Lindsey's personal life suffered the pains of celebrity. He married and divorced four times, once to a woman 25 years younger than he was, and was rumored to have had numerous extramarital affairs. He rarely talked about any of this except in veiled hints, and details were hard to come by. But his books stayed in print for so long that you could follow his family life just by looking at the various back-cover shots. He was rumored at one time to be worth some $42 million.

While working for the U.S. Fish and Wildlife Service in the 1940s, Rachel Carson began the observations and research that would lead her to write 1962's *Silent Spring*. The book was a grave warning about the far-reaching and potentially devastating effects of pesticides and other chemicals.

At roughly this same time, in 1968, Erich von Däniken brought out his immensely popular *Chariots of the Gods?*, the book that sparked what has since become known as the "ancient alien theory." Von Däniken believed that various sophisticated technologies and religions of many ancient civilizations had not been devised by those humans alone but had been passed along to them by ancient astronauts, who had been welcomed as gods. The proof, he claimed, lay in the relics, stone monuments, and artifacts they'd left behind.

Writing about this phenomenon in his book *Supernatural*, best-selling author Graham Hancock had this to say:

It is a great mystery that people from many different cultures in many different epochs all report encountering supernaturals who are unwilling to be confined to supernatural realms and who, even while they initiate our shamans and bestow the "second sight" and healing powers upon them, seem to want to take something of our materiality, and incorporate it into their own non-physical lineage. As the first manifestations of these ancient supernatural forces in the technological age, UFO abductions and encounters with aliens have been subjected to an unrelenting campaign of ridicule and abuse by scientists who are strongly wedded to the materialistic paradigm. It has been said, however, that "the greatest trick the Devil ever played on us was to convince the world he doesn't exist." Living in societies elevated by technology to almost godlike heights, we have convinced ourselves, against the advice of our ancestors, that there are no supernatural intelligences, that spirits do not exist, that fairies are crazed delusions, and that aliens are just figments.

We may be wrong.

UFO sightings began in earnest in 1947. Kenneth Arnold, a private pilot flying near Mount Rainier in Washington State, reported seeing a group of nine high-speed objects moving at several thousand miles per hour. When he described them as objects that looked "like saucers skipping on water," the flying saucer craze began.

That same year, a rancher named W.W. "Mac" Brazel came across a mysterious 200-yard-long wreckage near an Army airfield in Roswell, New Mexico. After conflicting reports were filed, the U.S. military eventually issued a statement saying that it was just a weather balloon. But the public felt it knew better. The now-infamous Roswell incident still garners its share of TV and internet reports every year.

In 1959, even Swiss psychologist Carl Jung published a book about flying saucers. He called it *Flying Saucers: A Modern Myth of Things Seen in the Skies*. People were definitely looking to the skies, and they seemed ready to engage in what Jung called his "hope from the skies" theory. He believed that UFO sightings, which were very prevalent at this time, were connected to archetypal imagery and suggested that humans were looking for help from outside their perception realm.

> **In 1959, even Swiss psychologist Carl Jung published a book about flying saucers.**

Jung didn't talk about alien encounters, but he studied the fact that more and more people were reporting objects associated with what he called the "collective unconscious." He believed flying saucers to be archetypes of gods—the product of a universal change taking place in the human psyche. Jung taught that the collective human mind undergoes changes from time to time. People begin to view the world differently. These changes take place roughly every 2,160 years, he said, coinciding with the astrological signs of the zodiac.

The Christian era that began two thousand years ago is identified with the constellation Pisces, the sign of the fish. According to Jung, it was no accident that early Christians chose a fish as a symbol for their new faith, just as it was no accident that the Christian story identifies the first followers of Jesus as fishermen. According to the Bible, Jesus bid his disciples to follow him to become "fishers of men." During the Age of Aquarius, the age we are now beginning, people will start to move up out of the "water" that was the home of Pisces, the fish. The "water bearer," Aquarius, will begin the work of lifting people up to new heights.

So it was that after the explosion of the first atomic bomb taught everyone the futility of the path technology had been following, after two thousand years of wars and rumors of wars, after the Christian age began to deteriorate into denominational bickering and institutional persecution, humankind began the journey into a new realm. Looking up from the mud and sludge that we had suddenly noticed was pulling us down into the earth, we lifted our gaze to the skies. And what did we discover? The Rapture and the return of Jesus. Flying saucers! Chariots of "gods" from a different realm. Help from above!

If it was a cult, it was a really popular one. And it is still with us.

THE CHURCH OF SCIENTOLOGY

Quick trivia quiz:

According to the *Guinness Book of World Records*, which author has published the greatest number of books?

Who is the most translated author in the world?

Who holds the record for largest number of audiobooks sold?

The answer to all three questions? L. Ron Hubbard. Most of his books are categorized as science fiction, and many of them are about journeys into space. You may have read some of them.

But Hubbard is not best known as an author. His main claim to fame is as the founder of Scientology, some of whose most famous followers are Tom Cruise, Kirstie Alley, John Travolta, Chick Corea, Nancy Cartwright, and Erika Christensen.

Lawrence Wright, whose book *Going Clear: Scientology, Hollywood, and the Prison of Belief* was made into a TV documentary in 2015, makes the claim that most of what makes up Scientology's "theology" about how the world began and where the human race is headed comes from those science fiction books Hubbard wrote before he got famous. That includes the central word, "clear," that he uses within the religion itself to describe a person who is free of traumas and unwanted emotions.

Some very successful people declare that Scientology is a life-saving religion. Others call it a business. Still others swear it is a cult.

It has been investigated by government agencies, international parliamentary bodies, academic scholars, religious authorities, and law experts, sometimes on the basis of fraudulent business practices but more often for employing cult-like techniques. After enduring extensive litigation, Scientology has attained legal status as a religious institution within the boundaries of the United States, Australia, and Italy. Germany specifies that it is an "anti-constitutional sect." France claims it is a dangerous cult.

> **Scientology has attained legal status as a religious institution in the United States, Australia, and Italy. Germany specifies that it is an "anti-constitutional sect." France claims it is a dangerous cult.**

So, what is it? Here's some history. Decide for yourself.

Lafayette Ronald Hubbard was born in 1911. At the age of 27, he dropped out of George Washington University and began a career writing pulp fiction, for which he was paid a penny a word. According to official records, he became an officer in the Navy Reserve. He served during World War II and eventually attained the rank of lieutenant before he was mustered out in 1950. His own statements about his service don't quite jibe with Navy records.

He claimed, for instance, that he earned multiple medals during major battles in the war. But his military records seem to indicate that during most of his service he was stationed within the continental United States.

He claimed to have sunk two Japanese submarines. Navy records claim he opened fire on what turned out to be a floating log and dropped depth charges on two submerged magnetic rocks. Then, after mistaking a Mexican island for an enemy target and opening fire, he was relieved of his command.

His second wife, Sara Northrup, recalled that he told her he spent weeks on a raft after his ship was sunk in the Pacific, suffering from a broken back and being blinded by the sun. Navy records indicate the only injuries he ever reported were arthritis and conjunctivitis.

After resigning his commission, Hubbard moved to Los Angeles and became a friend of Jack Parsons, an engineer who was involved in Ordo Templi Orientis, a black magic cult. The friend-

> **He claimed to have sunk two Japanese submarines. Navy records claim he opened fire on what turned out to be a floating log.**

ship became strained, however, when Hubbard ran off with Sara, Parsons's girlfriend. The two were married in 1946 and later had a daughter together, eventually winding up in Elizabeth, New Jersey. It was there that, in 1950, Hubbard began to write the book *Dianetics*, the basis of Scientology.

Its basic principle is that our brains record every experience, both good and bad, that we have in life. The bad experiences are called "engrams." Those are the experiences that rise up unbidden to hurt us if they are somehow triggered. A trained "auditor" can "clear" someone of these engrams, producing a perfectly functioning mind.

It sounds like a noble goal, and many people believe it to be true. But Hubbard's first wife had a different recollection of why *Dianetics* came to be written. In the 2015 HBO TV documentary *Going Clear: Scientology and the Prison of Belief*, Hubbard is said to have told his wife that "the only way to make any real money was to have religion." She said that was what *Dianetics* was all about. If he could obtain an income based on a religion, "the government wouldn't take it away from him in the form of taxes."

If he ever said that, it turns out that he was right. *Dianetics* became a cultural phenomenon. In 1950, Hubbard went on a cross-country tour, teaching people how to cure their psychological ills for the low, low price of only $500. The response was so great that Hubbard apparently began be-

L. Ron Hubbard, photographed in Los Angeles in 1950, the year he published Scientology's foundational work, *Dianetics*.

lieving his own press clippings. According to his wife, "He began to believe he was a savior and a hero, that he was really this God figure." She soon threatened to divorce Hubbard if he didn't get psychiatric help.

Hubbard's response was to grab his daughter and flee to Cuba. Not feeling competent to raise the child himself, he gave her over to a local woman who might have been mentally challenged in some way. Reportedly, she placed the child in "some kind of cage."

Again according to Sara, "He called me and told me he killed her. He said he cut her into little pieces and dropped the pieces in a river and that this was my fault. Then he'd call back and say she was still alive. And this went on and on and on."

The ordeal came to an end in 1951. Hubbard divorced his wife, and she was awarded custody of the child, who was, indeed, very much alive. "When I left him, he cleaned out all the joint bank accounts so I wouldn't have any money," she later declared.

If Hubbard did "clean out all the joint bank accounts," there must not have been a lot of money in them, because a year later, he was broke and desperate. *Dianetics* had provided his 15 minutes of fame, but it was beginning to fade in popularity. He had a book but did not yet have a religion to go with it. Then, in 1952, Hubbard even lost the rights to *Dianetics* in bankruptcy proceedings.

Thus it was that Scientology was born. In the book *Bare-Faced Messiah: The True Story of L. Ron Hubbard*, author Russell Miller describes how Hubbard got started on his way to success as a cult-type guru.

Hubbard first pitched Scientology to 38 people gathered in a room. Upon payment of a fee, they could rise up through various

> By the late 1960s, the IRS was looking into Hubbard's finances. He responded by moving offshore.

levels of teaching. It was a success. The church has since grown to more than 50,000 adherents.

That kind of growth encourages investigations. By the late 1960s, the IRS was looking into Hubbard's finances. He responded by moving offshore. There he began a ship-based operation he called Sea Organization, or Sea Org, a sort of floating boot camp for what was to become Scientology's clergy. Those who declared unity paid a price, of course. Those who didn't, or who circumvented the rules, were accused of what Hubbard called "ethics." They were put off the boat if they were found to be "in the wrong."

It was not long before Hubbard's boats were no longer permitted to dock in Mediterranean ports, so he snuck back to Florida and, practically speaking, hid from the IRS for the rest of his life.

Others who flew under his banner were not so lucky. In 1979, as a result of FBI raids, 11 senior people in the organization were convicted of obstruction of justice, burglary of government offices, and theft of documents and government property. In January of 1986, Hubbard died of a stroke. He was 74 years old.

Because he left no heir apparent, a power struggle ensued, after which David Miscavige emerged as president. Under his leadership, the organization underwent tremendous growth. It is currently a tax-exempt church that has amassed a fortune, holding real estate that is worth, by some estimates, hundreds of millions of dollars.

What is Scientology all about? How has it managed to convince so many very famous people to fork over a lot of money to practice the religion?

No religion can be adequately described in a brief format, but here are some of the basics. Scientology teaches that we are immortal, spiritual beings, called Thetans, which are resident in human bodies. Thetans have lived many past lives. Secret Scientology texts, available only to advanced practitioners, reveal that before taking up residence on earth within humans, Thetans were extraterrestrials.

Anyone who undergoes an "audit" by an accredited Scientologist teacher will eventually recount a rather typical series of previous events. Most of these events refer to an extraterrestrial called Xenu. Some 70 million years ago, Xenu was the ruler of a confederation of planets and was responsible for bringing billions of alien beings to Earth. They were then killed by thermonuclear weapons.

This information is kept secret from most followers, not being revealed until they have advanced enough to be "clear." The only reason I can report it here is that there are some folks who learned all this as Scientologists but have now left the fold and reported the information to various media outlets, including the aforementioned HBO special. But this forms the basis of the central mythological framework of Scientology. When it was finally revealed by a few former members, the organization became the subject of a lot of ridicule. It still suffers from the revelations.

Scientology may not be constantly in the news these days, but it refuses to go away, sometimes coming to the surface in surprising ways.

Martha Ross, for instance, of the Bay Area News Group, reported in a December 2020 article that Tom Cruise, known to be a rather advanced Scientologist, brought the group into focus during the filming of the seventh *Mission: Impossible* movie, *Dead Reckoning*. In the midst of the COVID-19 pandemic, the megastar caught some extras on the set who were not distancing themselves correctly. In a profanity-laced rant, he told them in no uncertain terms to shape up or they would be shipped out.

He was immediately lauded worldwide for supporting proper pandemic procedures. But then things got interesting. Some Cruise critics reminded their readers of his involvement with the Church of Scientology.

As Scientology's highest-profile convert, Tom Cruise has become an occasional lightning rod for the organization's detractors.

Mike Rinder, a former Scientology leader who had by then become a well-known critic of the organization, was quoted on his Twitter account: "This abusive side of TC is not often seen." In his opinion, Cruise was imitating the way

David Miscavige, who still heads up the organization, used to harangue his subordinates. "He learned from his buddy David Miscavige," Rinder said. "Sounds just like him—same language, same inflection, same 'I have the world on my shoulders and you are (expletive) me over' routine."

Investigative journalist Yashar Ali, who writes for the *Huffington Post* and *New York Magazine*, went even further. "Please remember as you're praising the audio of Tom Cruise yelling at crew members who don't follow Covid restrictions, that he's the chief enabler of a criminal organization that has destroyed people's lives, bankrupted and separated families, and led to people being imprisoned."

He went on, saying that Scientology reportedly broke up Cruise's marriage to Nicole Kidman because she wouldn't join the church, and that Scientology has "forced women to have abortions against their will, led people to die after being forced to follow dangerous pseudoscience, led former members to be chased all over the country/world by private investigators ... and those are just the broader issues." Ali concluded, "Tom Cruise is evil."

The battlegrounds were now firmly set. "Covidites" against "non-Covidites." Cruise backers against Cruise critics. Marlow Stern, who writes for the *Daily Beast*, even suggested the whole thing might have been set up by the Church of Scientology to raise its public image by supporting pandemic guidelines. This was no doubt brought about because a spokesman for the church told the *Tampa Bay Times* that it enforced social distancing and decontamination practices at its facilities, using the "most powerful and aggressive decontaminant available."

As often happens when it comes to reporting about Hollywood stars, the voices quoted were loud, boisterous, and gobbled up by the public.

So, we return to our original statement: Some very successful people declare that Scientology is a life-saving religion. Others call it a business. Still others swear it is a cult.

Which is it? You'll have to be the judge.

RAËLIANS AND THE ELOHIM: INTELLIGENT DESIGN FOR ATHEISTS

There is no God, only the Elohim. They are a group of extra-terrestrial scientists who intelligently designed the human race. One of the Elohim is named Yahweh. In 1973, he revealed himself to Claude Vorilhon (b. 1946), a sports car journalist from France. According to the book *Intelligent Design*, written by Vorilhon after the encounter, Yahweh gave him a message: "Listen to me carefully. You will tell all human beings about this meeting, but you will tell them the truth about what they are, and about what we are." He then gave Vorilhon a new name, Raël.

Following instructions to the letter, Raël began his mission. It was the birth of the Raëlian movement, which is now the biggest UFO-based religion in the world. Raël's second book, *Les extra-terrestres m'ont ammené sur leur planête* ("Extraterrestrials took me to their planet"), describes his actual encounter with the entire group. In this book, he recalls how he was given certain insights that were needed to enable humans to fully blossom. He was introduced to the mysteries of cloning. He even had the opportunity to watch as his own double was being manufactured in a vat containing some kind of liquid. The Elohim taught him about their system of government, "geniocracy," which consists of a kind of pecking order in which geniuses rule with benevolent love.

Raëlians began their work in France, established headquarters in Geneva, Switzerland, and opened up branch offices in Canada and eventually more countries. In the United States they took root first in Hawaii, South Florida, and Southern California. They now claim 60,000 members in 90 countries around the world, with Japan being the most popular.

Their chief claim to fame is that in 2002, they announced to the world that they had produced the world's first human clone. Their claim, however, was never proved to be true.

Who are these people? There certainly are a lot of them. What is the great attraction?

Let's start with the basics. Their official title is the International Raëlian Movement (IRM), or the Raëlian Church, de-

> In 2002, they announced to the world that they had produced the world's first human clone. Their claim, however, was never proved to be true.

pending on who you talk to. Raël is most definitely in charge. The story about his rise to power is a fascinating one. It goes something like this.

In the ancient past, the Elohim, an extraterrestrial species, created humanity using what to us is advanced technology. The name "Elohim" is found in the Bible. It is one of the names of God used in the Pentateuch, the first five books. So is "Yahweh," but in the original language of the Bible it is spelled YHVH. Jews believed the name of God too sacred to pronounce, so whenever they wrote it down in Hebrew, they left out the vowels to ensure the reader wouldn't say it aloud by mistake. (Even today in English, some Jews spell God "Gd" or "G-d.") In most English Bibles the name is usually translated as "Jehovah" or "THE LORD."

Raël considered this a mistranslation. "Elohim," he said, actually means "those who came from the sky." When the Bible tells us that God made humans "in his own image," it is actually referring not to God or to a god but to Elohim "from the sky," or ancient aliens.

Mistaking "Elohim" for gods was an understandable error. The Elohim were so advanced that early humans mistook them for gods and wrote about them as such. But Raëlians are, by their own admission, atheists.

The Elohim created 40 Elohim/human hybrids who, over the centuries, served as prophets. The Buddha, Jesus, Muhammad, and Joseph Smith were only a few of them. These prophets were born through unions between one of the Elohim (the singular is "Eloha") and a mortal woman, chosen for her "virgin DNA." Down through the ages, their job was to prepare humanity for the shocking news about their origins. Raël is the fortieth in line, and the last.

In 1945, when the United States dropped an atomic bomb on Hiroshima, Japan, the human race entered what is called the Age

In Japan, an alien character mascot does public outreach for the Raëlian Church. Raëlism teaches that prophets of the past were human-alien hybrids created by the Elohim, or visitors from the sky.

of "Apocalypse" or "Revelation," and its existence was threatened by a technology they were not yet equipped to control. This event was prophesied by Jesus, who, two thousand years before, warned humanity what would come to pass.

The job now, and it is an urgent one, is to find a way of harnessing new scientific and technological development for peaceful purposes. Once this is done, the Elohim will return to earth, share their technology with humanity, and establish a utopia. To accomplish this, they first need us to build an embassy that will include a landing pad for their spaceship and a hotel to make them comfortable. This complex will, hopefully, be built in Israel, where the Elohim will descend with the 39 previous prophets. There they will meet with representatives of the world's various nations. For this project there is no immediate rush, however. The Elohim are not expected to land until 2035.

Until then, and to speed the process along, Raëlians are encouraged to participate in daily meditation. Their future includes immortality through human cloning and a system of ethics that includes, as often seems to be the case, a strong emphasis on sexual experimentation.

This vision for the future was first presented in Raël's 1974 book, *Le Livre qui dit la verité*, or "The book that tells the truth." Following its release, Raël started an organization called MADECH (*Mouvement pour l'Accueil des Elohim, Créateurs de l'Humanité*, or Movement for Welcoming the Elohim, Creators of Humanity), which never really got off the ground. Just two years later, he disbanded it and began the Raëlian Church. This is the one that caught on. It contains an internal command structure of seven levels, which soon began to attract enough of a following that the group was able to afford an estate in France.

When Raël returned to earth from his trip into space, he attempted to form a French political party called la Geniocratie. Its purpose was to create a one-world government, with leadership positions based on intelligence tests. It didn't help its cause that the group's symbol was a swastika inside a star of David—both potent symbols with a lot of earthly baggage. That led to accusations that the Raëlians were preaching a form of fascism. Some of the Raëlian leaders were arrested, held for questioning, and had their documents seized. Raël responded by abandoning the group's political project. Soon, they migrated to Québec, Canada.

> It didn't help their cause that the group's symbol was a swastika inside a star of David.

In 1998, Raël established the Order of Angels. This group consisted solely of women, who are generally sequestered from the surrounding society. Their task was to be trained "properly" (no one on the outside seems to know exactly what that means) so that they could become future consorts of the Elohim.

A second internal group, begun a year later, was called the Clonaid, directed by Brigitte Boisselier. It was engaged in the science of human cloning and announced in 2002 that it had been successful in its endeavors. The baby was named, of course, Eve. But Eve has never been identified, much less tested. So for the present, the world has to take the word of the Raëlians that she exists and is now a young adult. She will be revealed when the time is right.

Unfortunately, this announcement brought the organization under a lot of governmental scrutiny, to say nothing of protests that were staged by women's and gay rights groups, as well as anti-nuke-testing advocates. Journalists, former Raëlians, and other anti-cult groups, including many religious scholars, joined in the fray.

The key to participating in the church is the practice of meditation. When Raël visited the Elohim's planet, he was taught a meditation technique that was intended to activate his brain potential while developing sensuality. All this was to gain access and connection to the Infinite. With this came the ability to become infinite himself. He outlined the technique in a tract called *Raël's Sensual Meditation*, which he published in 1980. It forms the basis for the group's work.

Over the years, various reporters have infiltrated what Raëlians call their open-to-the-public "Happiness Academies." Opinions vary as to what goes on at these meetings. Reports of nude dancing are common, although denied by members.

If such reports are true, though, it should come as no surprise. Raël himself has initiated an annual "Go Topless" protest, a street demonstration that takes place every year in late August, in several cities around the United States and in other countries. He is quoted by multiple sources as saying, "As long as men can go topless, women should have the same constitutional right, or men should also be forced to wear something that hides their chests."

> Raël himself has initiated an annual "Go Topless" protest, a street demonstration that takes place every year in late August.

Nudity by itself, of course, is certainly not proof of cult activity, as much as some conservative religionists would like to insist that it is. Raël also instituted Women's Equality Day, which sounds like a noble goal. Still, many members make light of the whole topic.

Some Hindu beliefs seem to peek out occasionally from Raëlian doctrine. This is especially seen in his use of the word *maya*, or "illusion." According to Raël, everything around us is an illusion. This especially includes things such as religion, nationality, color, and gender. Even democracy is an illusion, according to the doctrine, because it "changes nothing."

Reporters, even those who criticize his beliefs, seem to be pretty much in agreement that Raël is a gifted orator. When he appears before an audience wearing his white robe, he seems to know how to convey his message. A Raëlian organizer named Houari, who helps run various Happiness Academies, summed it up well: "Raël fits the perfect modern-day criteria of how you would act if someone would say, 'I need you to relay this message to humanity, go ahead and do it.'"

Susan Palmer, however, has a slightly contrasting view. She is a sociologist who has written 12 books on new religious organizations. One of them is *Aliens Adored: Raël's UFO Religion*. She spent 15 years watching and writing about the movement and has earned a reputation as one of the world's foremost outside authorities on Raëlians. In her opinion, "[Raël] is not a very well-educated person, and he doesn't write very well either. But he certainly has leadership qualities. He's very intense and enthusiastic, and actually very creative."

Vishnu demonstrates *maya* to a sage by appearing as an infant on a fig leaf in a deluge. After experiencing other vivid visions, the sage realizes everything was an illusion.

Raël is now well into his 70s, having been born in 1946. He leads one of the most fascinating, certainly the most controversial, and probably the biggest UFO cult in the world. What happens next is, of course, anyone's guess, but the group does not show any indications of fading anytime soon. Probably it will thrive until at least 2035, when the Elohim return. And if they don't show up, who can tell what will happen?

INTO THE UNIVERSE: LATTER-DAY SAINTS AND THE COLONIZATION OF THE COSMOS

In 2011, *The Book of Mormon*, a musical comedy by Trey Parker, Robert Lopez, and Matt Stone, opened on Broadway. It offered a satirical look at the beliefs and practices of the Church of Jesus Christ of Latter-day Saints—commonly called the Mormons.

The church, naturally, pushed back right away about how some of its beliefs were misconstrued and ridiculed. One of them was the idea that someday, every Mormon will be given their own planet to rule.

At issue was a song that mentioned Kolob, which an Associated Press writer explained is the "planet or star closest to the throne of God." It is referred to in the Book of Abraham, a book of scripture included in *The Pearl of Great Price*, written by Joseph Smith, the founder of the religion. In the musical, a fictional Mormon missionary sings about the Mormon doctrine in which he fervently believes: "I believe that God has a plan for all of us. I believe that plan involved me getting my own planet. I believe that God lives on a planet called Kolob."

It probably doesn't help at all that the popular TV series *Battlestar Galactica* features a planet called "Kobol." *Battlestar Galactica* was created by a Mormon.

> **Although Kolob is named in a Mormon hymn, nowhere is it implied that it is the place Mormons will go when they die.**

Although Kolob is named in a Mormon hymn, nowhere is it implied that it is the place Mormons will go when they die. It comes from one rather obscure verse in Mormon Scripture, and it is by no means described in any kind of vivid detail. Matthew Bowman, an assistant professor of religion at Hampden-Sydney College, assures his students that "even most Mormons aren't sure what exactly to make of the reference."

But truth doesn't stop a good rumor.

So the church called the presentation in the play a "cartoonish image" and published a series of articles trying to explain what Mormons believe and what that belief is based on. Still, the statements issued by the church didn't seem to quite deny that there is something behind the accusation: "While few Latter-day Saints would identify with caricatures of having their own planet, most would agree that the awe inspired by creation hints at our creative potential in the eternities." It went on to say that "the expectation of exaltation is more figurative and ambiguous than boiling it down to living on one planet.... Church members imagine exaltation less through images of what they will get, and more through the relationships they have now, and how those relationships might be purified and elevated."

The statement certainly sounds theological, but what does it mean? Who are the Latter-day Saints, really?

In 1820, the little town of Palmyra, New York, was typical of the many towns and villages that flourished along the Erie Canal. Religious revival hit the area, the impact of which can still be seen in the small town that is famous for the fact that a church of a different denomination stands on each of the four corners of its main intersection. They surround what was—until a few decades ago, at least, when I lived there—Palmyra's only traffic light, which sparked some interesting theological debates on Sunday mornings at about 11 o'clock.

A young man named Joseph Smith (1805–1844), whose family had migrated down from Vermont, was caught up and confused by the religious questions of the day. Every preacher seemed to claim that his own church was the "right" church. Methodists vied with Presbyterians for new converts, and many other long-forgotten sects all added their voices to the spiritual mix. It was typical of the American melting-pot kind of frontier revival of the early nineteenth century.

Smith decided he needed to go right to the source for guidance. He began to pray for help in knowing God's will concerning which church he should join: "In the midst of this war of words and tumult of opinions, I often said to myself, What is to be done? Who of all these parties are right; or, are they all wrong together?"

In a small grove of trees now called the Sacred Grove, which is visited by many tourists every year, Smith received his answer. He later claimed that God the Father and Jesus Christ appeared to him, warning him not to join any church. Just as God had appeared to Moses and Paul in former times, he appeared to Smith with a message. The times were changing. Something new was about to happen.

In a stained-glass window from 1913, Joseph Smith is depicted receiving his first vision from God the Father and Jesus.

Instructed to climb Hill Cumorah, a small glacial drumlin just north of Palmyra on the way to the little village of Manchester, Smith did so and met the angel Moroni, son of the great prophet Mormon, who showed him where golden plates were buried that would answer Smith's questions. They were written in a language Smith described as "Reformed Egyptian Hieroglyphics," and he was able to translate them because along with the plates he discovered a pair of "translating spectacles" that allowed him to read the lost language. When translated, they became the Book of Mormon, Another Testament of Jesus Christ.

The story they told changed Smith's life. When Jesus Christ walked the Galilee, he organized his church to be the vehicle whereby God, the Heavenly Father, would reveal himself to humanity and welcome them into heaven. The apostles continued this tradition and preached the Gospel during their lifetimes. They were the saints of the former days. But gradually the church pulled away from the Gospel. It became apostate, and God withdrew the church from earth. Now, in these latter days, it was to be restored according to the prophecy given by the apostle Peter in Acts 3:19-21:

> Repent, then, and turn to God, so that your sins may be wiped out, that times of refreshing may come from the Lord, and that he may send the Messiah, who has been appointed for you—even Jesus. Heaven must receive him until the time comes for God to restore everything, as he promised long ago through his holy prophets.

Mormon, the author of the golden plates and one of the last of the prophets of ancient America, had buried the record there in Hill Cumorah centuries before. It described how Lehi, a prophet who had lived in Jerusalem some 600 years before the birth of Christ, had sailed with a small group of people from the Mediterranean Sea all the way to the Americas. They had built a great civilization in Central America while trading, and eventually warring, all the way north to the place of present-day Palmyra.

After his resurrection in Jerusalem, Jesus Christ appeared in the Americas, preaching the Gospel to his "sheep of another fold." This reference is from John 10:16: "And other sheep I have, which are not of this fold: them also I must bring, and they shall hear my voice; and there shall be one fold, and one shepherd."

Alas, the people in America were no different from those in other places of the world where the Gospel had been preached and rejected. God raised up prophets, but they were ridiculed. War broke out. The last great battle between God's faithful and the apostate armies took place at Hill Cumorah. The descendants of those who had fought were the people Americans later called Indians. Although remnants of history and snatches of language remained to hint of the events that had taken place so many centuries before, the story was lost.

Lost, that is, until Smith translated the Golden Plates and revealed what had taken place there. He was able to do so, he said, because God was restoring the saints in these latter days, fulfilling the prophecy and preparing the way for the return of Jesus Christ.

Moroni concluded his book with a great promise. He said those who read his words and sincerely prayed about their meaning would be shown by the Holy Ghost that the message was true and that God's promise was being fulfilled.

No one was allowed to see the plates except Smith, although he did later reveal them to two different groups of witnesses so they could testify to their existence.

The Book of Mormon is not meant to replace the Bible. It is to be used as a companion to what Christians call the Old and New Testaments. Mormons claim it predicts the history of the Americas for some 2,500 years. It prophesied the voyage of Christopher Columbus, the fate of Native Americans, the coming of the Puritans, the Revolutionary War, and much more.

> **On April 6, 1830, the Church of Jesus Christ of Latter-day Saints was organized in Fayette, New York. It now boasts over 11 million members around the world.**

On April 6, 1830, ten years after Smith received the plates, translated them, and began to preach the newfound Gospel, the Church of Jesus Christ of Latter-day Saints was organized in Fayette, New York. It now boasts over 11 million members around the world.

The church experienced persecution right from the beginning. Threatened and finally driven out of town, Smith led his followers west, joining the great migration taking place at the time. In 1844, both Joseph Smith and his brother were killed by a mob while they were imprisoned in Carthage, Illinois, awaiting charges for the destruction of an anti-Mormon newspaper press.

Brigham Young (1801–1877) took control. Leading the people across more than one thousand miles of unsettled prairie, he finally arrived, in 1847, at the great Salt Lake Valley of present-day Utah. This, Young declared, would be the scene of the New Jerusalem. Salt Lake City was born. From this base, Mormon communities were established in Utah, Wyoming, Idaho, Colorado, New Mexico, Arizona, Nevada, California, north to Canada, and south into Mexico. They were united by the Bible, the Book of Mormon, and the Thirteen Articles of Faith that Smith had summarized concerning the beliefs of the new church.

Although the official name of the church is the Church of Jesus Christ of Latter-day Saints, they are often called Mormons, after the name of the one of the authors of the text translated by

Smith. They are a Christian church in that they follow Jesus Christ, but they do not consider themselves to be Protestant because they feel that by the time of the Protestant Reformation of the sixteenth century, the true church had long since been withdrawn from the earth. Restored in the time of Joseph Smith, it now awaits the literal gathering of Israel and the restoration of the Ten Tribes, "lost" since the Assyrian invasion of Israel beginning in 732 BCE.

Zion, the New Jerusalem, will be built on the American continent, where Jesus Christ will someday return to rule planet Earth.

Brigham Young took up leadership of the young church after Joseph Smith's murder in Illinois, leading the Latter-day Saints into the West.

It is probably very frustrating to church leaders that, in light of all this history and theology, people seem to ask the same two questions time and again.

The first is probably more prurient than theological: "What is the Mormon position regarding polygamy?"

The church now forbids plural marriage. Its official position is that at various times in the past, God commanded a few men to take more than one wife. Abraham, Isaac, Jacob, Moses, David, and Solomon all did it. When Joseph Smith and Brigham Young were told to take more than one wife, they questioned the practice, but were faithful to God and followed his will. Since 1890, however, when Mormon president Wilford Woodruff received a revelation from God that the practice had to cease, it has been forbidden by official church policy.

> **Do some Mormons still practice plural marriage? Of course. There are fundamentalists in every religion who believe their church has become too liberal and refuse to follow suit.**

Do some Mormons still practice plural marriage? Of course. There are fundamentalists in every religion who believe their church has become too liberal and refuse to follow suit. But polygamists are excommunicated by the officially recognized church, the greatest punishment the church can deliver.

Some fundamentalist Mormon sects still operate, however. They have been disfellowshipped by the main church, but sometimes they still manage to make headlines.

One such event took place at the Yearning for Zion Ranch, a community made up of members of the Fundamentalist Church of Jesus Christ of Latter-day Saints, also known as Fundamentalist Mormonism, near Eldorado, Texas. In May 2008, police followed up on an alert from someone named "Sarah," an alleged 16-year-old girl, who claimed to be a member of the church. She had tipped off the authorities to the sexual abuse of children on the ranch by adult men.

It turned out that "Sarah" was, in fact, woman named Rozita Swinton, who later swore she had placed the call as a joke. Swinton had been arrested for such hoaxes in the past. But police, not knowing all this, raided the compound and placed 412 children in the temporary custody of the State of Texas.

Although there were multiple cases of polygamy at the ranch and a few of the children had minor bone fractures, there were no signs of sexual abuse in any of the children. After a legal battle, the Texas Supreme Court ordered the children to be sent back to their mothers, finding that there was not enough evidence of abuse to remove the children.

Governments and individual citizens tend to assume the worst when it comes to cults. Even so, the church denounced polygamy after the children were returned, and since then there has been neither an uproar nor an outcry.

The second question comes as a result of recent lawsuits involving people researching their family trees: "Why does the Mormon Church keep such extensive genealogical records?"

Mormons believe in baptism by immersion. That's not much different from some Protestant churches. But according to Mormon theology, you can baptize the dead by proxy, so to speak. You can stand in for them at the temple and be baptized in their stead. To identify deceased family members in order to baptize them, Mormons have established a huge genealogical databank.

This project has caused some interesting news reports. Mormons have put prison inmates in Utah to work transcribing, from German records released since the Holocaust, the names of Jewish people the church wants to baptize by proxy. This practice has raised serious church-state separation problems, to say nothing of the fact that living Jewish relatives don't want their ancestors being baptized. They feel it is disrespectful. A class-action lawsuit was supposed to have put an end to the practice, but it was recently discovered, according to Jewish complainants, that deceased Jews were still being baptized by proxy. The Mormons had apparently broken their word.

The church has stated that these people were baptized accidentally, claiming that the transcribers could not always tell whether the deceased were Jewish just from their names.

The LDS Church performs baptisms for the dead by proxy in dedicated temples, such as the Salt Lake Temple, home of this elaborate baptismal font.

The principle at stake is this: Mormons believe families are united forever, even after death. It is very important for them to discover who their family is and to make sure they are baptized, thus fulfilling God's requirements on earth.

Meanwhile, a lot of Gentile genealogists, given free access to Mormon computer files, are at least happy with the result of the doctrine, regardless of their religious beliefs.

Mormons have endured quite a bit of persecution, yet most who come into contact with them as a group come away with nothing but good things to say. The Mormon Tabernacle Choir is one of the most respected vocal ensembles in the world. Residents of Palmyra, New York, who each summer face an influx of thousands of Mormons arriving to attend the famous Mormon Pageant, a reenactment of the Mormon story that is held on Hill Cumorah, are unanimous in their praise of Mormon visitors. Townspeople claim Mormons are always well dressed and well behaved, and they never drink or smoke. The church erects beautiful buildings and maintains an extremely polished website and visitor center. Its members strive to be polite and helpful.

Some conservative Christians, however, ridicule the religion, labeling it a dangerous cult. Articles have addressed the faith's past ban on Black men in their clergy and the early history of polygamy.

Way back in 1832, Alexander Campbell published *Delusions: An Analysis of the Book of Mormon.* In it he pointed out that the golden plates seem to have anticipated and given a definitive "answer to just about every error and truth discussed in New York for the last ten years." In other words, according to Campbell, the book was a hoax written by Smith, conveniently kept secret by not allowing witnesses to watch the "translation" process, and designed to answer the current theological dilemmas of the day.

The idea that Native Americans were descended from the ten Lost Tribes of Israel was a popular one, and it had been around for a long time. The late Vernal Holley, after a comprehensive study of the geography of the Book of Mormon, claims that a map of the "Holy Land according to Joseph Smith" can be placed right over a map of present-day New York. The two, he claims, are identical, including place names, rivers, lakes, and historic landmarks.

Some who have "come out" of the church insist the public image and theology is a cover for a domineering sect that controls the lives of its members and teaches a totally different set of beliefs from those published for public consumption.

Even Sherlock Holmes enters the picture. In Sir Arthur Conan Doyle's first adventure featuring the famous detective, *A Study in Scarlet* (1887), Mormons are the evil enemy the fledgling detective has to defeat.

While the church has faced persecution since its inception, it continues to flourish and grow. Any visit to its newly completed visitor's center in Palmyra is a treat. Its television cable network is always informative. And its magnificent choir will no doubt continue to make definitive choral recordings for a long time.

It is very common, especially in these days of social media when virtually anyone can obtain a few minutes of fame at the stroke of a button, for critics to latch on to the most outrageous or unique aspects of religions. That might be why the perception of Mormons inheriting their own planets became widespread.

On the other hand, the words of Isaiah 9:10 still raise an eyebrow:

> Of the increase of his government and peace there will be no end. He will reign on David's throne and over his kingdom, establishing and upholding it with justice and righteousness from that time on and forever. The zeal of the LORD Almighty will accomplish this.

Does an eternally expanding universe imply a constantly growing number of habitable planets for people to carry out the mission of Jesus? Since Jesus came here, will his "brothers and sisters," who have been told to mimic his work even if it means "picking up their own cross and following him," travel to those planets, to accomplish there what he did here? Is Earth a training ground for future saviors of worlds unknown? God only knows.

HEAVEN'S GATE: HELP FROM ABOVE?

On July 23, 1995, amateur astronomers Alan Hale and Thomas Bopp, working independently, observed for the first time in recorded history a comet that now holds their name. It was the most distant comet ever to be discovered by amateurs.

Little did they know that their sighting, once the news of its discovery was spread abroad, would two years later play a part in the suicide deaths of Marshall Herff Applewhite (1931–1997) and 38 of his followers, all members of the religious UFO cult called Heaven's Gate.

It all started in May of 1931. Applewhite was born in the town of Spur, Texas. There was no indication at the time that his life would lead to one of the most famous mass suicides in American history. By all accounts, he was pretty normal. After an uneventful childhood, if any childhood can really be called uneventful, he graduated from Austin College in 1952, got married, and then spent two years in the Army Signal Corps. All regular stuff.

Long before his own foray into religious leadership, Applewhite attended the Presbyterian-affiliated Austin College in his home state of Texas.

At first, his talents led him toward a life on stage. He had a good baritone voice and enjoyed singing opera. A talented public speaker as well, he spent time in New York City during the 1960s hoping to succeed as an actor. But like so many artists who try to grab that particular brass ring, he failed in his attempts. Moving to the University of Alabama, he conducted singing groups for a while, and he eventually returned to Texas, where he headed up the music department at a university in Houston.

It was there, back in his home state, where things started to fall apart for him. Following a divorce in 1968, reports began to circulate that he was struggling with his sexual identity. Two years later, he quit his job in the midst of what might best be described as a nervous breakdown.

It is at times such as these when people are most apt to have a religious conversion, and Applewhite was no exception. The one who was there to guide him through it all was Bonnie Lu Nettles (1927–1985), who had a good background in the Bible and was devoted to a spiritual path.

The biblical Book of Revelation describes life at the end times of human history, just before Jesus returns. It speaks of two witnesses who will prophesy at this tumultuous time:

> I was given a reed like a measuring rod and was told, "Go and measure the temple of God and the altar, with its worshipers. But exclude the outer court; do not measure it, because it has been given to the Gentiles. They will trample on the holy city for 42 months. And I will appoint my two witnesses, and they will prophesy for 1,260 days, clothed in sackcloth." They are "the two olive trees" and the two lampstands, and "they stand before the Lord of the earth." If anyone tries to harm them, fire comes from their mouths and devours their enemies. This is how anyone who wants to harm them must die. They have power to shut up the heavens so that it will not rain during the time they are

prophesying; and they have power to turn the waters into blood and to strike the earth with every kind of plague as often as they want.

Now when they have finished their testimony, the beast that comes up from the Abyss will attack them, and overpower and kill them. Their bodies will lie in the public square of the great city—which is figuratively called Sodom and Egypt—where also their Lord was crucified. For three and a half days some from every people, tribe, language and nation will gaze on their bodies and refuse them burial. The inhabitants of the earth will gloat over them and will celebrate by sending each other gifts, because these two prophets had tormented those who live on the earth.

But after the three and a half days the breath of life from God entered them, and they stood on their feet, and terror struck those who saw them. Then they heard a loud voice from heaven saying to them, "Come up here." And they went up to heaven in a cloud, while their enemies looked on. (Rev. 11:1–12)

According to some scholars from the Church of Jesus Christ of Latter-day Saints, these two witnesses were Joseph Smith and his brother Hyrum. The Bahá'í faith identifies the two witnesses as Muhammad, the founder of Islam, and Ali, the son of Abú Tálib. Most Evangelical Christians look to a future fulfillment. Applewhite and Nettles came to believe that *they* were the appointed ones to whom the passage referred. Hence, they were now engaged on an important spiritual mission. They took to the road and wandered the country, firm in their belief that they were called by God.

Earthly laws no longer applied to them. They were above such things. It was no surprise, then, that they were arrested for

> Earthly laws no longer applied to them. They were above such things. It was no surprise, then, that they were arrested for credit card fraud in 1974.

credit card fraud in 1974. The charges were subsequently dropped. This gave them even more motivation. Assured from heaven on high, Applewhite rented a car in St. Louis, Missouri, and never returned it.

This time God didn't come to his rescue. He was tracked down and sentenced to six months in prison. But like St. Paul of old, who, when imprisoned, used the time to study and write one-third of the New Testament, Applewhite spent his time studying and refining his theology. He became even more convinced that he and Nettles had a divine destiny to fulfill.

To make a long story short, he believed that he and Nettles came from a place he called a "Level Above Human." This was a physical place that the Bible describes as heaven. Like Jesus, he had been sent to earth to prepare the human race to reach this next level.

According to Applewhite, "The Evolutionary Level Above Human" (TELAH) is a "physical, corporeal place." It is another world in our universe, where residents live in pure bliss and nour-ish themselves by absorbing pure sunlight. At the next level, be-ings do not engage in sexual intercourse, eating, or dying—the things that make us "mammalian" here. He believed that what the Bible calls "God" is actually a highly developed extraterrestrial.

Not all extraterrestrials are good. Some mean us harm. "Lu-ciferians" are evil aliens, posing as God while conspiring to keep us from developing spiritually. They are advanced beings, practicing advanced technology. They possess spacecraft, which are seen from time to time, and are capable of space and time travel, telepathy, and in-creased longevity. They use holograms to produce fake miracles. Because they are flesh-and-blood beings, with gender, they stopped trying to achieve the kingdom of God thousands of years ago. All religions currently on earth have long since been corrupted by them.

Applewhite theorized that human-ity was being visited by near-om-nipotent extraterrestrials, including some who meant us harm.

After developing this theology, Ap-plewhite began to refer to his body as a ve-hicle. To achieve ascension, people had to separate their true selves from all that was "human," meaning earthly needs and desires. He further believed that a UFO would return him to the next level after he and Nettles had completed their earthly mission.

Upon release from prison, now that he had a better understanding of who he was and why he was on earth, Applewhite and Nettles hit the road again, speaking at informational gatherings organized wherever they could muster a crowd. He was the talented talker; she was his spiritual source of strength. A few people listened, and they developed a following.

By 1975 they had attracted about 20 followers. After a meeting held in Oregon, they caught the attention of the national news. The next year, they were the subject of a book called *U.F.O. Missionaries Extraordinary* by Hayden C. Hewes and Brad Steiger.

Applewhite and Nettles didn't like their increased public scrutiny. From then on, when they sent their followers out as missionaries to evangelize the country, they instructed them to keep a low profile. As a result, even at the height of their influence, there were never more than a few hundred members of their group. Only their most dedicated and obedient followers were allowed to stay on in the fold.

Various spiritual practices were begun, including unusual diets and sex practices. One of the most extreme was that Applewhite and a few other male members were castrated. Drinking and smoking were forbidden. Lying and breaking the rules were major offenses. Uniformity in dress became important. Members wore baggy clothing, and all wore short hair to camouflage their gender and sexuality.

Applewhite taught that one of the ways extraterrestrials communicate with humans is by staging a "walk-in." A walk-in can best be defined as "an entity who occupies a body that has been vacated by its original soul." Applewhite explained that "an extraterrestrial walk-in is from another planet."

The whole idea behind a walk-in is to transform the individual host. Applewhite and Nettles believed they had experienced this and were working with clean slates thereafter. They had taken on a new life, as James R. Lewis described it in his book

Odd Gods: New Religions and the Cult Controversy, having managed to "erase their human personal histories as the histories of souls who formerly occupied the bodies of Applewhite and Nettles." The walk-in who took up residence in Applewhite was the same one who had inhabited Jesus 2,000 years ago. "Jesus" was just the name of the body of an ordinary man who had held no sacred properties. But the walk-in had, in essence, delivered next-level information to him.

By the 1980s, the group rented houses in various regions near Dallas. A few of them got outside jobs using counterfeit names. But in 1985, disaster struck. Nettles died of cancer. Without the source of his spiritual strength, Applewhite began to flounder.

That, finally, brings us back to the comet Hale-Bopp—its identification in 1995, and the prediction that it would become visible to earthlings two years later. Applewhite saw the comet as physical proof that a spaceship was coming, hiding from view in the comet's wake, to take them to the next level. Within a year, the group used its successful computer business, housed in an exclusive neighborhood in Rancho Santa Fe, California, to produce videos that advertised their beliefs and encouraged others to leave with them. Their motto was that this was the "last chance to evacuate Earth before it's recycled." The videos were called *Beyond Human—The Last Call*. They included information about the group and the next level where they were headed. They took out ads worldwide, including *USA Today*, which ran an article with the headline "UFO Cult Resurfaces with Final Offer."

The comet Hale-Bopp, seen here over Zabriskie Point in Death Valley, April 1997, played a crucial role in the tragic end of the Heaven's Gate cult.

By 1997, excitement about the comet was reaching a fever pitch. It was now plainly visible to the naked eye, and it seemed as though everyone was talking about it. On March 21, the group ate a Last Supper-like communion meal at a local restaurant. They all ate the same thing: turkey pot pie, cheesecake with blueberries, and iced tea. It wasn't bread and wine, but it served the same purpose.

On March 26, their bodies were found, all dressed the same, covered with purple shrouds. They had taken their own lives, drinking a mixture of vodka and barbiturates.

The news of the mass suicide rocked the nation. Media outlets ran clips from a video that Applewhite had made shortly before his death, explaining his mission while encouraging others to follow along. Most members had recorded exit videos. But, needless to say, that did little to comfort family, friends, and a fascinated public.

What seems especially strange, emphasizing the lengths to which people will go to adjust their beliefs to physical reality, is that the group was against suicide. How could that be? Well, all you have to do to make it make sense is to redefine what you mean by "suicide."

Suppose you reason that "suicide" means death to your soul, not to your external vehicle, or body. As a matter of fact, you might have to "disable" your external vehicle in order to free your soul so it can attain the next level. Real suicide would consist of not allowing your consciousness to leave your human body in order to ascend. Remaining alive instead of participating in the group suicide would be suicide of your consciousness, and that would be a sin. So killing yourself in order to live is not suicide. *Not* killing yourself—your body—is.

> **Heaven's Gate, the name Applewhite and Nettles used for their group, was very much into ancient alien theory.**

Heaven's Gate, the name Applewhite and Nettles used for their group, was very much into ancient alien theory. This is the idea that extraterrestrials visited planet Earth in the distant past. Applewhite believed—again, as explained by Lewis—that "aliens planted the seeds of current humanity millions of years ago, and have come to reap the harvest of their work in the form of spiritually evolved individuals who will join the ranks of flying saucer crews. Only a select few members of humanity will be chosen to advance to this transhuman state. The rest will be left to wallow in the spiritually poisoned atmosphere of a corrupt world."

The individuals who chose to join Heaven's Gate, follow Applewhite and Nettle's belief system, and make the sacrifices required for membership were allowed to escape human suffering. For the rest of us, it seems, our suffering will just have to continue.

PROPHETS OF THE END TIMES: TELLING THE FUTURE FOR FUN AND PROFIT

Technically speaking, a prophet is one who is believed to speak for God. But generally speaking, when people hear the word "prophet," they tend to think of one who sees the future. In popular parlance, "prophesying" and "telling the future" are the same thing.

People have done this seemingly forever, using all kinds of methods:

- ◆ Aeromancy refers to seeking the future by looking upward toward the skies. Weather forecasters do this all the time, of course, but the craft also includes watching the patterns of birds and butterflies.

- ◆ Sometimes people "draw straws." This is called belomancy.

- ◆ If you have ever opened the Bible—or any book, for that matter—hoping for a message found in the first words you read, you are practicing bibliomancy.

- ◆ In olden days, prophets used to carve symbols on small bones, cast them on the ground, and determine the future by their positions. This is called astragalomancy.

◆ When you use special decks of cards to seek messages, it is called cartomancy. The phrase "it's in the cards" comes from this practice.

◆ Palmistry is the art of telling the future by reading creases on the open hand.

◆ Casting lots means to throw, or cast, objects such as dice or marked sticks to see how they land. If you use dice, it is called cubomancy. This is probably what the Jewish prophets did when, in Bible stories, they utilized the "urim and thummim" to determine God's will in a particular situation.

◆ A conjuror consults the spirits of the dead to foresee the future. A necromancer actually divines the future by reading dead bodies.

◆ Sometimes people follow advice given them in dreams. This is called oneiromancy.

◆ Dowsing with pendulums, forked sticks, or "L" rods is technically known as rhabdomancy.

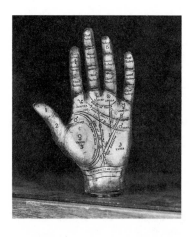

Of all the major methods to tell the future, palmistry is one of the most personal, connecting a person's physical characteristics directly to their fate.

◆ Finally, and most important to the subject of cults, we come to theomancy. This is when an oracle, speaking for God, declares a message from a deity that foretells what "must come to pass." Usually, the message is a bit complicated, and if the future doesn't unfold quite the way it was supposed to, the fault lies in the interpretation, not the prophet.

Here, for instance, is a prophecy illustrating theomancy from the Hebrew Scriptures:

See, the day of the Lord is coming—a cruel day, with wrath and fierce anger—to make the land desolate and destroy the sinners within it. The stars of heaven and their constellations will not show their light. The rising sun will be darkened and the moon will not give its light. I will punish the world for its evil, the wicked for their sins. I will put an end to the arrogance of the haughty and will humble the pride of the ruthless. I will make people scarcer than pure gold, more rare than the gold of Ophir. Therefore, I will make the heavens tremble; and the earth will shake from its place at the wrath of the Lord Almighty, in the day of his burning anger. (Isaiah 13:9–13)

And this, from the Apostle Paul, in the New Testament:

But mark this: There will be terrible times in the last days. People will be lovers of themselves, lovers of money, boastful, proud, abusive, disobedient to their parents, ungrateful, unholy, without love, unforgiving, slanderous, without self-control, brutal, not lovers of the good, treacherous, rash, conceited, lovers of pleasure rather than lovers of God—having a form of godliness but denying its power. Have nothing to do with such people.

They are the kind who worm their way into homes and gain control over gullible women, who are loaded down with sins and are swayed by all kinds of evil desires, always learning but never able to come to a knowledge of the truth. Just as Jannes and Jambres opposed Moses, so also these teachers oppose the truth. They are men of depraved minds, who, as far as the faith is concerned, are rejected. But they will not get very far because, as in the case of those men, their folly will be clear to everyone. (2 Timothy 3:1–5)

For every passage of Scripture, there are probably at least two, and sometimes many, different interpretations. The same is true for other prophets whose words have been recorded and passed down through time. Sometimes these prophets and alleged prophets, even long after they are dead, develop a cult following. It is worthwhile for our purpose, then, to learn just what these prophets proclaimed.

We begin this section with the prophets who authored the Christian Bible.

FROM 666 TO THE "SEVENTY SEVENS": WHAT DOES THE BIBLE REALLY SAY ABOUT THE END?

People tend to find in the Bible what they expect to find there. Arguments to the contrary seldom make a difference. Many so-called experts have made a living out of interpreting what the Bible says about THE END—that is, the end of this world. But there is no standard of agreement. Take, for instance, the most argued-over number in the Bible—the famous 666.

> The [false prophet] also forced everyone, small and great, rich and poor, free and slave, to receive a mark on his right hand or on his forehead, so that no one could buy or sell unless he had the mark, which is the name of the beast or the number of his name.

> This calls for wisdom. If anyone has insight, let him calculate the number of the beast, for it is man's number. His number is 666. (Rev. 13:16–18)

These are surely among the most enigmatic verses in the Bible. They are certainly at the core of many a conspiracy theory. The numbers have caused so many fears that some people refuse to use any check numbered 666. Highways in both Arizona and Texas have had their official numbers changed due to complaints from Fundamentalists. Urban legends spread like wildfire, usually through people who claim they know people who are related to people who, for example, have had Social Security checks snatched out of their hands by bank tellers mysteriously claiming that these checks were not yet supposed to be issued.

Millennia of controversy have surrounded the passage in Revelation connecting the number 666 with the coming of a false prophet.

It is entertaining to speculate on the possibility that all this sound and fury might have been expended on the wrong number. A papyrus manuscript fragment discovered in Egypt sheds a different light on the issue of the number. It is purported to be a very early copy of a portion of the book of Revelation that lists the number as 616, not 666. If 616 is indeed the original number used by the author of Revelation, it would change much of the numerological speculation surrounding the interpretation of this passage.

> **A papyrus manuscript fragment discovered in Egypt sheds a different light on the issue of the number. It lists the number as 616, not 666.**

Whether or not the findings support the traditional text, what do the numbers really mean? Do they point to a yet-to-be-revealed antichrist, an ancient figure known to the original author of the book of Revelation, or a metaphysical power lurking behind the scenes of world history?

The many theories about the number 666 generally fall into one of three categories.

Past-Historic School of Biblical Interpretation: Authors espousing this view include such New Testament scholars as Marcus Borg and Dominic Crossan. This is the interpretive scheme that insists the original authors of Holy Writ must have been writing in terms their readers could have understood. If 666 refers to a man, it must have been a coded reference to someone who was alive at the time. Perhaps Nero, or one of the other Caesars, might fit the bill. After all, it was a time of persecution for the early church. Maybe the antichrist from "Babylon" was really Caesar from Rome.

Futurist School of Biblical Interpretation: Those espousing this view include popular authors such as Tim LaHaye, Jerry B. Jenkins, and Hal Lindsey. This school of thought, followed by most modern Evangelical Christian writers, believes that even if the prophecy has a meaning grounded in the past, it awaits a greater fulfillment in the future. They insist that the number refers to a man and to a system of economic control that will someday, just before the Second Coming of Jesus and the battle of Armageddon, engulf the whole earth. New 666 candidates are introduced every year, but so far no one person or bureaucratic system has been positively identified.

Intuitive/Metaphysical School of Biblical Interpretation. The author credited with popularizing this kind of theology is Walter Wink, who was a professor of biblical interpretation at Auburn Theological School in New York City. His approach is more difficult to understand. Some background in both biblical interpretation and history is required to fully grasp the ideas he puts forth.

In 1984, Walter Wink published the first volume of what eventually became a trilogy, examining the language of power in the New Testament. His thesis was that first-century writers intuitively understood realities they couldn't fully explain, at least in language familiar to our modern academic culture. They understood, for instance, that human organizations, such as governments, seem to operate under forces quite beyond their own control, taking on a personality that is bigger than any individual.

In the United States, for example, it often doesn't seem to matter much whether Democrats or Republicans are at the helm. Policies may vary somewhat, but the Washington mindset grinds on. "Pork" projects, filibusters, back-room deals, and heavy spending continue unabated. Similarly, in the private sector, the entire board of directors of General Motors could be replaced, but the company will continue as before. And, of course, the military will lumber forth in their familiar fashion long after its current commanders are gone. Change can be effected, but it requires a herculean effort. Even smaller institutions manifest this syndrome. Churches, for instance, or universities, develop "personalities" that seem to last for generation after generation.

Wink believed that the New Testament writers recognized this fact. They called the "powers" that control these forces "angels" and "principalities," among other descriptive terms. He quotes from the book of Revelation, for instance, where Jesus addresses comments not to the "church of Laodicea" but rather to "the *angel* of the church of Laodicea."

By this Wink doesn't mean that some fallen angel fluttered by and took control of the organization. Instead, he argues that human organizations actually develop traditions and customs that are so strong that they take on an almost metaphysical life of their own. To change the institution, the "angel," or spirit of tradition—the metaphysical reality of the institution—has to be changed. Whether the original authors *intellectually* understood all this modern psychology doesn't make any difference. They *intuitively* recognized the reality of it, and they gave it a name.

How does this kind of thinking relate to the battle of Armageddon and the number 666?

> **The author of Revelation does not say that the number 666 refers to "a" man. He says that "it is man's number." In other words, it symbolizes humanity, not one distinct individual.**

The author of Revelation does not say that the number 666 refers to "a" man. He says that "it is man's number." In other words, it symbolizes humanity, not one distinct individual. Six is one short of seven, the number of perfection, assigned to God throughout the Bible. Thus, 666 represents either fallen humanity or humans striving to become more than they are. Because God is a trinity, humans fall three times short of perfection. As such, 666 represents a human system, not a particular human.

But what system? It must represent an *economic* system because the number is associated with "buying and selling." As Revelation 13:17 says, "No one could buy or sell unless he had the mark." Perhaps the early writers intuitively understood, even two thousand years ago, that whoever controlled the economy controlled the population.

The current economic system of Western civilization that has spread around the entire planet began, it is thought by many conservative biblical scholars, some six thousand years ago, probably in Mesopotamia. It started with the Agricultural Revolution, a developmental leap that brought us writing, cities, job specialization, warfare over territory, male-dominated society, gods, and religions. The time before the Agricultural Revolution is called pre-history. The time after the invention of writing, originating as a result of this revolution, is called history.

In other words, "history" and the "buying and selling" economy that marks modern life began about six to eight thousand

Western history began with the development of writing in Mesopotamia, a fertile region also linked with the start of agriculture and many other civilizational advances.

years ago, at least according to this school of thought. This is also approximately when the Bible says the world began, if we take Genesis dates literally.

Perhaps the biblical writers really referred to the beginning of "our" world, not "the" world. This is when Adam and Eve walked out of the Garden of Eden and began to earn their bread by toiling at agriculture, following God's command in Genesis 3:19, "By the sweat of your brow you will eat your food."

Ever since the Agricultural Revolution, humanity has lived by trade. Civilizations rise and fall, but commerce is at the root of it all. Economic systems have been put in place. They all revolve around who controls the means of production—who can "buy or sell." But they all have one other thing in common. In each civilization, the rich tend to get richer and the poor tend to get poorer, until, eventually and inevitably, the civilization falls and something new replaces it. A spiritual, or metaphysical, economic power is in place. It demands of each of us that we participate. No one can really go it alone anymore. We all have Social Security numbers. We all carry credit cards. We have numbers, fingerprints, files, and tracking data. We cannot "buy or sell" without them.

As Walter Wink might well ask, is this what the biblical authors intuitively recognized, even two thousand years ago? Do we all wear the "mark of the beast"? As such, does "Armageddon" really refer to the demise of a six-thousand-year-old social system that carried, at its root, the seeds of its own destruction? When the Agricultural Revolution began its long ascendance, did fallen humanity, who unwittingly invented it, place on their hand and forehead the "mark of the beast"?

What, after all, does "antichrist" really mean? According to the author of 1 John, everyone who fails to acknowledge Jesus the Christ is an antichrist: "Who is the liar? It is the man who denies that Jesus is the Christ. Such a man is the antichrist."

> **Those who subscribe to the intuitive/metaphysical school of biblical interpretation believe that an "Armageddon" will mark the destruction of the economic system that has been in effect for six thousand years.**

In other words, those who subscribe to the intuitive/metaphysical school of biblical interpretation believe that an "Armageddon" will mark the destruction of the economic system that has been in effect for six thousand years. It is contrary to the commands of Jesus. He ordered us to "give a cup of cold water" in his name, to "turn the other cheek" and "walk the second mile." Jesus insisted that "true religion" meant giving, not hoarding. He never suggested anyone ever save for a rainy day.

To people who read the Bible this way, Armageddon represents spiritual warfare against the "Prince of this world," who has held sway ever since the Agricultural Revolution. We "fight not against flesh and blood," says Paul in Ephesians 6:10, "but against the rulers, against the authorities, against the powers of the dark world, and against the spiritual forces of evil in the heavenly realms." Those powers are not "beings" who were created by God and subsequently fell from grace. They are metaphysical powers inherent in a human invention, now called modem economics.

Fed by greed and avarice, sins that are contrary to Christ, or "antichrist," they have now grown so big as to take over our very lives. So great has their power become that we now take such powers for granted. But in the end, according to the biblical prophets, they will destroy us.

This is a totally different way of interpreting the book of Revelation and its depiction of the battle of Armageddon than those offered by biblical systems advanced before Wink's work in the 1980s.

So, there is no single "Christian" view of the future. Christians have divided and subdivided many times over the subject. Often within the same local church, even the same Bible-study circle, many different opinions will be aired. Still, we can categorize these differing views in a general way, understanding that shades of meaning exist within each category.

LIBERAL, NONLITERAL VIEWS

Liberal Christianity tends to read the end-of-history Bible passages as metaphors, written for specific people who lived at a specific time. According to this view, Jesus of Nazareth was a first-century Jew who understood the old Hebrew concept of the Divine in a fresh way. He attempted to teach his insights, was

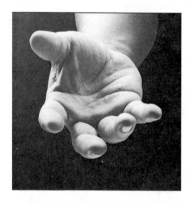

arrested by his detractors, and was crucified by the Roman government. But his ideas did not end with his death. All that he taught, all that he represented, all that he was—his very spirit—lived on in his followers after the Crucifixion. He will not literally return in a physical body. Rather, the church, his earthly body, carries on his ministry of love, reconciliation, and spiritual growth. Seen in this perspective, Armageddon—the final confrontation between good and evil—is not a future war. It is a constant battle against institutional power, human sin, and entrenched evil.

A nonliteral interpretation of Jesus's teachings may lead believers to stop waiting for (or seeking) literal battles and focus instead on how they can improve themselves spiritually.

Some Christians who hold views of this kind envision a gradual evolution of human spirituality. Others think there will have to be a revolution. They believe that humans may have to go to the very brink of Armageddon before they shape up.

Some liberal Christians believe that the Second Coming is personal, experienced whenever the spirit of Jesus becomes a living reality for an individual. That person is then converted to living life "in the spirit" rather than simply in the material world.

Others see the Second Coming as a metaphorical way of describing a quantum leap of the whole human race into universally recognizing the spiritual nature of life rather than the material. Many believe that spirituality is the normal human condition and was practiced by our ancestors. The evidence, they say, lies in stone circles like Stonehenge, the pyramids and ziggurats, and other megalithic monuments that were built because our ancestors were in tune with something we have forgotten.

This "great forgetting" is symbolized by the biblical story of Eden. We have been cast out of the metaphorical garden. The Second Coming of Jesus symbolizes the future "great remembering," the turning back to a spirituality the human race experienced before Eden, in a time when "God saw all that he had made, and it was very good."

CONSERVATIVE, LITERAL VIEWS

The conservative camp has quite a different understanding of the end times, but it, too, has some subdivisions. Many carefully nuanced theologies exist, each with very vocal proponents. They are similar in that their expositors are waiting for an actual, physical return of the same Jesus Christ who was born in Bethlehem and whose story is told in the New Testament Gospels. Most agree that God has already decreed a day that will mark the end of the present age. Most agree that there will come a time of great tribulation. Where they disagree, sometimes even violently, is about the timing and order of events.

These are mentioned in the chapter about the Christian Rapture, but here they are again, with some additions, in summary form.

Pre-tribulationism: This school of thought holds that, at any moment, true believers will be changed into spiritual beings, or "raptured," snatched up to be with God. A seven-year period called the Tribulation will follow, during which the antichrist will rule. Eventually he will be defeated at the battle of Armageddon when Jesus returns to earth. Christ will then reign for a thousand years, or a millennium. At the end of that time, Satan, having been "bound" following the battle itself, will be released. He will raise an army that will again be destroyed by Jesus Christ. The world will then enter into eternity, wherein "time shall be no more."

Mid-tribulationalism: The events are the same; only the timing changes. The Rapture will not occur *before* the Tribulation, but rather at the *halfway* point. Three and one-half years after the start of the Tribulation period, the faithful will be snatched up to be with God. Then all hell will break loose on earth until the Second Coming.

Post-tribulationalism: Again, same events, different timing. The faithful will have to endure the entire seven years of Tribulation before the return of Christ. Then they will be "raptured" at the Second Coming, ending the Battle of Armageddon.

Pre-millennialism: All three of the preceding views make up the "premillennial" position. The Rapture, the Tribulation, and

Those wishing to literally interpret the messages of the Bible have found their meanings as slippery as the IRS tax code. Though full consensus isn't likely, most agree on one thing: one way or another, Jesus will someday physically return to this world.

the Second Coming all occur before the thousand-year, or millennial, reign of Jesus Christ on earth.

Post-millennialism: This viewpoint is different from any of the others. Postmillennialism envisions either a literal or a symbolic thousand-year period on earth during which the words of the Lord's Prayer, "Thy kingdom come ... on earth as it is in heaven," will be fulfilled. This school of thought tends to view the Rapture and Tribulation as metaphors, rather than actual events. But some of its adherents teach otherwise, purporting that the Second Coming of Jesus, again viewed literally or symbolically by different camps, will take place at the end of the Millennium.

A-millennialism: Amillennialists generally consider the thousand-year (or so) "millennium" to be a metaphor for a long period of time. There will be no literal Millennium, just as there will be no literal Rapture, Tribulation, or Second Coming. In amillennialism, metaphor and symbol are key words to remember when reading biblical texts.

Pan-millennialism: What started out as a seminary joke has, over the years, become a catchword that expresses the confusion and frustration many Christians feel when hearing all the arguments for and against a specific biblical position. Each millennial position has its proof texts and proponents, who can be quite forceful when they expound their particular position. "Panmillennialism" supposedly came about because a seminary professor was asked by his students which millennial position he espoused, "pre-, post-, or a-"?

"None of them," he said. "I'm Pan-millennial."

"What's that?" his students asked.

"Everything will pan out in the end!"

The joke has been told now for decades, in every seminary throughout the land. It has been repeated so many times and passed on by so many students that there are actually some ministers who, understanding it or not, hold to this position.

How does all this fit in with the voice of the prophet and the vast web of people who, in cult-like fashion, follow their favorite Bible teacher? To answer that question, we have to go next to a key biblical passage from the book of Daniel, in the Hebrew Scriptures. Every Bible teacher worth his or her salt has to have this arrow in their exegetical quiver.

> While I was speaking and praying, confessing my sin and the sin of my people Israel and making my request to the Lord my God for his holy hill—while I was still in prayer, Gabriel, the man I had seen in the earlier vision, came to me in swift flight about the time of the evening sacrifice. He instructed me and said to me, "Daniel, I have now come to give you insight and understanding. As soon as you began to pray, a word went out, which I have come to tell you, for you are highly esteemed. Therefore, consider the word and understand the vision:
>
> "Seventy 'sevens' are decreed for your people and your holy city to finish transgression, to put an end to sin, to atone for wickedness, to bring in everlasting righteousness, to seal up vision and prophecy and to anoint the Most Holy Place.
>
> "Know and understand this: From the time the word goes out to restore and rebuild Jerusalem until the Anointed One, the ruler, comes, there will be seven 'sevens,' and sixty-two 'sevens.' It will be rebuilt with streets and a trench, but in times of trouble. After the sixty-two 'sevens,' the Anointed One will be put to death and will have nothing. The people of the ruler who will come will destroy the city and the sanctuary. The end will come like a flood: War will continue until the end, and desolations have been decreed. He will confirm a covenant with many for one 'seven.' In the middle of the 'seven' he will put an end to sacrifice and offering. And at the temple he will set up an abomination that causes desolation, until the end that is decreed is poured out on him. (Daniel 9:20–27)

This is one of the most disputed passages in the Bible. Translations differ at key points, making it very difficult to decide exactly what the original author was saying. The reason the translations differ is that the ancient manuscripts with which the translators work are not in agreement with one another. To further complicate the problem, the Western calendar we use today was not in use when Daniel was written, and even our modern calendar has been adjusted a few times over the centuries, clouding the calculations about times and dates that signify the end of history.

But those who say that the Bible's prophecies await future fulfillment agree that this is a key passage of Scripture. It reveals dates that give us clues about the timing of the end of history. Every cult prophet uses this particular passage to some degree. To put it mildly, interpretive controversy prevails more often than not.

WHAT DO THE CULT LEADERS BELIEVE?

Although I cannot outline the technical details of every position, which becomes very involved and demands a lot of biblical familiarity, what follows is the position held by probably the majority of futurist Evangelical scholars today and encompasses the theology of most futuristic cult-style "prophets."

As the chapter opens, the Hebrew prophet Daniel is studying the biblical book of Jeremiah. He realizes that Jerusalem will lie desolate for 70 years as a punishment for her sins. Daniel was a young man when Jerusalem was torn down by Nebuchadnezzar and the Babylonian army. He was taken prisoner in that captivity and led to his present place of residence in what became known as Persia. He was very familiar with the event, so it took only a quick calculation to discover that the timed punishment is almost over.

But he cannot discover anywhere in his Bible what is scheduled to happen next. So he prays for the next 19 verses and is interrupted in the middle of his heartfelt exhortation by no less a heavenly messenger than the angel Gabriel, the same angel who will later appear to Mary and announce the birth of Jesus, and, even later, to Muhammad, to whom he will dictate the Qur'an.

Gabriel says: "Daniel, I have now come to give you insight and understand-

In his painting *Jeremiah Lamenting the Destruction of Jerusalem*, Rembrandt depicts the prophet whose story Daniel would later come to puzzle and pray over.

ing. As soon as you began to pray, an answer was given, which I have come to tell you, for you are highly esteemed. Therefore, consider the message and understand the vision: Seventy 'sevens' are decreed for your people and your holy city."

First of all, what does "seventy sevens" mean?

Some translations use 70 "weeks." It is generally explained that God was referring to "weeks of years," or 70 periods of seven years. In other words, 70 X 7, or 490 years.

Many interpreters stop right there and insist that this is already a pretty big interpretive leap. But that doesn't deter those who are bound to move forward where even the angel Gabriel might fear to tread. So, we continue.

The purpose of these 490 years, according to Gabriel, was to allow time for the completion of the items on God's priority list. Again, in the words of Gabriel, this time was "decreed for your people and your holy city."

Notice the two separate entities. First are Daniel's "people," the Jews. Second is the "holy city," or Jerusalem. Six things were going to happen during this time period:

1. To finish transgression

2. To put an end to sin

3. To atone for wickedness

4. To bring in everlasting righteousness

5. To seal up vision and prophecy

6. To anoint the most holy (or "the most holy place," or even "the most holy one"; translations differ)

Again, we run into problems with translations and interpretations. But at least a pattern seems to be developing. God is devoting a certain period—490 years is as good a guess as any—to accomplish a set of objectives. If we can figure out when that period starts, we can then figure out when it will end.

Gabriel now becomes even more enigmatic: "Know and understand this: From the issuing of the decree to restore and rebuild

Jerusalem until the (or 'an') Anointed One (the ruler) comes, there will be seven 'sevens' (or 'weeks'), and 62 'sevens' (or 'weeks')."

The "decree to restore and rebuild Jerusalem" is generally thought to be the one given by Artaxerxes in Nehemiah, chapter 2. The British theologian and Bible scholar Sir Robert Anderson, in his book *The Coming Prince*, asserted that this chapter refers to a decree issued in 445 BCE. This is the date most Evangelical scholars use when marking the beginning of God's clock for the 490-year period. Because Nehemiah claims that the command was given during the month of Nissan, in the Hebrew calendar, it is generally thought that the prophecy period began during the month of March, 445 BCE.

It marked, according to Gabriel, the beginning of a period of "seven sevens (49)" and "sixty-two sevens (434)." When we do the math, we come up with 483. In other words, according to this interpretation, 483 years after the command to restore Jerusalem was given in 445 BCE, the Anointed One would come.

But these, according to Sir Robert, were Hebrew years, which were based on a lunar calendar rather than our solar one. Each month of the ancient Hebrew calendar consisted of only 30 days.

> **Consulting charts, graphs, and astronomical data, Anderson finally deduced that the 483 years ended on, according to our calendar, Palm Sunday, April 6, 33 CE.**

Consulting charts, graphs, and astronomical data, Anderson finally deduced that the 483 years ended on, according to our calendar, Palm Sunday, April 6, 33 CE. His thesis was that when Jesus entered the city on that day, he offered the people a kingdom. If they had received him, the final seven years of the prophecy would have unfolded.

The prophecy, remember, was for 490 years, but only 483 had transpired before the coming of the Anointed One. This left seven to go.

As described in the Book of Luke, Jesus rode into Jerusalem, greeted by crowds singing "Hosanna."

According to the Gospel of Luke, the people began to sing the psalm reserved for the coronation of the Messiah—Psalm 118: "Hosanna in the Highest! Blessed is he who comes in the name of the Lord!"

Anderson believed that Jesus knew very well this was the promised day because, when the Pharisees told him to "rebuke his disciples," his reply was, "If they keep quiet, the stones will cry out" (Luke 19:37–40). Jesus even went on to say to the people of Jerusalem, "If you, even you, had only known on *this day* what would bring you peace. But now it is hidden from your eyes" (emphasis mine).

Gabriel had spoken the truth, according to this interpretation. God allowed a period of 490 years to redeem the earth. The clock began to tick when the Jews came back from the Babylonian captivity. With seven years left to play in the game, Jesus rode into Jerusalem to offer the people a kingdom. They refused, and he was crucified.

At that point the Heavenly Referee stopped the clock but let the teams go on playing. Like a great parenthesis, the Church Age was dropped into the slot between the first 483 years of the prophecy and the last seven. But the time will come when the Church Age will end. That's what the Rapture is all about.

When that happens, the clock will begin again. The Jews will be back in Jerusalem, just as they are right now. A European emperor, this time called the antichrist, will again be in control. No one knows who he is yet.

The final years are called the Tribulation. They begin when a peace treaty, a "covenant with many," is signed to bring peace to the Middle East.

In the middle of the Tribulation, the antichrist will "put an end to sacrifice and offering." Desolation, or the Great Tribulation, will continue until the battle of Armageddon brings the whole game to a screeching halt, and time runs out.

> **Is this the correct interpretation of Daniel 9? Probably not. It is simply the most popular right now.**

Is this the correct interpretation of Daniel 9?

Probably not. It is simply the most popular right now. But many liberal Hebrew and Christian scholars believe the whole concept is out of bounds. They believe Daniel was writing about events that happened during his own time.

Others, while still believing in the future fulfillment of prophecy, disagree over this particular interpretation because they have different views on what the "sevens" mean and when the prophecy began to unfold in history.

But if you want to start a prophetic cult and establish a cult-like following, this is where you have to begin.

FROM NOSTRADAMUS TO EDGAR CAYCE AND BEYOND

Cults tend to form when a self-appointed messenger of God declares he or she has been given a message, usually about the future. The prophet gathers a small following, and a cult is born. This is also generally when the money starts flowing in, or at least a hierarchical power structure is developed.

Not all so-called prophets have developed cults, but many have developed at least a cult-like following. Some of them exist to this very day. As an example, let's start with two of the most famous prophets outside those of the Bible, the Qur'an, and the Book of Mormon.

THE FAMOUS NOSTRADAMUS

Michel de Nostredame (1503–1566), widely known as Nostradamus, is certainly the best known, and arguably the most extraordinary, Christian prophet since the completion of the Bible in the first century of the Christian era. His final prophecies, published two years after his death, have been widely studied and are the source of many controversial interpretations. He has developed, over the years, quite a cultish following.

Most of his prophecies were written as quatrains, or four-line poems. They are marked by double entendre and symbolism, and their meanings are often obscure. Scholars claim that many of them name specific historic people and events. They believe that although quite a few of his predictions have come to pass, others are so obscure that no one has yet interpreted them correctly, so perhaps they refer to events still in the future.

Nostradamus was born into a Jewish family in 1503 in Saint-Rémy-de-Provence. Since this was the time of the French Inquisition, which labeled non-Christian beliefs heretical and severely punished those who held them, his family felt forced to convert to Roman Catholicism. Most Jewish families of that time practiced their traditions quietly at home while publicly following the Christian faith.

During his lifetime, the new Protestant movement was gaining momentum, so Nostradamus was probably influenced by both Protestant and Roman Catholic Christianity, as well as Judaism. Erika Cheetham, in her book *The Final Prophecies of Nostradamus*, claims that he particularly disliked Protestants, believing their ideas caused too much of an uproar. The printing press had been invented in the mid-fifteenth century, making the Bible available to everyone who could read, and Nostradamus probably had read it in Latin, as well as the original Greek and Hebrew, by the time he was a teenager.

This portrait of Nostradamus, the prolific seer whose prophecies have become synonymous with long-range fortune-telling, was painted posthumously by his own son.

As a boy he was sent to his maternal grandfather to be educated. Besides learning to read Latin, Greek, and Hebrew and studying mathematics, he was also steeped in astrology. It became a passion he held all his life. His parents, however, disapproved. Astrology was not on the accepted academic curriculum of the Inquisition.

After the death of his mother's father, the boy was sent off to his paternal grandfather's home to complete his education. He eventually entered the university at Avignon, where he studied grammar, philosophy, and rhetoric. There he became known for his interest in astronomy and astrology. He went on to the University of Montpellier to study medicine and became a very good doctor, curing many people of the bubonic plague by advocating cleanliness, running water (as opposed to well water), and fresh air. More important, he defied tradition by refusing to bleed his patients. But by doing so, he alienated himself from his more traditional colleagues.

He traveled all over France, becoming quite popular, and was sought after by many people who were ill. Fame, however, did nothing to improve his standing with jealous fellow medical practitioners.

Nostradamus settled down long enough to marry and have two children, but he lost his young family to the scourge of the plague. The pain of their deaths sent him off traveling again. He had lost the trust of many of his patients, who felt that if he could not save his own family, he probably could not cure theirs.

Nostradamus defied tradition by refusing to bleed his patients.

During this round of travels he began to gather an audience by publicly prophesying. One famous story tells of his coming upon a young shepherd and suddenly kneeling before him. When the astonished young man asked why, Nostradamus told him that he would one day be crowned pope. In 1585, almost 20 years after Nostradamus's death, the young man did indeed become Pope Sixtus V.

Nostradamus eventually came to the attention of Queen Catherine de' Medici. He spent a lot of time with her, giving her prophecies concerning the fate of her husband, King Henry II, and six children. He was well paid, and most of these dictions seem to have worked out as he described them.

Eventually, Nostradamus settled in Salon-de-Provence and remarried. In his new home, he designated the attic as his study and declared it off limits to everyone else. There he spent many hours staring trancelike into a bronze bowl set on a tripod and then writing down the visions he saw in the water. These became the basis of his *Almanachs*, published in 1550.

Though many of his predictions did not come to pass during his lifetime, the books were successful enough to encourage him to write *Prognostications*, which was also very well received.

In one of his quatrains, Nostradamus, as translated by Erika Cheetham in her collection *The Final Prophecies of Nostradamus*, described his solitary nighttime vigils: "Sitting alone at night in secret study, it rests solitary on the brass tripod. A slight flame comes out of the emptiness, making successful that which would have been in vain."

> **Nostradamus not only saw visions in the bowl of water; he heard sounds and voices as well, making him a clairaudient as well as a clairvoyant.**

It was not until after his death that Nostradamus's wife and his protégé, Jean-Aymes de Chavigny, published his last volume of prophecies. Nostradamus had intended to publish one thousand predictions, divided into ten books of *centaines* ("centuries"), which were sets of 100 four-line quatrains. When the visions were published in 1568, Century Seven had only 42 quatrains, and Centuries Eight, Nine, and Ten were missing. It is probable that he died before reaching his goal of a thousand.

Nostradamus not only saw visions in the bowl of water; he heard sounds and voices as well, making him a clairaudient as well as a clairvoyant. He seemed to see wars being fought with weapons he did not comprehend. He described famine and drought. He saw things happening to people he neither knew nor had heard about:

> Pau, Verona, Vicenza, Saragossa,
> Swords dripping with blood from distant lands.
> A very great plague will come in the great shell,
> Relief near, but the remedies far away.
> (*Cheetham*, Final Prophecies of Nostradamus)

Pau, Verona, Vicenza, and Saragossa are names of European cities Nostradamus would have recognized. But some interpreters have asked if the "great plague" referred to HIV/AIDS. Could the "great shell" be a vehicle delivering a virus during some kind of germ warfare?

Some of his interpreters insist that whatever he saw, it was not of his time. Others see no reason to look beyond Nostradamus's era. The bubonic plague was widespread in his day, and it often began with the arrival of ships ("great shells"?) in port cities. And even earlier, the Bible mentions plagues in Matthew, Mark, Luke, and Revelation. Perhaps that was what inspired him to write these words.

Many quatrains appear to touch on either aerial or submarine warfare. For example:

> Through lightning in the ship, gold and silver are melted,
>
> The two captives will devour each other.
>
> The greatest one of the city is stretched
>
> When the fleet travels under water.
>
> (*Cheetham,* Final Prophecies)

Could Nostradamus have seen, and not understood, the reactor in a nuclear submarine? He had to interpret his visions through the lens of his own time, and many things from our present day would have made little or no sense to him.

Here are two of Nostradamus's most controversial "Armageddon" prophecies. He believed there would be three antichrists, followed by 27 years of war. In the first quatrain, again translated by Erika Cheetham in *Final Prophecies,* he seems to be predicting a global war:

> The third Antichrist soon annihilates everything,
>
> Twenty-seven years of blood his war will last.
>
> The unbelievers dead, captive, exiled with blood,
>
> Human bodies, water and red hail covering the earth.

The second, translated by the Nostradamus enthusiast David S. Montaigne, actually mentions a date:

> The year 1999, seventh month,
>
> From the sky will come great king of terror.
>
> To revive the great king of the Angolmois,
>
> Before and after Mars reigns by good luck.

Although many of the seer's devotees entered the year 1999 with great trepidation, nothing much happened. Two years later,

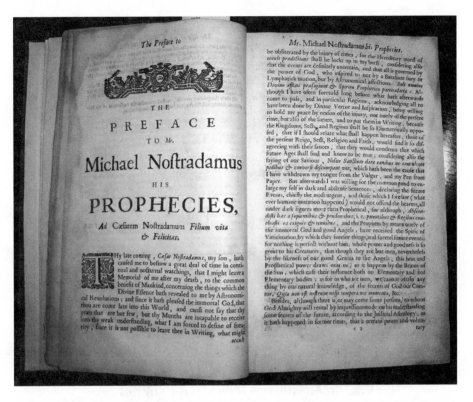

Nostradamus's definitive work, *The Prophecies*, was released posthumously by his wife. Theophilus de Garencières later translated the volume into English in 1672.

however, many of these same disciples quickly decided that this quatrain actually describes the September 11, 2001, attacks on the World Trade Center in New York.

The "seventh month" is not September, and the year is wrong, but most believers in Nostradamus would argue that these are not large errors, considering the prophecy was written more than 400 years before the event.

Of course, these are hardly the only interpretations possible for such a cloudy piece of writing. Some of the faithful, for example, point out that the word *Angolmois* is an anagram for "Mongolias." David Montaigne believes that the quatrain predicts the rise of the Middle East and China, areas he thinks will challenge a coalition of the United States, Europe, and Russia, bringing about a global war that will end the world as we know it. He predicted that these events would transpire in 2002, however, so we need to take them with a grain of salt.

As a Christian scholar and doctor, Nostradamus probably grew up steeped in biblical lore. He would have been aware of the prophecies concerning the end of time and the Second Coming. These were important issues in his day. The book of Revelation probably played a large part in his thinking. With this in mind, it is easy to imagine that he believed he was seeing the end of time in his visions. But the images of his quatrains remain tantalizingly out of reach.

Clarity and obscurity overlap in utterances that might mean almost anything. It makes for a fascinating, if controversial, field of study, and there is no end of ideas from those who form a probably harmless Nostradamus cult.

Another prophet who has established quite a cult following is a bit more contemporary, although he and Nostradamus are often studied by the same people.

THE ONLY REAL MODERN CHRISTIAN PROPHET?

Born on a farm near Hopkinsville, Kentucky, Edgar Cayce (1877–1945) became, according to many of his followers, the only real Christian prophet the United States has ever produced. As a child Cayce experienced visitations from what he called the "little people." (His parents dismissed these as imaginary playmates, which they may well have been.) As a teenager, he claimed, he was twice visited by an "angel" who asked him what he wanted to do with his life. His answer was that he wanted to help others, especially children. The angel told him that he must be true to these aspirations. Cayce was a very serious and religious young man, and these visits would guide him in his future.

He grew up in the Christian Church. An elderly Black man who had once saved him from drowning gave him his first Bible. As a young man, Cayce taught an adult Bible-study group, became a deacon of his church, and always carried a Bible with him. He continued to teach and carry his Bible throughout his life. He was never good in school, however, and he suffered his father's wrath for not being able to learn from his books.

One night, after being left at the table to continue studying until he had mastered the assigned lesson, he fell asleep on his book. According to family lore, when he awoke, he knew every word in the book. His parents, of course, were amazed and tested him by having him fall asleep on other books. Soon word got out about his strange talent, and his schoolmates came to think of him as a freak. This was more than the sensitive young man could handle, especially when he was spurned by an attractive young lady because of what was being said about him. He left school at the age of 16 and went to work to help support his family.

Edgar Cayce in 1910, in a photograph that appeared on the front page of the *New York Times*.

The famous Evangelical preacher Dwight L. Moody visited Hopkinsville in 1898, and he and Cayce met by accident in a field not far from Cayce's home. Cayce went to hear him preach and was apparently very impressed. During Moody's visit, the two continued to meet in the same field. Cayce poured out his heart to the preacher as he had to no one before. He told Moody of the little people and of the visits by the angel. He was shocked when Moody told him that others had come to him with similar stories. The preacher recounted places in the Bible where God had spoken through humans. He also told Cayce of a powerful, mystical experience of his own. The two men never saw each other again after that visit, but Moody appeared to Cayce in dreams throughout Cayce's life.

While he was in trance, an entity from another dimension spoke through him.

During that same year, a traveling "Mesmerise," or hypnotist, came to Hopkinsville and guided Cayce into a trance. What followed was the beginning of a very turbulent time in Cayce's life. While he was in trance, an entity from another dimension spoke through him. Cayce himself had no idea what was being said in these sessions, and he seemed to be amazed when he read the transcripts or was told what had transpired. Cayce would lie down on the floor or a couch and be guided into a trance by a partner, who would then ask the "Source," as the entity was known, questions about the health of some other individual. The Source would recommend a treatment for that person. Without any medical training, Cayce had no idea how this was all transpiring. Only his faith in God and his belief that this work was somehow what God wanted him to be doing kept him at it.

Cayce would spend many years going from job to job and town to town, often being taken advantage of by partners who had only their own selfish interests at heart. He did not have a direction or focus for his talent. He was often confused and troubled. At one point, he had laryngitis for months. Finally, he agreed to do a reading on himself. The Source guided him through to a cure, and when he awoke, he could speak again. The laryngitis recurred from time to time—according to Cayce, whenever he strayed from the path of using his talent only to help others.

It was during this troubled period that he married his long-time fiancée, Gertrude. He was working as a photographer and had become successful enough to feel that he could support a wife and family. Gertrude was uncomfortable with the attention her husband was getting. She wanted to live the quiet, Christian life the two had often talked about, and she did not trust all of his partners. The stranger who spoke through him frightened her. The trances took Cayce's focus away from his family. He was often gone for long periods, giving readings for people all over the South and Midwest.

Eventually Cayce met two men who helped give him the direction he needed. One, Arthur Lammers, suggested that he build a hospital, where people who received his readings could get the recommended treatments. The other, David Kahn, helped him raise money for the project. After years of travel and fundraising, the hospital was built in the then sleepy town of Virginia Beach, Virginia. Cayce set up the headquarters there for the Association for Research and Enlightenment, which is still in existence today.

Cayce's readings soon began to take new directions. The Source began to talk about people's past lives and even of life on other planets, saying that human souls, between lives on earth, spent sojourns both on these planets and in other dimensions. As a Christian, Cayce found these ideas difficult to accept. Nevertheless, he found himself giving readings on astrology and its influence on human behavior.

> **The Source began to talk about people's past lives and even of life on other planets, saying that human souls, between lives on earth, spent sojourns both on these planets and in other dimensions.**

Cayce became known as both the "sleeping prophet" and the father of holistic medicine. He wrote many books and continued to give readings on health and related subjects up until his death in 1945. Many of his "patients" thought that his medical diagnoses and cures were right on target, and many believed they would not have lived but for the advice from the Source.

Cayce, of course, had more than a few detractors who judged him to be, if not an outright fraud, at least benignly deluded. His predictions of what might be regarded as end-of-the-world events did little to quiet his critics. Most of his end-time prophecies dealt with a reconfiguring of the continents. In trance, he reported that Atlantis would reappear somewhere near the Bahamas, most of the West Coast of the United States would fall away, land would appear off the East Coast, much of Japan would sink into the sea, and South America would be shaken from Colombia to Tierra del Fuego. Upheavals in the Arctic and Antarctic would set off volcanoes in the tropics and perhaps even cause the magnetic poles to shift. An inundation would stretch from Salt Lake City to Nebraska. All this was to be accompanied by a great deal of sunspot activity. At first, he predicted that these things would all take place in 1936. He later amended that date to 1998, but he did not live to see if his prophecies were fulfilled.

In spite of all this, Cayce's advice on how to prepare for the end seems to provide words to live by, with or without impending doom. When asked how best to prepare for the coming turmoil, his answer was: "Do thy duty today. Tomorrow will take care of itself. These changes in the Earth will come to pass, for the time and the times and half times are at an end, and there begin these periods for the readjustments. For how hath He given? 'The righteous shall inherit the Earth.'"

Nostradamus and Edgar Cayce—two prophets who lived centuries apart, neither of whom seemed particularly interested in profiting from their gifts. They have both established a fervent group of followers and scholars. Both believed their visions came from God.

Much different is another group of end-time prophets who are not religious at all. They claim their insight comes strictly from current events.

THE DOOMSDAY CLOCK

When the world first saw the devastation caused by the first explosion of the atomic bombs the United States dropped on Hiroshima and Nagasaki, Japan, it entered a new age. No one felt safe anymore. Mass destruction could literally be rained down on anyone, no matter where they lived.

A group of researchers who had participated in the Manhattan Project, the project that produced the weapon of mass destruction, drew together in an organization they called the Chicago Atomic Scientists. They began publishing a newsletter called the *Bulletin of the Atomic Scientists*, which depicted a clock on its front cover, conceived by Hyman Goldsmith and designed by artist Martyl Langsdorf. Thus was born the Doomsday Clock. It's been with us since 1947.

The clock was not invented to serve as a gauge that registers fluctuations of international power relations. It was designed to represent basic changes in the levels of danger in which humankind lives in the nuclear age. Environmental changes due to human technology figure in as well, as do developments in politics, non-nuclear energy and weaponry, and diplomacy.

In January 2007, the bulletin's governing board decided to modernize the design a bit. Michael Bierut, a member of the board,

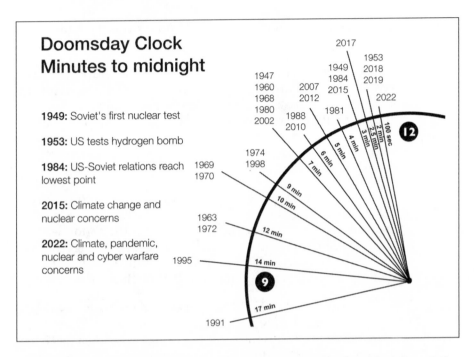

Since the Doomsday Clock's birth in 1947, its hand has bounced back and forth through the minutes leading up to midnight, the hour signifying global catastrophe. It reached its most promising setting of 17 minutes to midnight in 1991, and it has never been so close to midnight as right now, showing 100 seconds left to Doomsday.

was chosen for the task. Two years later, the *Bulletin* became the first publication in the United States to break away from print and become completely digital. A Doomsday Clock Symposium is held periodically to update the information. The Fifth Doomsday Clock Symposium was held on November 14, 2013, in Washington, D.C. It consisted of a daylong event that was open to the public and featured panelists discussing various issues on the topic "Communicating Catastrophe." An evening session followed, called "Damage Control: Art and Destruction since 1950."

The clock has been adjusted some 24 times since its inception, when it was then set at "seven minutes to midnight." Since 2020, it has read "one hundred seconds to midnight."

It's easy to say "midnight" and think nuclear war. But it has a much broader meaning. Think "global catastrophe." That might include nuclear war, but it also encompasses energy disruptions, diplomacy, climate science, bioterrorism, and even the misuse of artificial intelligence.

On January 24, 2018, for instance, scientists moved the clock to two minutes to midnight based on growing threats in the nuclear realm. Scientists were disturbed by the political decisions of Kim Jong-Un in North Korea and the administration of Donald Trump in the United States. Their opinion was that "hyperbolic rhetoric and provocative actions by both sides have increased the possibility of nuclear war by accident or miscalculation."

In 2019, due to the twin threats of nuclear weapons and climate change, plus the problem of those threats being "exacerbated this past year by the increased use of information warfare to undermine democracy around the world, amplifying risk from these and other threats and putting the future of civilization in extraordinary danger," the clock was left unchanged.

Then, on January 23, 2020, the Doomsday Clock was altered again, this time placing it at its current position of 100 seconds before midnight. That's the most worrisome position it had occupied since 1947. According to Jerry Brown, the *Bulletin*'s executive chair, "the dangerous rivalry and hostility among the superpowers increases the likelihood of nuclear blunder. Climate change just compounds the crisis."

What does all this have to do with cults? Simply this. When people are frightened, when they feel threatened by events they cannot control, they look to others for help. They are more susceptible to messages from the lips of those who claim to know "the answer"—especially those who occupy pulpits or podiums. Cults have flourished in this environment. Preachers and politicians have taken advantage of the situation to increase their own power base. Harmless religions that once sought to comfort the afflicted switch to afflicting the comfortable.

"THE END is near," shouts the cultist, and a fearful, even terrified, public is ripe and ready for the pitch.

Doomsday Clock watchers may not yet be a cult, but the opportunity is certainly there, ready to be manipulated by those who seek power and authority.

It is important to remember that religion is not the only basis for prophesying about the end of the world. Secular thinkers do

> ## "THE END is near," shouts the cultist, and a fearful, even terrified, public is ripe and ready for the pitch.

it, too. Philosophy, for instance, usually doesn't offer predictions about what the future holds. Philosophers are good at synthesizing the past, not predicting the future. They deal with ideas, not numbers and dates.

Nonetheless, in 1989 an astrophysicist named Brandon Carter noticed something in a philosophical argument that proved to be quite disturbing. Although he didn't publish his finding, the philosopher John Leslie did. Leslie called this doctrine the "doomsday argument" because it seemed to demonstrate, by inescapable mathematical logic, that the human race may be in its last days.

Carter's complicated argument has since proved very difficult to dispute. As many refutations have been published as have refutations of the refutations. Simply put, the problem is this: If you were to die and be reincarnated anywhere within the span of human existence, from the first human to the last, would the chance of your being reincarnated in the first third of human existence be greater or less than that of being reincarnated in the last two thirds?

Statistically, the answer is obvious. There is a greater mathematical chance of being reincarnated in the last two thirds because that's when most people would have lived.

Now take away the idea of being reincarnated. Simply consider the fact that you have been born somewhere, sometime, into the human race. This, of course, is exactly what has happened to you. You were born at a particular time and place and have no idea where that spot is on the time scale of human existence.

Now ask yourself the original question. Are you more likely living in the first third or the last two thirds of human existence?

Brandon Carter is credited with first describing the Carter Principle, also known as the Doomsday argument.

Just as before, the odds are greater that you are living in the last two thirds. The mathematical probabilities remain the same.

Here's where the problem comes in. Given the history of human population growth, about 60 billion people have lived since the first human ancestor. Suppose we assume the earth's population will someday have to stabilize at 20 billion people, all having an average life expectancy of some 75 years. (These numbers are guesses, but a few years, or a few billion humans, one way or another, won't make a great deal of difference in the final result.)

If this is true, and if you are indeed among the last two-thirds of all humans who have ever lived, as probability suggests, then the human race will be extinct in roughly 500 years.

Most people, when they first encounter this argument, intuitively feel that there ought to be some maddeningly simple way to refute it. But it proves to be very difficult indeed. Many have tried. As yet, they have not succeeded.

Given all this theory and these relatively harmless examples of prophets who saw the end of the world coming soon, what happens when the whole world of prophecy turns ugly and dark? Can it get dangerous?

In a word, yes!

ROCH THÉRIAULT AND THE ANT HILL KIDS

February 1979. That's when the world was supposed to end. Obviously, God didn't get the memo. Or maybe God wasn't using the right calendar.

Of all the cults we have surveyed so far, by far the worst, most outrageously evil group, and the one that seems to have absolutely no redeeming features, was dubbed the Ant Hill Kids, founded by convicted murderer Roch Thériault in 1977. Like so many other cult leaders we have described, he, too, got his start in the Seventh-day Adventist Church, but he was disfellow-shipped in 1978.

Thériault was a self-declared prophet who, like so many before him, claimed to have received a divine message that doomsday was right around the corner. Taking the name Moïse, he somehow convinced a small group of followers—four men, nine women, and four children—to divest themselves of their earthly possessions and set up a communal existence to await the coming apocalypse. His story is both familiar in its overview and unique in its details.

Born in Québec, Canada, in 1947, Thériault claimed he was regularly abused by his father throughout his entire childhood. His father denies the accusations. He dropped out of school at the age of 13 and began to intensely study the Bible, especially the sections that dealt with the end of the world. Some people later claimed he was obsessed. He also developed what some call an unhealthy interest in any Bible passages that talked about masculine authority, both within the family and in society in general.

Although he was born into a Catholic family, he left the church and converted to the Seventh-day Adventist Church. He adopted all the rules and regulations of membership, giving up alcohol, tobacco, and processed foods. But when he tried to become an official Adventist, he was denied membership. Apparently, even then, his disturbing beliefs and personality were recognized.

Before leaving the church, however, he had still somehow managed to attract a following. By the middle of the 1970s, Thériault had convinced himself and his small group of followers that he was anointed by God to become the savior of the world. God had declared that Thériault was to save humankind from evil and guide true believers through the maze of the Apocalypse that was soon to begin. To that end, he would

Thériault's intense study of the Bible seems to have inspired both his obsession with the apocalypse and his extreme views on his authority as a prophet.

create a free-thinking commune where his acolytes could listen to his teachings and live as equals.

> **By the middle of the 1970s, Thériault had convinced himself and his small group of followers that he was anointed by God to become the savior of the world.**

Thériault managed to convince his small group of followers that the world, their families, and their friends were corrupt in the sight of God. They abandoned their homes, left their families, and moved to the woods to establish a commune consisting of tents and log cabins near the Gaspésie tourist region in Québec, near the village of Saint-Jogues. They called their new home "Eternal Mountain." His followers accepted him as God and believed his prophecy that the world would end in February of 1979.

Needless to say, it didn't. Like the members of so many doomsday cults that have come and gone throughout North American history, Thériault's followers experienced severe disappointment when the date arrived and nothing happened. But, just like other prophets before him, he came up with a good reason. As it turned out, Thériault hadn't figured in the difference between the Israelite calendar and the Roman Catholic calendar.

Nevertheless, after that, things deteriorated quickly. To make his flock grow, Thériault impregnated all the women in his commune. He fathered 20 children by nine women.

As the children began to grow, what can only be described as pathological punishments became the order of the day. In 1981, for instance, two-year-old Samuel Gilguere was experiencing difficulty urinating. Thériault cut open his penis. The boy wouldn't stop crying after his "surgery," so Thériault ordered one of his followers, a man named Guy Veer, to beat the young boy, who soon died from the punishment. To conceal the death, Thériault had the boy's body burned. But as punishment for the severe beating, Thériault castrated Veer and then ordered his followers to say that Veer had been trampled by a horse.

Rumors began to circulate, and the police soon raided the commune. They discovered young Samuel's charred body. Thériault and eight of his followers were arrested and charged with criminal negligence causing bodily harm.

For some reason, they were all released.

But after experiencing such a close call, Thériault and the group decided they needed to move to a new location. They reestablished their commune near Burnt River, Ontario.

Thériault's hold over the group remained strong. Their numbers now included 26 children, most of whom were his own, and the small number of followers who remained. They had been, for whatever their reasons, loyal to him while he was in jail.

To refurbish their reputation, the group tried to blend in with the population of the small town nearby. They produced maple syrup, preserves, bread, and smoked fish. They were so industrious that Thériault compared them to ants working on an anthill. Thus, "The Ant Hill Kids" were established.

Plans to integrate into the community, however, didn't work, because by this time Thériault's drinking was influencing his leadership. Violence was the order of the day. Cruelty reigned supreme, and his followers couldn't seem to break away. They were forbidden from speaking, even to each other, without first receiving his permission.

He began to stage what he called "gladiator tournaments," in which his followers were forced into fighting with each other. Paranoia was rampant. He obviously was becoming more and more mentally unstable. He first struck his devotees with his belt and then graduated to hammers and the flat side of an axe.

If he suspected that one of them was thinking about leaving the commune, he would punish them by hanging them from the ceiling, and worse. They were forced to prove their loyalty by breaking their own legs. The cruelty became unspeakable.

Finally, it escalated to murder. A mother hid her baby out in the cold during a blizzard. Later testimony revealed that she had done it to protect the child from one of Thériault's violent outbursts. The baby froze to death. This led to an investigation, and in 1987, 14 children were removed from the commune and placed into foster homes. Because Children's Aid was primarily interested in saving the children, not seeking justice for the others, life at the commune continued, but by now the numbers had dropped to two men and eight women.

All this made Thériault even more violent. When he was drunk, he had the idea that he was a doctor who could perform operations on his followers. These were simply too gruesome to describe in detail. Suffice it to say that things came to a head in 1988. One of the women in the group, Solange Boilard, was killed during one of these supposed "medical procedures."

Thériault, however, claimed he could bring her back to life. His complicated procedure, which involved ejaculating into her opened skull, failed to bring about a resurrection.

When another woman, Gabrielle Lavallée complained about a toothache that November, Thériault pulled out a number of her teeth with pliers. Somehow, the group continued. Lavallee even briefly escaped the cult but decided she couldn't live without it, so she returned. The rest of the members were either too ill, too frail, or too mentally spent to resist.

> **Finally, however, after another crisis involving Gabrielle Lavallée, this one involving a meat cleaver and the removal of her arm, she somehow managed to escape.**

Finally, however, after another crisis involving Gabrielle Lavallée, this one involving a meat cleaver and the removal of her arm, she somehow managed to escape on August 16, 1989. She hitchhiked to a hospital near Toronto. There she became the first of the commune to completely tear the cover off what was going on.

Thériault was arrested and pleaded guilty to three counts of aggravated assault and one count of unlawfully causing bodily harm. He received a sentence of 12 years in prison.

Thériault's first prosecution landed him in prison for 12 years, which was bumped up to a life sentence after an additional murder came to light. While imprisoned at New Brunswick's Dorchester Penitentiary, the cult leader met his end when shivved by his cellmate.

When another member of the group led authorities to the body of Boilard, Thériault was further charged with second-degree murder. He pleaded guilty and was sentenced to life in prison, with no possibility of parole.

He didn't last long in prison, however. In February of 2011, Thériault was stabbed to death by his cellmate. He is now considered to have been one of Canada's most notorious criminals.

What could possibly have caused a group of people to follow such a pathological leader? The stories are mixed. Most, undoubtedly, really believed he was God, at least for a while. After that, fear, confusion, shame, and illness, both physical and mental, took over.

It is easy for those of us on the outside of such a cruel existence to say we would never accept being treated this way. But we have never experienced it, so we just don't understand. These were, by all accounts, once normal, ordinary people. Yet they endured endless torture from a liar, a drunk, and a psychopathic sadist, just because their religious beliefs were the same as his.

Obviously, charisma and fanatic religious fervor can make a man
into a leader in the eyes of at least a small percentage of the population. The "Ant Hill Kids" are gone, but who knows what future
leaders are still out there, waiting to express their self-awarded
divinity to a gullible following?

THE RISE OF RACIAL RELIGION CULTS AND SOCIAL MEDIA

Americans take great pride in claiming that their nation is a melting pot. Various ethnic flavors from all over the world flow together, blending into one.

This is, of course, nonsense. America is not so much a melting pot as it is a soup or stew, wherein individual pieces of meat and vegetables simmer together in a rich broth, each lending its own individual flavor while retaining its own unique identity.

Even our language exposes the fault in the "melting pot" analogy. We talk about African Americans, Native Americans, Irish Americans, Japanese Americans, German Americans, and Jewish Americans. We have elderly Americans and young Americans. All these compound labels reveal that we may be in the same soup, and we may certainly complement one another, but we have not exactly melted together. Just the opposite. From time to time, we have even hated one another. From institutionalized slavery to signs reading "no Chinese" or "no Irish need apply" to the Trail of Tears, the "separate but equal" doctrine, and Japanese American concentration camps, Americans have, most assuredly, never fully assimilated.

There is one category of Americans who have consistently managed to keep the upper hand, however, by controlling the

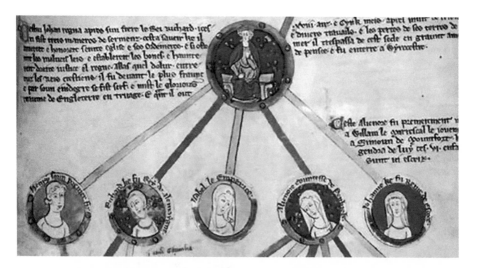

In a coincidence as revealing as it is baffling, 42 of the first 43 U.S. presidents shared as a common ancestor John, King of England, pictured here with his children in a thirteenth-century family tree.

courts and the laws to a formidable extent. I am referring, of course, to White, Anglo-Saxon, Protestant Americans, abbreviated as WASPs. Generally speaking, with a few notable exceptions, the more of those letters that you can check on your résumé, the better your chance to succeed. Take, for example, one conspicuous position of service—that of the leadership of the country that espouses the phrase "Give me your tired, your poor...." Note that:

- All the U.S. presidents but one have been white, and the one exception wasn't elected until 2008.

- A recent bombshell of a genetics discovery made by 12-year-old BridgeAnne d'Avignon was hailed by both the *Daily Mail* and *New York Daily News* when she announced her discovery that 42 out of the first 43 U.S. presidents shared King John of England as a common ancestor.

- In the field of religion, all the U.S. presidents have been Protestant except for two. The first of them wasn't elected until 1960, and the second in 2020.

- I need to add here that there is one important letter missing from the WASP acronym. That letter is M, for male. The United States has yet to elect a woman president.

The whole idea of America being a melting pot, especially in terms of the religious heritage to which we pay such lip service, is associated first with the Pilgrims who stepped off the *Mayflower* in 1620. But we need to remember that the Pilgrims were an offshoot cult called Separatists when they left England. By the time they took root and began to prosper, the former cult had become the established religion of much of the Northeast. It is not by accident that their religious brand soon became known by the derogatory adjective "puritanical." Anyone who didn't fit the image, be they Quakers, Shakers, Jews, or Catholics, were ushered out of town on a rail. Yet somehow, they managed to enshrine the idea of religious freedom in the very halls of Congress.

> **The Pilgrims were an offshoot cult called Separatists when they left England.**

The idea of Manifest Destiny carried America's lip-service religious ideals from sea to shining sea, but it took an Indian Removal Act by Congress, a Trail of Tears, various exterminations, and an unprovoked war with Mexico, resulting in the annexation of Texas and California, to accomplish it. Meanwhile, even a Civil War couldn't end the domination of dark-skinned people by light-skinned ones.

Somehow in the midst of all of this, a strange thing happened in the religious community. Jesus, a first-century Jew, was adopted by the WASP community. His portraits changed. He managed to morph into the kind of Savior anyone would have been proud to bring home to dinner, even though he had upset the established religion of his own day. His hair color lightened along with his skin tone. Sometimes his Mediterranean dark eyes became blue. Along the way, he turned into a kind of warring leader who hated Native Americans and anyone who wanted to have fun. Then he turned against Jews and Catholics. Later, by stages, he became a bit of a Democratic "hippie," and later still an establishment Republican. Then he allegedly fronted a political insurrection that, in 2021, led the charge against a "corrupt" United States government that, his true believers claimed, somehow stole an election.

On April 6, 2022, the *New York Times* published an article titled "The Growing Religious Fervor in the American Right: 'This Is a Jesus Movement.'" The article, written by Elizabeth Dias, described how a large portion of the Evangelical church has coalesced with various racial power groups and social far-right organizations, forming a coalition that has managed to merge politics with religion, especially conservative Evangelical religion.

According to Dias, "Rituals of Christian worship have become embedded in conservative rallies." Apparently, pop praise music and prayer have become the new norm. Trump rallies "open with an invocation, summoning God's 'hedge of thorns and fire' to protect each person" present. "They call for testimonies, passing the microphone to anyone with 'inspirational words that they'd like to say on behalf of our J-6 political prisoners,' referring to people arrested in connection with the Jan. 6, 2021, attack on the Capitol."

She describes a rally in Phoenix, Arizona, in vivid detail:

Holding candles dripping wax, the few dozen who were gathered lifted their voices, a cappella, in a song treasured by millions of believers who sing it on Sundays and know its words by heart:

"Way maker, miracle worker, promise keeper

Light in the darkness, my God

That is who you are ..."

This was not a church service. It was worship for a new kind of congregation: a right-wing political movement powered by divine purpose, whose adherents find spiritual sustenance in political action.

There is no doubt that politics and religion have been joined for decades. But the phenomenon has grown almost exponentially since the rise of the Trump era. Elements of Christianity have been a part of the political scene ever since the first politician learned he could get an "Amen" when he closed his stump speech with "God bless America." But real worship—with prayers, songs, and testimonies—was generally reserved for church. These days, however, you are apt to see many of the same believers who cry at the drop of a "Jesus" reference do the same thing when they sing "America the Beautiful." A significant portion of believers feel they must attend rallies because they want to bring God's kingdom to earth. For them, right-wing political activity has become a sacred act.

The dedication many followers show to Donald Trump can easily be compared with religious fervor.

At a Trump rally in Michigan, for instance, a local pastor offered a public prayer that stated, "Father in heaven, we firmly believe that Donald Trump is the current and true president of the United States." He prayed, in the name of Jesus, that precinct delegates at an upcoming Michigan Republican Party convention would support Trump-endorsed candidates, whose names he listed. The crowd responded, "In Jesus's name!" They went on to ask God to metaphorically topple the walls of government and to end vaccine requirements. Such devotees to the Republican "faith" seem to share a belief that the United States is on the cusp of a spiritual and political revival.

Ché Ahn, the pastor of Harvest Rock Church in Pasadena—the same church that successfully sued Governor Gavin Newsom of California for temporarily prohibiting in-person, indoor worship in Los Angeles County during the COVID-19 pandemic—put it this way: "We are seeing a spiritual awakening taking place. Christians are becoming more involved, becoming activists. I think that is a good thing, because the church has been slumbering."

And to think that Jesus was brought here, to America, first by Catholics in Florida and California and then by Puritan cultists in New England! It was quite a journey. How did "gentle Jesus, meek and mild," turn into a cheerleader for, among others, White Nationalism? We'll begin the story with a quick survey of what is perhaps the best-known cult America ever produced.

FROM THE KU KLUX KLAN TO WHITE NATIONALISM

When the American Civil War ended in 1865, the North, technically, may have won the horrible, chaotic conflict. The Union was preserved, and the enslaved were freed. But words on a piece of paper do not necessarily correspond to thoughts within the heart, to say nothing of social actions.

So it was within the heart of the Confederacy. Racism was not over. Indeed, the battle had only begun.

When six Confederate veterans gathered in Pulaski, Tennessee, following Appomattox, they were not ready to give up the fight they had fought for so long. Their purpose was to create what was to become known as the Ku Klux Klan, a vigilante cult that went on to mobilize a campaign of violence and terror against the progress of Reconstruction. Members were recruited from every level of white Southern society. Where possible, they wrote laws and utilized judges, local police, and courts to accomplish their mission, which was to prevent recently freed African Americans from voting or holding political office. But their greatest weapon was terrorism.

The Klan and sympathetic white Southerners, for instance, engaged in a violent campaign of deadly voter intimidation during the 1868 presidential election. Thousands of formerly enslaved African Americans were killed in Arkansas and Georgia. Lynching was common. Tarring and feathering, rape, and other violent attacks on those challenging white supremacy became the Klan's proud hallmark.

> **They called themselves an "invisible empire," and secrecy only added to their mystique.**

Led by its first "grand wizard," the popular ex-Confederate general Nathan Bedford Forrest, the Klan organized, solidified its membership, and terrorized the Black population. Using a hierarchy sporting such titles as "imperial wizard" and "exalted cyclops," Klan members would show up in the dead of night, wearing hooded costumes and carrying torches. They called themselves an "invisible empire," and secrecy only added to their mystique.

This period of the Klan's history is now called its "first era," and it galvanized both North and South to action. When it became evident that Jim Crow laws would ensure white supremacy across the country, the Klan cut back on overt physical terrorism and turned to the courts to accomplish its goal of complete and absolute segregation.

But its ranks never completely dissolved. The "cult of the Lost Cause," as it came to be known, continued. Led by the work of the sometimes-ferocious Daughters of the Confederacy, white Southern heroes were enshrined by the erection, decades after the Confederacy's loss, of statues raised in public spaces as a constant reminder of the resentment and lingering racial hatred that continued, never far below the surface.

To this day, those statues remain a contentious reminder of Civil War hatred. On July 9, 2020, Tennessee's State Capitol Commission voted to remove the bust of KKK grand wizard Nathan Bedford Forrest from the state Capitol Building. It was subsequently removed on July 23, 2021, and placed in the Tennessee State Museum. But the removal only antagonized far-right extremists, who showed up in large numbers to protest the action.

The "second era" of Klan activity began in 1915, when it was revived by white Protestants near Atlanta, Georgia. Some new opponents came under the Klan's agenda—mostly Catholics and Jewish immigrants. Communism was added to the mix as well, broadening the Klan base throughout the South and into the Midwest, with particular emphasis in Indiana.

A bust of Nathan Bedford Forrest, Civil War general and KKK grand wizard, was added to the Tennessee State Capitol in 1978 by resolution of the state senate. In 2021, the bust was moved to a museum.

In 1925, when its followers staged a historical march in Washington, D.C., the Klan boasted as many as four million members and in some states had amassed considerable political power. Only a series of sex scandals, coupled with internal battles brought about because of newspaper exposés, managed to reduce the group's influence.

The cult's "third era" began in the 1960s, fueled by those who opposed the civil rights movement, especially the attempt within the Supreme Court, under Chief Justice Earl Warren, to overturn "separate but equal" rulings that had been in effect since 1896. Bombings and other attacks by the Klan took a great many lives. Murders committed by Klansmen during the civil rights era included four young girls killed in 1963 while preparing for Sunday services at the 16th Street Baptist Church in Birmingham, Alabama, and the 1964 murder of civil rights workers Andrew Goodman, James Chaney, and Michael Schwerner in Mississippi.

Throughout the second and third eras of the Klan, many Black Americans left Southern states in what is now called the Great Migration. They moved north to improve their economic condition or social opportunities. They were also hoping to escape the racial terror enforced by the Klan's ideological stronghold in the South. More than six million Black Americans took part in this migration, and the U.S. demographic profile shifted dramatically. But the Klan, solidly entrenched, remained strong.

> **A series of court cases aimed at bankrupting the Klan and closing down the group's paramilitary training camps served to weaken the white supremacist cult, but internal fighting and government infiltrations did even more damage.**

A series of court cases aimed at bankrupting the Klan and closing down the group's paramilitary training camps served to weaken the white supremacist cult, but internal fighting and government infiltrations did even more damage. The group was successfully stymied. Given the Klan's insistence on remaining an "invisible empire," it is difficult to estimate how many active members were left. But enough must have remained to resurrect it yet again, for when the Vietnam War ended in 1975 and American soldiers began to come home, several key leaders rose up within the Klan's membership.

Louis Beam was a Vietnam veteran who joined the Alabama-based United Klans of America upon his return from East Asia. He began a teaching program consisting of what he called "leaderless resistance." He also introduced the Klan to the computer age and modernized their media presence. By making use of new, emerging technologies, he managed to bring together previously divided neo-Nazi and Klan groups, and he helped organize what is now known as the white power movement.

In the same way, beginning in 1975, following the same principles while using new techniques and employing the added benefit of a more media-friendly persona, David Duke, the founder of the Knights of the Ku Klux Klan, maintained a distinctly anti-Semitic hatred. The ideology of both the Klan and neo-Nazis thus overlapped. The gap was bridged, and a new movement began in earnest. It is called white nationalism.

"White nationalism," "white power," and "white supremacy" don't mean quite the same thing. There is a subtle difference between them that is both linguistic and historical.

"Nationalism" generally means support for a particular country. Sometimes it is used interchangeably with the word "patriotism." This describes those citizens in the United States who want to put "America first." "White nationalism" is close to this kind of nationalism, with the twist that advocates of white nationalism see America as composed primarily of and for white people. This links up with what is sometimes called the "Aryan" nation. According to this view, the word "United" in the name United States really means "white." People of color are considered to be inferior. They are accepted as long as they "know their place." This is really important. White nationalism is, at root, deeply anti-democratic.

"White power" is not limited to one country. It doesn't regard borders very much at all. It simply believes that white is white the world over. Brenton Tarrant, the shooter who murdered people at a mosque in Christchurch, New Zealand, is thus connected to Dylann Roof, the man who murdered people at a prayer meeting in Emanuel African Methodist Episcopal Church in South Carolina.

That leads, in turn, to "white supremacists." In a way, the white power movement provides a home for white supremacists. Tehama Lopez Bunyasi and Candis Watts Smith, in their book *Stay Woke: A People's Guide to Making All Black Lives Matter*, state that white supremacists believe "that white people are inherently superior to people of color and should dominate over people of color." White supremacy is "the systematic provision of political, social, economic, and psychological benefits and advantages to whites, alongside the systematic provisions of burdens and disadvantages to people who are not white." It is not just an ideology expressed in opinions and words. It actually exists as a clandestine political movement, having been used to build government and create policy in the real world. And it is not new. In a 2016 article for *Vox*, Jenée Desmond-Harris wrote that it has been "a constant throughout history" that not only ensured the enslavement of Black people and the genocide of Native Americans, but it constantly kept people of color out of jobs, limited their enrollment in universities, and sought to keep them from any kind of political power. What that means is that everyone, regardless of personal beliefs, lives in a white supremacist system.

When we see militia groups arming themselves and claiming that their freedoms are being taken away while marching with neo-Nazi slogans and Confederate battle flags, we are watching a cult-like ideology unite these three heretofore separate movements. When politicians on the far right, probably out of ignorance of American history, not only acknowledged, but glorified, these three ideologies, with which they sought to build a political base, adherents surfaced once again in what some have called a "fourth era." We have yet to see where it will end.

THE NEW MILITIA MOVEMENT

There is a loose but growing affiliation in America that has come to be known as the militia movement. Its members primarily espouse a far-right-wing ideology, like to call themselves "patriots," and believe with cult-like fervor that the federal government has been infiltrated and is now occupied by a shadowy conspiracy called the "Deep State," which is trying to strip

American citizens of their constitutional rights, the most important of which is gun ownership. Members see themselves completely in line with the minutemen who launched the American Revolutionary War and the southerners who fired on Fort Sumpter to begin the Civil War. These militia groups include such subgroups as the Oath Keepers, the Proud Boys, the Three Percenters, and others. Some observers also place antifa activists within the new militia movement, although the focus for anti-fascist ("antifa") activists is not on the right to bear arms but on opposition to fascism, racism, white supremacy, and other far-right ideologies.

OATH KEEPERS

Thanks to their participation in the insurrection at the Capitol Building in Washington, D.C., on January 6, 2021, perhaps the best-known group of people in this movement are the Oath Keepers, who fancy themselves "Guardians of the Republic." They are a large group of right-wing, anti-government extremists who focus specifically on recruiting well-trained military personnel and veterans, law enforcement representatives, and first responders.

The underlying idea is that these people, besides being highly trained, all swear an oath to defend the United States Constitution "from all enemies, foreign and domestic"—hence the name "Oath Keepers." By reminding them of this promise, the Oath Keepers ask members to honor their original pledge and to disobey any orders from current superiors that they might perceive as "unconstitutional."

The enemy perceived by the Oath Keepers is primarily domestic, but it exists worldwide. If new recruits are ever issued any orders that explicitly, or even implicitly, contradict militia-related conspiracy theories, such as mass gun confiscation or the arrest of white Americans for the purpose of confining them in concentration camps, such orders are countermanded by the oath they swore to uphold the Constitution as they interpret it. Thus, the Oath Keepers urge military and law enforcement personnel to step up, remember their primary oath, and oppose the real, Deep State "conspirators."

Who are the Oath Keepers? How did they gain their new-found fame?

The Oath Keepers played an important role in invading the U.S. Capitol on January 6, 2021. Here, a crowd of Trump supporters marches on the Capitol, ultimately leading to the invasion and several deaths.

Stewart Rhodes, a former Montana attorney and U.S. Army veteran who worked in the office of Libertarian Ron Paul during his presidential run in 2008, founded the Oath Keepers in 2009 and, until his 2022 arrest, acted as its main spokesperson. His idea was to update and modernize an organization called Police Against the New World Order, which had been started by a retired police officer named Jack McLamb.

McLamb believed that a post–Cold War world was being undermined and occupied by mysterious members of what he called the New World Order. This, he said, was an elitist-controlled organization run by global oligarchs (a term often interpreted as "Jewish") who were bent on destroying America's constitutional republic.

By 2014, the Oath Keepers were at the forefront of an armed response to confrontations between ranchers, miners, and federal agencies at what is now called the Bundy Ranch standoff in Nevada, the culmination of a two-decade land management dispute. When group members dispersed out of fear of possible drone strikes, the group suffered a blow to its reputation among other groups of anti-government extremists. This probably inspired them to take a more public stand.

So in 2020, the Oath Keepers participated in various protests against temporary workplace and school closings related to the COVID-19 pandemic, and they provided what they called vigilante-style "security" for local communities and businesses during the Black Lives Matter protests that spread throughout the country after Minneapolis police officer Derek Chauvin murdered George Floyd, a Black man suspected of passing a counterfeit twenty-dollar bill. They began to warn everyone who would listen that the country would soon be undermined and overthrown by the "Marxist left" during the upcoming election.

> **By mid-2022, at least 29 people who were associated with the Oath Keepers were charged with conspiracy in connection with January 6th activities.**

This highly publicized and inflammatory stance caused Twitter to "de-platform" the group, which only caused its members to become more convinced than ever that they were right. Their opinion was further strengthened when some of the group's members were arrested in connection with a wide range of criminal activities, including various firearms violations, conspiracy to impede federal workers, possession of explosives, and threatening public officials. And by mid-2022, at least 29 people who were associated with the Oath Keepers were charged with conspiracy in connection with January 6th activities.

Rhodes had warned during the Trump administration about a possible "Benghazi-style attack" that would target then-President Trump. He promised that the Oath Keepers would station its "best men" outside Washington, D.C., during the time of the 2020 presidential election, because he anticipated the government would enable a coup against Trump. He discussed the possibility of a second Civil War and promised that his "battle-hardened" supporters were prepared to fight the "street soldiers" of the "radical left."

Estimates as to the size of the organization varies between one thousand and three thousand members, but no one, including the Oath Keepers, really knows how many people follow their banner.

There is no official list of the "rights" the group says are being "taken away," but certainly, all evidence to the contrary, the elimination of the "right" they fear most is centered in the Second Amendment to the U.S. Constitution: the right to "keep and bear arms." According to Oath Keeper propaganda, this is the first thing that will happen when the New World Order comes to power. Apparently, they have a lot of public support for this fear. Quite literally, every time there is a mass shooting, the sale of guns throughout the United States skyrockets.

Obviously, any theories about the New World Order and the impending takeover of the government need facts to back them up. Here are some of the "facts" quoted by the Oath Keepers in their public literature:

> **Oath Keepers urged President Trump to declare that there was an ongoing Marxist insurrection led by antifa and Black Lives Matter activists and to call the militia into federal service to suppress the "rebellion."**

There is an impending takeover of the United States by the Marxist left. According to Twitter, which has barred the Oath Keepers from its platform, the Oath Keepers declared that there is a "Marxist rebellion against the United States, with the oft-stated intent to overthrow its government under the Constitution." Using social media, Oath Keepers sent messages to President Trump, urging him to declare that there is an ongoing Marxist insurrection led by antifa and Black Lives Matter activists and to call the militia into federal service to suppress the "rebellion." They called the Democratic Party "a Marxist-Islamist organization, where an unholy alliance of communists and jihadists aim to defeat their common enemy—Western Civilization." The reason Democratic leaders support gun-control legislation, according to published Oath Keeper documents, is to allow for easy gun confiscation, which will make the American people dependent and vulnerable to a takeover. Oath Keepers have made numerous claims that antifa is an organized arm of the Democratic Party and that the two entities are working together toward the goal of a socialist takeover.

Impending martial law is a reality. One of the most prominent Oath Keeper theories is that a large-scale pandemic, natural disaster, or terrorist attack will give the government an excuse to impose martial law resulting in (but not limited to) door-to-door gun confiscation, the ban of interstate travel, and the detainment of U.S. citizens in concentration camps. Some Oath Keepers claim that the government may secretly stage a terrorist attack or other incident as an excuse to declare martial law. The coronavirus "scam" is viewed as a government plot to accomplish those ends.

The Second Amendment is under assault. Oath Keepers call for the nullification of all gun ownership laws and view any gun control measures as schemes designed to dismantle the Second Amendment. The purpose of the Second Amendment is to "preserve the ability of the people, who are the militia, to provide for their own security" and "to preserve the military capacity of the American people to resist tyranny and violations of their rights by oath breakers within government."

The United Nations is bad. Oath Keepers view the United Nations (UN) as a tool of the New World Order, a movement that attempts to undermine American sovereignty by imposing a "globalist" agenda. The UN intends to implement global taxation and a global currency that would end the use of the dollar. A UN Small Arms Treaty will be implemented to bypass the Second Amendment and prohibit private ownership of firearms. UN sustainable development plans, such as Agenda 21 and the 2030 Agenda for Sustainable Development, will be used to take away private property and civil liberties in the name of sustainability.

Like many on the far right, Oath Keepers regard the United Nations with distrust.

The Oath Keepers have published a list called "10 Orders We Will Not Obey."

1. We will NOT obey orders to disarm the American people.

2. We will NOT obey orders to conduct warrantless searches of the American people.

3. We will NOT obey orders to detain American citizens as "unlawful enemy combatants" or to subject them to military tribunal.

4. We will NOT obey orders to impose martial law or a "state of emergency" on a state.

5. We will NOT obey orders to invade and subjugate any state that asserts its sovereignty.

6. We will NOT obey any order to blockade American cities, thus turning them into giant concentration camps.

7. We will NOT obey any order to force American citizens into any form of detention camps under any pretext.

8. We will NOT obey orders to assist or support the use of any foreign troops on U.S. soil against the American people to "keep the peace" or to "maintain control."

9. We will NOT obey any orders to confiscate the property of the American people, including food and other essential supplies.

10. We will NOT obey any orders which infringe on the right of the people to free speech, to peaceably assemble, and to petition their government for a redress of grievances.

To give credit where credit is due, besides showing up at protests, the Oath Keepers do public service work through what they call Post-Disaster Responses. In October 2013, for example, they announced the formation of "civilization preservation cells," now called Community Preparedness Teams, or CPTs.

Although the Oath Keepers demonize the Federal Emergency Management Agency (FEMA) and its response to natural disasters and are quick to point out problems that the agency experienced in dealing with Hurricanes Katrina and Harvey, they have, since 2017, assisted in the wake of natural disasters across the United States and Puerto Rico, providing bottled water and food. They cleared roads and helped with rescue missions. Their Facebook posts document disaster relief after five hurricanes, and they have issued calls for action following floods, tornadoes, and wildfires. The press coverage from these activities hasn't hurt their cause any.

Since 2015, various CPTs have sponsored militia-like training sessions, covering topics as varied as weapons use, patrolling techniques, first aid, emergency communications, and disaster management.

The advent of the COVID-19 pandemic in early 2020 and beyond offered a mixed bag of responses. Oath Keepers have long believed that a manufactured pandemic would be used as a pretense to infringe on American liberties, so in 2014 they highlighted the outbreak of the Ebola virus in West Africa and criticized the Obama administration's response to it. They wondered whether the epidemic would be an excuse to justify medical martial law in the United States.

> At the beginning of the pandemic, they claimed the virus was worse than government officials were saying. They pushed people to keep themselves safe, including wearing masks, because the government wouldn't help them.

In January 2020, they provided advice and information regarding COVID-19 to their followers. At the beginning of the pandemic, they raised a concern that the virus was worse than government officials were saying. They pushed people to do whatever they needed to do to keep themselves safe, including wearing masks, because the government wouldn't help them. Their website declared that the government had failed to contain the virus. It was now a global pandemic. The Oath Keepers called on then-President Trump to immediately shut down all commercial airline traffic, as well as schools and public places, to slow the spread of the virus. By April they were calling for lockdowns.

Other militia groups, however, were taking a much different approach. They opposed *any* public health efforts to curb the pandemic. Lockdowns were seen as Orwellian violations of liberty. The Oath Keepers then recanted their earlier advice and urged their members to defy any and all official measures, especially the use of masks.

In one way, the Oath Keepers broke ranks with then-President Trump. He had briefly promoted the use of hydroxychloroquine to fight the virus. Oath Keepers believed that substance to be a Chinese bioweapon and refused to endorse its use.

On and on it went. For a while, it seemed as though the narrative changed almost week by week. Black Lives Matter was part of Marxist program. Antifa was "a loose collection of groups, networks and individuals who believe in active, sometimes aggressive, opposition to far right-wing movements." They were the modern-day "Brown Shirts." The "Deep State" was an alleged network of institutions and bureaucracies within the federal government that was trying to undermine, and even destroy, the Trump administration.

On January 13, 2022, founder Stewart Rhodes was arrested at his home in Texas. During a virtual court hearing, he pleaded not guilty to charges of participating in the plans for the January 6, 2021, insurrection in Washington, D.C. Not only had he spent thousands of dollars stockpiling a huge arsenal of weapons and ammunition, but he had also built a series of escape tunnels and spider holes to hide in if the authorities ever came for him. The court was afraid he might disappear if he were released, so he was held without bail, awaiting trial in the fall of 2022.

In early September, however, before the trial could even be held, the Anti-Defamation League Center on Extremism obtained leaked documents that revealed more than 38,000 names of alleged members, including 370 people it believed worked in law enforcement agencies, many of them current police chiefs and sheriffs. It also identified more than 100 people who were active members of the military, hundreds of U.S. law enforcement officers, elected officials, and more than 80 people who were running for office in the 2022 midterm elections. Much of this information was compiled in a database subsequently published by the Distributed Denial of Secrets, a "transparency" collective.

Simply appearing in an Oath Keepers database does not, of course, prove that a person was ever an active member of the group or even once shared its ideology. When contacted directly by the Associated Press, some people on the list claimed past membership but said they were no longer affiliated.

The revelation, so long after the attack on the Capitol, caused many people to wonder exactly how far the reach of the Oath Keepers extended. Meanwhile, more than 21 months following their arrest for participating in the January 6th insurrection, more than two dozen people still awaited their trials.

PROUD BOYS

The Proud Boys were founded in 2016 by Gavin McInnes. Enrique Tarrio, the Florida director of Latinos for Trump, later took over as leader.

Unlike the Oath Keepers, the Proud Boys are exclusively male. Because their published literature, both in print and online, often espouses misogynistic, Islamophobic, and anti-Semitic views, the Southern Poverty Law Center has designated them as a hate group.

Why, you might ask, did a homophobic group ever come up with a name so open to ridicule as "Proud Boys"? McInnes himself explained in a YouTube video where he got the idea:

> We're called Proud Boys because I went to one of my kids' music recitals and some ponce got up there and while everyone's playing the piano and the violin and doing stuff they tried, he gets up and he goes, "Proud of your boy, I'll make you proud of your boy." It's some song from *Aladdin*. And I was looking around for the dad because I thought there's no way this dad is proud of his boy, and of course, he was the child of a single mom—duh! His mother told him, "Yes, sing a song, that's a talent," and there was no dad to say, "No you're not, play the piano, for Christ's sakes."

At protests the Proud Boys stand out because they wear distinctive black-and-yellow uniforms. In 2020, President Trump

A group of Proud Boys, including chairman Enrique Tarrio (in ball cap and sunglasses), participate in a January 2020 Second Amendment rally held in Richmond, Virginia.

himself offered them a shout-out among other white nationalist groups when he said, "Proud Boys, stand back and stand by."

And stand by they did, right through the storming of the Capitol Building on January 6th, 2021. After that, they grew disillusioned with the president. Trump not only quickly distanced himself from the riot, but he declined to offer immunity to those who were involved.

The Proud Boys' leader, Enrique Tarrio, had been arrested two days before the attack on charges of property destruction and illegally hoarding weapons. This, of course, caused a bit of a leadership vacuum. The Proud Boys responded by changing their tactics. They dissolved their national leadership and were henceforth run exclusively through local chapters.

Since they no longer wanted to be identified with Trump and no longer attended his rallies, they couldn't accomplish much on a national level. So they went local. They began to appear, in all their intimidating glory, at town council gatherings, school board presentations, and health department question-and-answer sessions across the country. Their presence at these events was part of a deliberate strategy to attack on a different front. They brought their brand of menacing politics to the local level.

In an article dated December 14, 2021, Sheera Frenkel reported in the *New York Times*:

> Away from the national spotlight, the Proud Boys instead quietly shifted attention to local chapters, some members and researchers said. In small communities—usually suburbs or small towns with populations of tens of thousands—its followers have tried to expand membership by taking on local causes. That way, they said, the group can amass more supporters in time to influence next year's midterm elections.
>
> "The plan of attack if you want to make change is to get involved at the local level," said Jeremy Bertino, a prominent member of the Proud Boys from North Carolina.

In other words, although they seemed to be dissolving, just the opposite was true. Using the internet and encrypting their messaging on the Telegram app, new channels have now sprung up all over. Their published membership, about 31,000 followers, is probably much larger now. Local Telegram groups numbered in the hundreds in 2022.

A lawsuit brought by the District of Columbia's attorney general sued both the Proud Boys and Oath Keepers, alleging that they attacked the Capitol Building on January 6th, but it's hard to identify groups that don't keep records and have no central authority. Again according to Frenkel:

> "We've seen these groups adopt new tactics in the wake of Jan. 6, which have enabled them to regroup and reorganize themselves," said Jared Holt, a resident fellow at the Atlantic Council's Digital Forensic Research Lab who researches domestic extremist groups. "One of the most successful tactics they've used is decentralizing." ... But as local chapters flourished, he said, the group "increased their radical tendencies" because members felt more comfortable taking extreme positions in smaller circles.

One area of such activity has centered on mask requirements and vaccination policies, particularly related to public schools, designed to protect the public during the COVID-19 pandemic. The Armed Conflict Location and Event Data Project, a nonprofit that monitors violence, credited the Proud Boys with about 140 protests and demonstrations a year. But that doesn't include school board meetings and local health board meetings, where they can have a huge terrorist-like effect simply by showing up and looking menacing.

In the words posted by one anonymous member, "Think local, act local." They have threatened community leaders, sometimes simply by standing silently, armed where legal, and staring. Again quoting Frenkel:

> Last month, the school board in Beloit, Wis., said it canceled classes because some of the Proud Boys were at a local protest over mask requirements. In Orange County, Calif., the school board said in September that it would install metal detectors and hire extra security after several Proud Boys attended a meeting and threatened its members.

The technique is intimidating, cheap, and highly effective against common, community-supporting people who just want to contribute to their local governing agencies after a long day at work.

Enrique Tarrio, along with four of his fellow members, was again arrested in June of 2022. They were indicted on new federal charges of seditious conspiracy for their activities on January 6th, and their trial date in federal court was set for December 12, 2022.

THREE PERCENTERS

The Three Percenters came into existence in 2008. They took their name from the fact that, supposedly, only 3 percent of American colonists took up arms against the British in the Revolutionary War. Members think of themselves as a modern version of those rebels, even though its website insists that the Three Percenters are not a militia. Their goal, they say, is not to overthrow the U.S. government but "to utilize the fail-safes put in place by our founders to rein in an overreaching government and

On January 6, 2021, a protestor wearing a Three Percenter flag stands with others on the Capitol grounds, about 90 minutes before crowds storm the building.

push back against tyranny." Just how different overthrowing a government is from reining one in can be debatable.

Like the Proud Boys, the Three Percenters are a rather loosely organized group that attained national prominence when some of its members provided "security" to far-right rallies around the country, notably the white supremacist Unite the Right rally in Charlottesville, Virginia, in August 2017. There they were infamously photographed wearing military-style combat gear while guarding the perimeter of the event. There was also a video of a white supremacist driving into a crowd of counter-protesters.

After the fiasco in Charlottesville that caused such bad publicity, the Three Percenters issued a "stand down order" urging members not to participate in future white supremacist events. The statement read, "We cannot have this organization tainted by new outlets as they will most certainly report that we have aligned ourselves with white supremacists and Nazis."

It didn't work.

Emily Claire Hari, a former sheriff's deputy who submitted a proposal to build Donald Trump's infamous border wall, was one of the group's leaders. (At the time she was named Michael B. Hari.) She was sentenced in September 2021 to 53 years in prison for masterminding the bombing of a Minnesota mosque in 2017. Fortunately, the attack didn't kill anyone. Its reported goal was to "scare" Muslims away from living in the United States. Later, in February 2022, she was sentenced to 14 years (to be served concurrently) for attempted arson related to a November 2017 attack on a women's health clinic in Champaign, Illinois.

After her arrest, it came out that Hari ran a group called the White Rabbit Three Percent Illinois Patriot Freedom Fighters Militia. Its website called Illinois a "failed state" and urged readers to take up "armed resistance" against the government. Such actions and evidence indicate that the group's efforts to distance itself from white supremacy and attempts at overthrowing the government haven't been very successful.

ANTIFA

Antifa is not a highly organized movement. But it's not just an idea, either. It consists of a loose affiliation of activists scattered across the United States and a few other countries, who are identified not so much for what they support as for what they oppose. They are against fascism, nationalism, far-right ideologies, white supremacy, authoritarianism, racism, homophobia, and xenophobia. Some denounce capitalism as well.

The term itself is short for "anti-fascist," and is used both by its adherents and its foes.

Mark Bray, who organized the Occupy Wall Street movement, is the author of *Antifa: The Anti-Fascist Handbook*, in which he outlines the ideology:

Despite the media portrayal of a deranged, bloodthirsty antifa ... the vast majority of anti-fascist tactics involve no physical violence whatsoever. Anti-fascists conduct research on the far right online, in person, and sometimes through infiltrations; they dox them, push central milieux to disown them, pressure bosses to fire them.... But it's also true that some of them punch Nazis in the face and don't apologize for it.

During public demonstrations, most antifa activists can be identified because they wear black from head to toe. Even before the COVID-19 pandemic, they sported face coverings.

There is no official national leadership. Followers have organized themselves into small, local cells that sometimes coordinate with other movements, such as Black Lives Matter. Some self-described antifa adherents have organized to confront organizations such as Patriot Prayer, the Proud Boys, and other far-right groups during public demonstrations, some of which have deteriorated into violence.

Although most antifa adherents try to keep a low public profile, some have developed websites and distinctive names. Rose City Antifa, for instance, was founded in Portland, Oregon, in 2007. According to its website, its main focus is "any work that prevents fascist organizing, and when that is not possible, pro-

A group identifying as Antifa participates in the Juggalo March in Washington, D.C., on September 16, 2017.

vides consequences to fascist organizers. This is supported by researching and tracking fascist organizations."

Antifa came to public attention following the infamous Unite the Right rally in Charlottesville, Virginia, in 2017. A white supremacist deliberately plowed his car into a crowd of counterprotesters, killing a woman named Heather Heyer. In his comments following the incident, President Donald Trump famously suggested that there was an equivalency between white supremacists on the political far-right and the "alt-left," including antifa protesters, on the other side.

"What about the alt-left that came charging at, what you say, the alt-right?" Trump asked. "Do they have any semblance of guilt? What about the fact they're charging with clubs in their hands, swinging clubs, do they have any problem? I think they do."

> **Antifa has also been accused of infiltrating the January 6 crowds, disguised as Proud Boys, in order to cast a negative cloud over their conservative enemies.**

Media coverage has since identified antifa activists as participants, and sometimes agitators, in clashes at numerous rallies and protests around the country, including a 2017 anti-hate rally in Berkeley, California, and a Patriot Prayer "freedom rally" in Portland, Oregon, in 2018.

Antifa has also been accused of infiltrating the January 6 crowds, disguised as Proud Boys, in order to cast a negative cloud over their conservative enemies. No corroborating evidence has yet been put forth to support this claim.

There is no doubt that militia groups will continue to spread for at least the foreseeable future. Are they cults, hate groups, or something else?

Well, that depends on the definition of "cult" we choose to follow. But whatever definition we choose, the victims of these groups don't really care what we call them. All they want is justice.

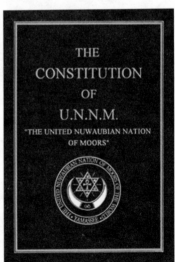

NUWAUBIAN NATION: FROM BLACK SUPREMACISTS TO UFOs

Historical trends swing on a metaphorical pendulum, from one extreme to the other. With the rise of the white nationalism, white power, and white supremacy movements, it was inevitable that an opposing backlash would develop. And it did.

The Nuwaubian Nation refers to an African American religious communal group that has existed under a variety of names. In 1967 it began as the Ansaar Pure Sufi. Later it was called the Nubian Islaamic Hebrew Mission, the Ansaaru Allah Community, the Ancient Mystic Order of Melchizedek, the Holy Tabernacle Ministries, the Yamassee Native American Tribe, and the Nuwaubian Nation of Moors.

The founder of these movements is Michael York. He, too, has taken on many names. In 1969 he was Amunnubi Rooakhptah. Later he became As Siddid Al Imaan Isa Al Haahi Al Madhi, Chief Black Eagle, Nayya Malachizodoq-El, and finally Malachi Z. York. The changing image of the group, and the shifting persona of its leader, has been a source of confusion while providing fodder for numerous critics.

York was born in 1945 and grew up in Brooklyn, New York. In the late 1960s, the Moorish Science Temple of America and the Nation of Islam, with its various offshoots, were on the rise. York served time in prison for a variety of offenses ranging from assault to possession of a deadly weapon. With the nation engaged in the Vietnam War and the draft seemingly fixed so that poor Black men were inducted

Published by York in 1992, the Constitution of the United Nuwaubian Nation of Moors is a fascinating document laying out the leader's principles and tenets.

into the army while white men of privilege had numerous ways to avoid service, it was a yeasty time for American race relations. Men such as the boxer Muhammad Ali, who refused induction, were considered heroes by the Black community. Civil rights activists Martin Luther King Jr., Medgar Evers, and Julian Bond were among their spokesmen. John Lewis and others went on to serve their nation with honor and distinction. It was a time that produced both great Americans and great suffering.

In 1967, a time of riots and civil unrest, Michael York decided that his career was going to be as a teacher. He took on the religious name Amunnubi Roakhptah and began to hold meetings of what was to become the Ansaar Pure Sufi organization in his New York apartment.

> **His followers began to be conspicuous for their black tunics, which set them apart as leaders.**

His followers began to be conspicuous for their black tunics, which set them apart as leaders. Through various name changes, the group continued to grow.

In 1970, York renamed his following the Nubian Islamic Mission. It was then that his followers agreed to live communally. They moved into a house in Brooklyn and opened a bookstore and meeting hall. As the group grew, they moved to larger and larger quarters over the next few years.

In 1972, York visited Sudan. There he developed an identification with the Sudanese military and religious leader Muhammad Ahmad Ibn Abdullāh, whose chief claim to fame came about when he organized and carried out a revolt against British rule. He eventually emerged victorious at Khartoum in 1885.

When York returned home, steeped in history, he changed his name to As Siddid Al Imaan Isa Al Haahi Al Madhi and began to claim he was the descendant of Muhammad Abdullāh, who, at least in New York, was also known as al-Madhi. York identified him as the True Madhi, who was the predicted successor to the Prophet Muhammad.

It was then that York separated his more dedicated believers, who wanted to build a new nation, from the rest of his followers, who loosely identified with the Islamic and African themes York preached but didn't really demonstrate what York considered to be the proper fervor.

From then on, he concentrated on only the sincerely committed. Throughout the decade of the 1980, this group was known as the Ansaaru Allah Community, and it soon spread to many major East Coast cities. The group expanded as well to the Caribbean, to Jamaica, Trinidad and Tobago, Puerto Rico, and Guyana. Members roamed the streets in Black communities, conspicuously dressed in white, and they sold York's books, which grew to more than 400 publications, and preached his message to anyone who would listen. That message varied widely, from topics such as UFOs to diet and personal hygiene.

York preached from the Bible, but he emphasized the Qur'an as well. Allah was the All, and Jesus was the Messiah. Muhammad, the last of the prophets in the lineage of Adam, passed his lineage to his daughter Fatima and son-in-law Ali. Adam and Eve were Nubian, or Black.

During the time of Noah, Ham, one of Noah's sons, committed sodomy after having come upon his father while naked. The story is told in Genesis 9:

Noah, a man of the soil, proceeded to plant a vineyard. When he drank some of its wine, he became drunk and lay uncovered inside his tent. Ham, the father of Canaan, saw his father naked and told his two brothers outside. But Shem and Japheth took a garment and laid it across their shoulders; then they walked in backward and covered their father's naked body. Their faces were turned the other way so that they would not see their father naked.

When Noah awoke from his wine and found out what his youngest son had done to him, he said: "Cursed be Canaan! The lowest of slaves will he be to his brothers."

He also said: "Praise be to the Lord, the God of Shem! May Canaan be the slave of Shem. May God extend Japheth's territory; May Japheth live in the tents of Shem, and may Canaan be the slave of Japheth."

After the flood Noah lived 350 years.

According to York, the punishment for Ham's sin was visited on his fourth son, Canaan, who was stricken with leprosy, thus acquiring a pale skin. Thus, the light-skinned races are descendants of Canaan.

Another important figure in York's theology was Noah's descendent Abraham, whose son Isaac and grandson Jacob were the ancestors of the Israelites.

The nation was enslaved for 420 years in Egypt. But from Abraham's other son, Ismael, came the Ishmaelites, or Nubians.

The Nubians include the Black people of the United States, the West Indies, and all other parts of the globe. York taught that it had been predicted that they would be in slavery for about 400 years, but because of their descent from Abraham, they are rightfully called Hebrews.

The year 1993 marked yet another time of transition for York's group. He changed his name to Malachi York and, along

with some 400 followers, bought a large parcel of land in Georgia and moved south. The group also took on some new names: The United Nuwaubian Nation of Moors, the Yamasee Native American Tribe, the Ancient Mystic Order of Melchizedek, and the Holy Tabernacle Ministries. With each new group name, York took on a different name himself. He was known as Chief Black Eagle, Nayya Malachizodoq-El, and Malachi Z. York.

In the early 1990s, York led many of his followers south to a large parcel of land in Georgia, where the community would build its quirky new home.

There is a significance to each name:

♦ The United Nuwaubian Nation of Moors identifies with the group's Arabic Sudanese and Abrahamic past.

◆ The Yamasee Native American Tribe claims to be related to the Yamasee, a Native American people who lived in Georgia. The Nuwaubians believe that the Yamasee were the original residents of Georgia. They came to North America from the Nile Valley long before continental drift caused the separation of the various continents. The importance of the Yamasee connection is that York believes the tribe signed over their lands to the United States in 1829. That fact allows the Nuwaubians to claim status as a separate, Indigenous nation, giving them autonomy—meaning that the laws of the United States do not apply to them.

◆ The Ancient Mystical Order of Melchizedek is a lodge found in the Masonic tradition. People who are considered Nubians, but who are not presently members of the United Nuwaubian Nation of Moors, may thus join up with the Masons, but their Masonic dues go to the Nuwaubians.

◆ The Holy Tabernacle Ministries is in charge of distributing the group's books and literature. It manages bookstores located in various cities and provides a steady flow of income.

The move to Georgia brought the Nuwaubians their first real publicity. Their new neighbors were concerned first by the sheer number of people who flocked to the area and then by the fact that it seemed like a long time before the group upgraded its various buildings to comply with legal codes. The new folks also stayed apart from the rest of the community. That aroused suspicion, which was confirmed when revelations of secret illicit behavior on the part of York and several close associates came to light.

In 2002, York was arrested on numerous charges of child molestation and a variety of additional associated charges stemming from his use of children for sexual purposes. After a four-year investigation, other members of the group were also arrested for participating in a cover-up.

York was convicted in federal court in January 2004 on charges of racketeering and transporting children across state lines for sexual purposes. Because he had previously confessed to a number of the child molestation charges, the scandal soon became public knowledge.

The Nuwaubian Nation of Moors is thus one of many religious groups, such as the Israelite House of David, the Alamo Christian Foundation, and the Unification Movement, that became involved in major illegal activity that resulted in prison times for their founders. But even after the smoke cleared and the founders were incarcerated, some followers remained loyal. To those remaining few, facts simply don't matter. They believed that the "chosen" ones were victims of religious persecution, period!

It is a hard fact of life that most human beings, despite their arguments to the contrary, choose to follow their beliefs rather than an obvious truth. But then again, as Commander Spock used to exclaim to Captain Kirk, who ever said that humans were logical?

SOCIAL MEDIA AND THE RISE OF HATE GROUPS

On January 6, 2021, a large group of protestors gathered to attend a rally scheduled to be held near the White House in Washington, D.C. They were there at the invitation of President Donald Trump. He claimed that the 2020 presidential election had been stolen, and he encouraged his supporters to be in Washington on that particular date because that was the day the Senate would ratify the results of the election. In Trump's words, "Big protest in D.C. on January 6th. Be there, will be wild!"

> "Big protest in D.C. on January 6th. Be there, will be wild!"

Some of them had come because they felt they were obeying the orders of their president. Many believed fervently that Jesus Christ had ordained the gathering and that they were carrying out the will of God. Others were members of groups such as the Proud Boys, the Oath Keepers, and, yes, the Ku Klux Klan. Some came in buses rented by local militia groups that had formed under the auspices of white nationalist, white power, and white supremacy organizations. Prayers were recorded throughout the crowd, most offered in the name of Jesus.

How was the event coordinated? How did the word get out? How were people from all over the country notified and alerted to what was going to happen?

In a word, the internet. Social media sites across the spectrum had championed the rally for weeks and provided exact details. In some cases, blocks of rooms had been reserved at local hotels and parking facilities arranged. It was all coordinated online, much of it under the auspices of various Evangelical churches.

This was certainly not the first time in American history that people, believing strongly that they were following the word of God, gathered in response to social media.

In April of 1775, for instance, Dr. Joseph Warren had summoned Paul Revere and given him instructions to ride to Lexington, Massachusetts, with the news that British soldiers stationed in Boston were about to march into the countryside northwest of town. Revere arranged to have a signal lit in the Old North Church, arguably the first use of social media in American history. He was ordered to alert local militias to gather in Concord. In the words of the American poet Henry Wadsworth Longfellow, "One if by land, and two if by sea." This was a reference to the secret signal meant to alert patriots about the route the British troops chose to advance toward Concord. As the minutemen—so called because they were to be ready at a minute's notice—followed their leaders to war, there was soon fired the famous "shot heard 'round the world." And the rest, as they say, is history.

It wasn't instantaneous, but it was a social media alert.

Founding Father Paul Revere is most remembered for his midnight ride, and somewhat less for being a pioneer in social media.

In 1904, organizers wanted to spread the word about the upcoming St. Louis World's Fair, which celebrated the Louisiana Purchase Exposition. They decided to use social media, and radio stations from coast to coast played the song that would last in memory long after the Fair was over:

Meet me in St. Louis, Louis,

Meet me at the fair,

Don't tell me the lights are shining

Any place but there,

We will dance the Hoochee Koochee,

I will be your tootsie wootsie,

If you will meet me in St. Louis, Louis,

Meet me at the fair.

In 1967, more than 100,000 people converged on San Francisco's Haight-Ashbury neighborhood to celebrate what became known as the Summer of Love. They had been notified through social media—in this case, a song played on radio stations all over the country that cautioned them, as the song title said, to "be sure to wear flowers in your hair."

But by 2021, times had changed. People no longer needed beacons or radio stations to learn where to be and when. They didn't need to use the cumbersome apparatus of phone trees or the church structure, which had proved so effective during the Civil Rights years. People could now be directed into action in real time. All participants had to do was check their smartphones to receive their marching orders, including up-to-the-minute reports about traffic patterns, escape routes, and where the action was hottest at any particular moment.

After the melee at the Capitol Building, further investigations proved that far-right groups maintained a vigorous online

> **Indeed, they had been publicizing the rally for weeks, even to the point of predicting violence, with extremists repeatedly stating their desire for chaos and destruction on that day.**

presence on social-media platforms such as Twitter, Parler, Gab, MeWe, Zello, and Telegram. Indeed, they had been publicizing the rally for weeks, even to the point of predicting violence, with extremists repeatedly stating their desire for chaos and destruction on that day.

Thousands of people traveled from across the country to join the protest that culminated in a riot. While many people were there to demonstrate peacefully, evidence of militia groups, white nationalists, and conspiracists was overwhelming. Video traffic on some far-right platforms became so overwhelming that the websites began to freeze up.

It soon became obvious that in the past, extremist groups had been kept in check by slow avenues of communication. But with the advent of internet and text communications, that hindrance was removed. Groups that once would never have met or, indeed, have even known about each other could now unite, publicize their views, and attract even more followers.

Facebook, Twitter, and their ilk, which had been designed to bring people together, had accomplished their task. But like every other evolutionary invention, they had a dark side. The "good guys" loved the new freedom of connection. But so did the "bad guys." The world would never be the same. Enter the "cult of social media," whose membership was open to anyone with a smartphone.

Enter also the web, the "deep web," and the "dark web," with all their temptations and hidden corners. But what are they, really? How do they work?

THE WORLD WIDE WEB

Most people use the words "internet" and "the web" interchangeably, but they are not the same thing. The internet is a vast network that connects computers all over the world. Anyone with access to the internet can communicate with anyone else who has a similar connection. They can bounce information off satellites or run it through cables, share information and emails, talk on social media sites, and all that. They are *on* the internet. But they connect *through* the World Wide Web (WWW). The web is actually just one of the many applications that are, in ef-

Tim Berners-Lee, considered the inventor of the World Wide Web, used his computer at CERN as the world's first web server.

fect, built on the internet. What happens, although this is a simplified explanation, is that a browser sends an HTTP (hypertext transfer protocol) message to a server. What the browser is doing, in effect, is requesting that information be sent to you. That information, along with all other subsequent communication, is sent across your internet connection using something called TCP/IP. (TCP/IP stands for transmission control protocol/internet protocol. It's basically a set of rules that all computers follow when they talk to each other. Are you still with me?) You then bring up, say, a company's website, where you can order a product in exchange for your name, address, and credit card information. But here's the problem. Everything is out in the open. HTTP does not encrypt your data while communicating with web servers. This means that a "hacker," who could be anyone with a computer and sufficient knowledge, can eavesdrop and read your messages. This brings us to the so-called deep web.

THE DEEP WEB

This is a term used to describe information that is not accessible by normal search engines such as Google, Ask.com, or Duck-

DuckGo. Content on the deep web requires sign-in credentials or what is called a paywall. This is usually a good thing. Doctors, for instance, want to share your medical information with each other, but they don't want anyone peeking at the state of your health. So they communicate through the deep web. Believe it or not, this part of the web is by far the biggest portion of the internet. It makes up more than 90 percent of the whole thing. The part you use every day is called the clear web.

Now we come to a portion of the deep web that can be really evil.

THE DARK WEB

The dark web is a kind of subset to the deep web, and it is intentionally hidden from casual users. No one knows for sure how big it is. Estimates generally run to about 5 percent of the total internet. To access it, you need a specific browser called Tor. It routes your web page requests through a series of proxy (intermediary) servers, which are operated by thousands of volunteers all around the world. That makes it virtually impossible to identify your internet protocol (IP) address—your internet location.

Note that the dark web is not totally sinister. Some people, for instance, use it in countries where internet access is criminalized. But its use by people who conduct illegal activities is legendary. You can buy guns, drugs, credit card numbers, counterfeit money, pornography, and lots and lots of stolen subscription addresses and phone numbers that allow you to break into other people's computers, giving you access to their bank records and much, much more. You can access the information needed to install RATs, or remote access trojans, and malware, whose sole purpose is to tangle up a computer so it doesn't work. You can conduct espionage. You can wreak all sorts of havoc. Navigating these depths is not easy. It takes dedicated, competent specialists. But it is a real concern, especially when we start to consider a new form of warfare on a global scale: cyber warfare. Why fire a bunch of missiles devoted to taking down power plants when you can accomplish the same thing by destroying an electric grid with the stroke of a computer key? Great damage can be done on a much smaller scale as well. Have you ever been "scammed"? Your information was undoubtedly obtained and sold to websites on the dark web. Law enforcement officials are getting better at finding and prosecuting owners of these sites, but it's a constantly evolving field.

With all this background, what we have seen in the last few years can only be called the birth of a social media cult. Perhaps even an internet cult. Still in its infancy, it is a growing danger and has perhaps recruited the vast majority of us. Whenever we wake up in the morning and turn on our computers to see what we've missed during the night, we exhibit our membership. Try unplugging for a few days and measure your level of anxiety. You might be amazed at what you discover about yourself.

> **Is the Social Media Cult destined to be the most dangerous cult of all?**

Is the Social Media Cult destined to be the most dangerous cult of all? Perhaps. It seems to be actually affecting the evolution of the human species in terms of reducing our attention spans, narrowing our world views, changing the way we process reality, and enhancing our ability to connect with people from the other side of the world at a moment's notice.

And it has only just begun.

SPOOFING THE MOVEMENT: FUN WITH CULTS

Peter McIndoe was an inventive student visiting friends in Memphis in January 2017 when he came across a protest march. Donald J. Trump had just been sworn in as president, and both pro-Trump and anti-Trump factions were going at each other. Watching the two groups brandishing their signs, he ripped a poster off a wall, turned it over and wrote on the back, in big letters, three random words that would change his life: "Birds Aren't Real."

Five years later, he would say, "It was a spontaneous joke, but it was a reflection of the absurdity everyone was feeling."

As luck would have it, his supposed earnestness was captured on video. That led to interviews with major news outlets. When asked what his sign meant, he spontaneously went into character and improvised an entire conspiracy theory about how he was part of an organization that had discovered that the U.S. government had destroyed all birds and replaced them with surveillance drones. They had been covering up this plot since the 1970s.

He even offered various "proofs," such as evidence of birds "recharging their batteries" while perching on power lines.

From impromptu prank to merchandise empire to actual conspiracy, Peter McIndoe's "Birds Aren't Real" campaign quickly took on a life of its own and continues to inspire grassroots flyering to this day.

He was so sincere, and he offered such a convincing line of made-up evidence, that the interviews went viral. Voila! A conspiracy was born. McIndoe managed to stay perfectly in character for the next five years, promoting an entire Birds Aren't Real conspiracy campaign that delighted the public, sparked by interviewers who never really quite got that he was acting. Even the crowds who started to show up at his rallies played their part, without ever letting on their pretense.

He finally came clean in 2022, but for a long time, he was really on a roll. He even dropped out of school to devote full time to the project.

It was no accident that McIndoe was the one who pulled the whole thing off. One might say he was born to play the part. Until he was 18 years old, he and seven siblings were homeschooled within the confines of a very conservative, religious family, first near Cincinnati, Ohio, and then in rural Arkansas. He was taught, in his words, that "evolution was a massive brainwashing plan by the Democrats, and Obama was the Antichrist." He learned that Hollywood produced anti-Christianity messages. Social media became his door into mainstream culture. "I was raised by the Internet, because that's where I ended up finding a lot of my actual, real-world education, through documentaries and You-

Tube," he later said. "My whole understanding of the world was formed by the Internet."

All this led to his spontaneous idea to concoct his own conspiracy. He didn't plan everything out. It just came to him and grew from there. Once it began, he simply went with it.

"I started embodying the character and building out the world this character belonged to," he said. Along with Connor Gaydos, a close friend, he wrote a fake history of the movement, developed hilarious, elaborate theories, produced fake documentation, and even hired an actor who claimed to be a former CIA agent and confessed to working on bird drone surveillance.

The interview garnered more than 20 million views on TikTok. Other actors claimed to be "bird truthers." Instagram exploded. They even protested outside Twitter's headquarters in San Francisco, demanding that the company change its bird logo.

"It basically became an experiment in misinformation," McIndoe said. "We were able to construct an entirely fictional world that was reported on as fact by local media, and questioned by members of the public."

The whole charade has made McIndoe a hero to the anti-conspiracy world. In one brilliant, intuitive move, he managed to prove three things beyond the shadow of a doubt:

1. Some people will believe anything.

2. Others will not believe but will carry on as if they do.

3. Still others will weaponize conspiracies, using them for their own gain.

"Dealing in the world of misinformation for the past few years, we've been really conscious of the line we walk," he said. "The idea is meant to be so preposterous, but we make sure nothing we're saying is too realistic. That's a consideration with coming out of character."

That's why he finally stepped out of the character he so carefully concocted, revealing that the whole movement was a convoluted parody. Mission accomplished.

Claire Chronis, a Birds Aren't Real member from Pittsburgh, explained: "It's a way to combat troubles in the world that you don't really have other ways of combating. My favorite way to describe the organization is that we're fighting lunacy with lunacy."

So Birds Aren't Real, as absurd as the movement is in both its content and unexpected popularity, actually has a purpose. How do you fight some of the crazy and dangerous conspiracies that dominate the internet nowadays? What McIndoe did—almost by accident, at least in the beginning—was to unite a young generation in fighting against something so big that they didn't know how to proceed. It gave them an outlet and a means to disarm the misinformation campaigns that are so prevalent today—Gen Z's attempt to disconnect the whole thing with absurdism.

"Birds Aren't Real is not a shallow satire of conspiracies from the outside. It is from the deep inside," McIndoe explains. "A lot of people in our generation feel the lunacy in all this, and Birds Aren't Real has been a way for people to process that."

QANON: POLITICAL CONSPIRACY AND RELIGIOUS ICONS

A vast field of conspiracy cults seems to thrive in the United States, and perhaps the grandaddy of them all is called QAnon.

You probably didn't know this, especially if you happen to be a Democrat, but in the presidential election of 2016, Donald Trump was running for president in part to expose a cabal of Deep State politicians, celebrity actors, medical professionals, and business tycoons who were engaged in satanic worship and pedophilia on a global scale.

This didn't become public knowledge until 2017, when an alleged top-secret governmental official who goes by the pseudonym "Q," reminiscent of Captain Jean-Luc Picard's nemesis in the television series *Star Trek: The Next Generation*, began to post online messages about the "truth" of what is "really" going on, not only in the United States but around the world.

This QAnon adaptation of the Gadsden flag changes the caption "Don't Tread on Me" to the QAnon slogan "Where We Go One We Go All."

As soon as Donald Trump became President Trump, he was going to order mass arrests and executions of members of the secret cult. This was going to happen on a day called either the "Storm" or the "Event." The alleged cabal was so worried about Trump winning the election that they masterminded a secret conspiracy involving Russia related to the election. QAnon supporters claimed that FBI director Robert Mueller's inquiry into Russian interference was really an elaborate cover story for an investigation into the alleged sex-trafficking ring, along with an attempted coup d'état by President Barack Obama, former secretary of state Hillary Clinton, and philanthropist George Soros, who were the ringleaders.

Somewhere along the line, "Q" learned of even greater plans. Deep research into George Soros and the wealthy Rothschild family—common targets of anti-Semitic conspiracy theories—allegedly revealed that Jewish instigators were at the bottom of the whole conspiracy, which used a well-known pizza chain as a front. Russian and Chinese state-backed media companies, along with the far-right Falun Gong–associated Epoch Media Group, were somehow in the mix as well.

There is, of course, not a shred of evidence in any of these claims. The day of the "Storm" came and went. Trump was elected, and no arrests were made. But that didn't make any difference to what is now often called the QAnon Cult. Facts simply don't matter. The bulk of the news is reported by the "Fake Media," and you can't believe anything they say. Therefore, you have to get your real news by way of social media sites, the only sources to be trusted.

Which social media sites, you might ask? Easy! The ones that agree with your opinions. All the rest are attempting to deceive you.

And how do you know you are receiving the truth? Well, you must be, because you have gathered around yourself a virtual community consisting of hundreds, if not thousands, of people who all reinforce your beliefs. And that many people can't be wrong. It becomes the main animating force in your life.

In 2013 a social media website called "Infinitechan" or "Infinitychan" was created. It was often pictured as ∞chan, employing the mathematical symbol for infinity, and this name became 8chan. It was a site that had been linked to white power groups, neo-Nazis, and other far-right organizations and anti-Semitic groups. Mass shootings from El Paso and Dayton to New Zealand had been advertised on the site, and it hosted child pornography chats as well. This was the site that first spread the missives of "Q" to the world and is thus the home of QAnon.

In 2015 the popular search engine Google deplatformed the site (that is, it stopped showing search results and links to the site), and in August 2019 the service that hosted 8chan on the so-called clear web (where indexed, common-access websites reside, as opposed to the dark web that hosts unindexed, hidden sites) stopped supporting the site. Banned from its home, 8chan vanished and then returned to the clear web as 8kun in November 2019, supported and funded by a Russian host provider.

"Q"'s often symbolic and cryptic posts became known as drops or Q drops. To say the least, they are enigmatic. Take this drop from 2019:

[C] BEFORE [D]. [C]oats BEFORE [D]. The month of AUGUST is traditionally very HOT. You have more than you know.

Jacob Angeli Chansley, known as the "QAnon Shaman," holds a QAnon sign in Peoria, Arizona, on October 15, 2020.

Once a message was dropped, it spread through private channels with amazing speed, posted and re-posted before search engines could catch up. It soon became a political tool, and Trump supporters began showing up at rallies with "Q Sent Me" placards. Trump himself began quoting Q drops on his Twitter feed.

The QAnon cult has even taken on a religious component. Jacob Angeli Chansley, labeled the "QAnon Shaman," made a name for himself by appearing at QAnon rallies dressed in animal skins and face paint and wearing a pair of bull horns on his head. He was easily the most identifiable character in any crowd, and cameras were frequently pointed in his direction. So it didn't help his cause when, as one of the first wave of people who entered the Capitol Building during the insurrection of January 6, 2021, he was photographed and easily identified. He had left a note inside the building that read "It's Only A Matter Of Time. Justice Is Coming!" Indeed, he was soon arrested, convicted, and sentenced to 41 months in prison for his part in the riot.

Christian conservatives and Evangelical pastors have weighed in on religion and QAnon.

The Reverend Jon Thorngate, for instance, is senior pastor at LifeBridge Church near Milwaukee. He is one of a small number of church leaders who will actually go on record about QAnon. Most fear backlash from their parishioners. He calls QAnon a "real problem" and recognizes that belief in conspiracy theories is a growing threat. Only five or ten of his church members have actually posted QAnon theories online, but many more—he doesn't know how many—are open to them.

Some of his members held meetings in which they viewed a short film called *Plandemic*, which puts forth the theory that the COVID-19 pandemic was a moneymaking scheme by government officials. The film has since been posted on common social media sites like Facebook. Some of his members also distributed a video, which has since been banned by mainstream social media sites, that promotes hydroxychloroquine as a cure for the virus.

Many QAnon believers have crossed the line between following and acting. In 2018, for instance, an armed believer named Matthew Wright blocked a bridge near the Hoover Dam. He later pleaded guilty to a terrorism charge.

Several former associates of President Trump, such as former national security advisor Michael Flynn, and two members of Trump's legal team, Lin Wood and Sidney Powell, have championed QAnon conspiracy theories. This led to a publicity crackdown on the movement and its claims, which only furthered the distrust between followers of "Q" and the media, who were accused of a political witch hunt.

> **Supporters have vowed there will come a day of reckoning, and many believe that arrests, convictions, and executions of prominent figures will yet take place.**

Supporters have vowed there will come a day of reckoning, and many believe that arrests, convictions, and executions of prominent figures will yet take place. Their slogan has become infamous: "WWG1WGA!" ("Where we go one we go all").

The movement most definitely has gathered political clout. Marjorie Taylor Greene, a U.S. congressperson from Georgia's 14th congressional district, was elected in November 2021. Since her election, she has quoted and championed a number of Q drops.

More than 21 past candidates for state legislatures have signaled their support for QAnon. Others, trying to be a bit more circumspect in their language, have decided simply not to condemn the organization publicly for fear of losing votes.

How many QAnon members are there? It's hard to guess. But QAnon-related traffic on social networking sites such as Facebook, Twitter, Reddit, and YouTube has exploded since the first

Q drop in 2017, and indications are the totals have risen even further during the coronavirus pandemic.

Various social media platforms have instituted rules about QAnon content and have banned hundreds of Q-supporting videos. But it's hard to stay ahead of a constantly evolving technology when so many users contribute to it with such growing technical savvy and political fervor.

Who is "Q"? No one knows for sure.

The *Washington Post* suggested it might be Ron Watkins, an administrator of the 8kun message board. The *New York Times* has entered the names of Paul Furber, an early follower of the movement, and Ron Watkins, who operated a website where Q drops began appearing in 2018. Watkins launched a campaign to run for Congress in Arizona in October 2021.

Frederick Brennan, the creator of 8chan, swears that his former business partner, Jim Watkins, Ron's father, is the culprit. Jim is a supporter of "Q." He began the QAnon Super PAC and wore a "Q" pin during his testimony before Congress about 8chan in 2019.

All candidates have denied responsibility.

Is QAnon a cult? Many claim it is. Just as many seem to claim it is simply a truth-telling organization. Tempers run high on both sides of the issue. It might be a while before this one is sorted out for the history books.

SEX IN THE CITY: THE DARK POTENCY OF CULTS

    Throughout this book, we have surveyed various cults that developed, in one way or another, a component of immorality and subjugation that involved sexual dominance and exploitation. Sad to say, this happens more often than not when cults idolize or otherwise revere a venerable leader. Temptation rears its ugly head, and the whole organization goes downhill.

    What is even worse is when a cult begins its mission with sexual exploitation in mind. It is hard to imagine how and why women, who are almost always the ones being exploited, fall into the clutches of real monsters such as the ones we are about to review, but it happens over and over again. It takes an experienced psychologist to explain the power of sexual exploitation, but it is a real phenomenon. It is hard to read about it. It is even harder to write about it. But if it helps even one person recognize the trap before it is sprung, it is worth the attempt.

BHAGWAN SHREE RAJNEESH: COMING TO AMERICA

In the 1960s and 1970s, Bhagwan Shree Rajneesh, who is also called Osho or Acharya Rajneesh and was originally named Chandra Mohan Jain, owned and ran a large ashram in Pune, India, that attracted thousands of visitors from around the world. Reports of violence and sexual aggression eventually accompanied the downfall of this ashram, and in 1981, Rajneesh moved to the United States. Soon after, he incorporated what he hoped would become a new city named Rajneeshpuram. The site was going to be built on an abandoned ranch near Antelope, Oregon. During the next few years, many of the people who had moved there with him, some of them his most trusted aides, packed up and left. Rajneesh himself came under investigation for multiple felonies, including arson, attempted murder, drug smuggling, and vote fraud. He plea-bargained guilty to immigration fraud and was deported from the United States, but he was refused entry to 21 countries before returning to Pune.

Who was this guy, and how did all of this happen?

Disciples meet with Bhagwan Shree Rajneesh in Pune, India, in 1977.

Rajneesh was born in 1931 in Kuchwada, India. When he was young, he lived first with his grandparents and then with his parents. Apparently, he was a handful, intelligent but rebellious—traits that would later earn him a living, a following, and a jail sentence. After graduating from high school, he attended college for a while, but at least one of his professors remembered him as being just as much of a handful to them as he was for his parents and grandparents.

In 1953 he took a year off from his studies to search for meaning and meditate, a common practice in India at that time. When he returned to school, he claimed to have reached enlightenment. He had come to believe that individual religious experiences lie at the base of spiritual growth and that such experiences cannot be organized into any one belief system.

He finally graduated with a bachelor's degree in philosophy and went on to study for a master's degree as well. After he graduated, he became a college professor, teaching philosophy at Raipur Sanskrit College.

Old habits are tough to break, however. His radical ideas got him fired, and he eventually moved to the University of Jabalpur. While still teaching, he began to travel throughout India, building a following by teaching some controversial ideas about spirituality.

> **What was so controversial that it caused his ideas to catch on? What else? It involved sex.**

What was so controversial that it caused his ideas to catch on? What else? It involved sex. He taught that sex was the first step toward achieving what he called "super consciousness." This was completely at odds with prevalent Hindu teachings.

By 1964 he was experiencing so much success conducting meditation camps and recruiting followers that he was able to fulfill almost every college professor's dream: he quit teaching.

Because of all this, he became somewhat of an outcast in academic circles and earned the nickname "the sex guru."

His following grew, and in 1970 he introduced a practice he called "dynamic meditation." It was a technique that, according to Rajneesh, enabled the practitioner to experience divinity. One can only assume the technique was inspired by practitioners who were heard to exclaim, "Oh God!" when they reached enlightenment. Or whatever.

Needless to say, Westerners began to flock to his ashram in Pune, India. They become known as *sannyasins*, disciples. Taking Indian names for themselves, they dressed in orange and red clothes and participated in group sessions that sometimes involved both violence and sexual promiscuity. Rajneesh taught them to renounce the world and practice asceticism. That's a common Hindu teaching. But in his system, they were trained to still live fully *in* the world. They were just not to become *attached* to it.

In a few years, the ashram was full to capacity, and Rajneesh was forced to look for new and larger quarters. Here, he ran into a problem. Local governments didn't want anything to do with him. By 1980, he had even survived an assassination attempt by a Hindu fundamentalist.

It seemed a good time to move, and America beckoned. He immigrated to the United States with 2,000 of his disciples and settled on a 100-square-mile ranch Oregon. Mixing East and West, he came up with the name Rancho Rajneesh.

> **By 1980, he had even survived an assassination attempt by a Hindu fundamentalist. It seemed a good time to move.**

Local authorities in the States, despite the sexually open reputation of America in the 1980s, still complained, however. That's what brought Rajneesh and his sannyasins to begin work on Rajneeshpuram.

To say the least, the neighbors disapproved. Local officials tried to shut the place down. Nearby churches didn't like it much, either. They joined forces to say that the burgeoning community violated Oregon's land-use laws. But Rajneesh emerged victorious in court and continued to expand the commune.

Now the story takes an especially dark turn. Rajneesh was upset. As is common for people who believe themselves above the law, subject only to God, he retaliated. Accusations of murder, wiretapping, voter fraud, arson, and a mass salmonella poisoning in 1984 that affected more than 700 people brought the situation to a boiling point.

Several of the commune leaders fled to avoid prosecution for crimes, and in 1985 police arrested Rajneesh, who was himself attempting to flee the United States to escape charges of immigration fraud. During his subsequent trial, Rajneesh pleaded guilty to immigration charges, realizing that a plea bargain was the only way he would be allowed to return to India.

When he finally came home, however, in 1986, he realized his following had dwindled away. It subsequently experienced

Rajneesh and his followers incorporated their ranch as the City of Rajneeshpuram, even building their own airport and creating their own airline, Air Rajneesh.

AMERICAN CULTS

ebbs and flows but never again reached its former heights. He wasn't exactly strapped for cash, however. Because he was an enlightened being, he chose to be seen in public only in a Rolls Royce. Not just one. He is said to have owned, at one time, 94 of them.

He continued his teaching, changed his name to Osho, and tried to keep going. But his health deteriorated, and he died of heart failure in 1990.

The remaining followers renamed their commune the Osho Institute and later re-renamed it the Osho International Meditation Resort. It attracts as many as 200,000 visitors a year, and some 750 Osho Meditation Centers have sprung up in more than 60 major cities around the world.

There's no doubt about it: sex sells.

KEITH RANIERE AND NXIVM: THE CASE OF THE SELF-STYLED REVERED ONE

In January 2021, *NXIVM* (pronounced "NEX-i-um") leader Keith Raniere was transferred to a maximum-security federal penitentiary in Arizona after a judge rejected his bid to remain in a New York facility. The reason was simple. The Arizona facility treated sex offenders. The prison in New York didn't. The 60-year-old sex-cult guru was serving a 120-year sentence for leading a secret master-slave cult based in Albany, New York, with satellite programs in Mexico, Canada, and South America, in which he mentally and physically abused dozens of young women.

The judge who presided over his sentencing also ordered Raniere to pay $3.4 million to 21 of his victims. Some of that money was earmarked for the removal of brands made with a cauterizing pen. The brands were of a symbol that, unbeknownst to the victims, was a stylized rendition of Raniere's initials. They were burned into the skin surrounding the pelvic region. While they were being branded, the women were required to be fully naked, while a cult "master" ordered a slave to film the procedure.

NXIVM was a combination of two kinds of cults. It was sex cult, certainly, but it was also a pyramid scheme, advertised under a "self-help" marketing program. Its alleged "courses" cost thousands of dollars each. Participants, called "NXIANs," were strongly encouraged to pay for additional classes as well, and to recruit others to take classes. With each new recruit they signed up, participants were able to rise in rank within the cult. It was a classic pyramid scheme technique.

Keith Raniere, founder of NXIVM

One of the most well-known group members was the actress Allison Mack, who appeared in more than 200 episodes of the popular TV show *Smallville*, in which she played the part of Clark Kent's friend Chloe Sullivan. After her trial, at which she pleaded guilty to two counts of federal racketeering, she was sentenced to three years in prison. She admitted to recruiting new members while participating in an inner circle of women who were subservient to Raniere.

This went on for more than 20 years. How could such a thing have happened in twenty-first-century America?

It began in 1990, when Raniere founded a program called Consumers' Buyline Inc. It offered big discounts on things like groceries and appliances, but, like all pyramid schemes, it made its money by recruitment. Raniere signed up members who then recruited more members, thereby earning massive commissions. Within only a few years, the company numbered more than 100 people, and it quickly grew to over 2,000 members. Raniere promised results, and people were willing to believe.

Consumers' Buyline was recognized as an illegal pyramid scheme and shut down by New York's attorney general in September 1996. But this only freed Raniere up to join with Nancy Salzman and expand into a company he called Executive Success Programs Inc. It consisted of a series of workshops that were designed to "actualize human potential."

As in most successful Multi-Level Marketing Cults (MLMs), results were spectacular at first. But it soon became obvious that something much more sinister was going on behind the scenes.

In 1998, Raniere and Salzman founded NXIVM, which was really a rebranding of Executive Success Programs Inc. Salzman was named president of the company, and cult members called her "Prefect."

She eventually paid a price for her position, however. When FBI agents staged a 2018 raid of her house in Waterford, New York, they found $520,000 in cash, stuffed in bags, envelopes, and shoeboxes. One shoebox contained more than $390,000. They also confiscated computers, data-storage devices, cameras, various mobile phones and BlackBerrys, and Mexican and Russian currency. Both she and her daughter, Lauren, were arrested, as well as her bookkeeper Kathy Russell, and Clare Bronfman. Bronfman was the half-sister of Edgar Bronfman Jr., who was head of Seagram's, the Canadian beverage giant, and owner of Universal Pictures.

In July 2018, the court found that Nancy and Lauren Salzman, Raniere, Bronfman, Allison Mack, and Kathy Russell were guilty of identity theft, extortion, forced labor, sex trafficking, money laundering, wire fraud and obstruction of justice. In addition, Salzman was found guilty of obstructing justice in a civil suit between NXIVM and a former member. She had "edited and removed portions of session videos to favor the appearance of the company."

> **NXIVM was declared to be a pyramid scheme that had exploited its recruits while conducting illegal human experiments.**

NXIVM was declared to be a pyramid scheme that had exploited its recruits while conducting illegal human experiments and making it "physically and psychologically difficult, and in some cases impossible, to leave the coercive community."

The subversion charge came about because of what NXIVM taught about people it called "suppressives." These were people who allegedly tried to impede progress within NXIVM—that is, people who saw what was going on and tried to become whistleblowers. They had undergone what Raniere called "the Fall" and were henceforth labeled "Luciferians, lost people for whom bad feels good, and good feels bad."

So what was going on for so many years that attracted so many people, and how did the cult manage to ensnare so many in its net?

The basis of it all was the claim that Raniere could help you "actualize" your "human potential" and learn an "ethical framework of human experience." The knowledge didn't come cheap. The first course of the Executive Success Program consisted of a five-day intensive workshop that cost, back in 1998, $2,700. It attracted more than 16,000 people over a five-year period who signed up to study a "scientific" method called "rational inquiry."

John Hochman, a forensic psychiatrist, analyzed the program in 2003 and determined it was mind-control, "aimed at breaking down his subjects psychologically." It boasted a 12-point public mission statement that was read at the beginning of each session. One of the points declared: "There are no ultimate victims; therefore, I will not choose to be a victim."

All who enrolled were required to sign a non-disclosure agreement, and they were subtly manipulated by ritualistic, cult-like practices. They were made to remove their shoes, for instance. They were given different colored sashes to wear, which revealed their rank within the hierarchy. They were made to stand when a higher-ranking member entered the room. Raniere was called "Vanguard," and anyone greeting him had to kiss him on the mouth.

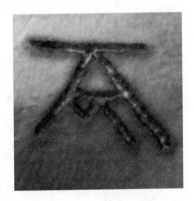

The structure was designed to drain students of energy and will. After a 17-hour day, participants felt quite cut off from the outside world. What is commonly called Stockholm syndrome, or dependence on one's captor, began to set in.

And this was just the beginning course of the program. High-ranking members of the cult lived together in commune-like housing. They instructed classes, usually without pay. There was an exclusive women's-only program called Jness. The

Among other abuses, Raniere ordered female followers to be branded with a symbol representing his initials.

men's-only course was called SOP (the Society of Protectors.) A program featuring physical fitness was labeled Exo/Eso.

Throughout the whole program, Raniere was hailed as an elusive, godlike figure. He was able, according to former participants, to help students overcome anxieties and phobias. Medical conditions such as obsessive-compulsive disorder and Tourette's syndrome were dealt with.

> **The Dalai Lama visited the cult in Albany in 2009 and gave it his recommendation.**

To add further luster to the group, the Dalai Lama visited the cult in Albany in 2009 and gave it his recommendation.

But all was not clear sailing. Rumors of less-than-stellar work began to circulate. As far back as 2003, *Forbes* magazine visited and came away less than impressed; contributor Michael Freedman wrote in its October issue: "Detractors say he runs a cult-like program aimed at breaking down his subjects psychologically, separating them from their families and inducting them into a bizarre world of messianic pretensions, idiosyncratic language and ritualistic practices."

Edgar Bronfman Sr., Clare's father, publicly called NXIVM a cult. But the organization managed to survive and even thrive for another 20 years.

In 2017, Raniere formed an exclusive, highly secret society for women within the cult. It was called DOS (Dominus Obsequious Sororium). Translated from Latin, it means, roughly, "Lord over the obedient female companions." This is the group that eventually led to all the bad publicity and lawsuits. It operated in a classic pyramid-scheme style. Women "slaves" were recruited by "masters." Slaves were then expected to recruit slaves of their own. That was how they became masters. They owed "service" not only to their own masters but also to masters above them in the DOS pyramid.

Raniere was the top of the pyramid. All other members were women. Mack was one of the women on the first level of the pyramid, right below Raniere.

Women were recruited by being told they were joining a women-only organization that would empower them and eradicate purported "weaknesses" that were "common in women." Raniere's place in the structure was not revealed to them.

Before joining DOS, women were required to provide "collateral." That included everything from nude photographs to damaging gossip about friends and family members. They were then told their collateral would be published if they told anyone about DOS's existence.

Sarah Edmondson, a Canadian actress who was an ardent supporter of the group for years, grew disillusioned after her initiation into DOS and filed a complaint with the New York State Department of Health. As part of her initiation, she had been required to send nude photos of herself as "collateral" to her "master." Blindfolded and called a "slave," she was led to a massage table, held down, and instructed to say: "Master, please brand me, it would be an honor." She was then branded. Following this experience, she was instructed to be "on call" 24 hours a day and punished by having food withheld if she did not respond to a text from her "master" within 60 seconds.

When the *New York Times* ran a story revealing all this in 2017, many participants seemed to suddenly wake up to what was going on. As they started to drop out, Raniere fled to Mexico. In 2018, a complaint was issued in federal court requesting an arrest warrant. Mexican authorities arrested Raniere in March and deported him back to New York. In June, the *Times Union* reported that NXIVM had suspended its operations due to "extraordinary circumstances facing the company."

The "Vanguard" himself was charged with crimes including sex trafficking and forced labor. He pleaded not guilty. At the same time, Allison Mack and Clare Bronfman were indicted for crimes including identity theft, extortion, forced labor, sex trafficking, money laundering, wire fraud, and obstruction of justice. They all pleaded guilty. Because of their voluntary plea, they were able to bargain for lesser sentences, but Raniere was found guilty and convicted by a Brooklyn jury of racketeering, sex trafficking, forced labor conspiracy, and wire fraud conspiracy. The jury debated for less than less than five hours.

Following this, a 2020 civil lawsuit was filed against NXIVM leadership by more than 80 plaintiffs who had at one time been members of the organization. Many of the plaintiffs filed under pseudonyms. The lawsuit alleged that Raniere, Salzman, Clare and Sara Bronfman, and Allison Mack, among others, conspired to systemically abuse, manipulate, and extort members of the organization.

Does NXIVM still exist? It seems highly doubtful, but rumors persist that it is still active in a limited capacity. In 2020, a group of dancers who called themselves "The Forgotten Ones" staged dances outside the Metropolitan Detention Center in Brooklyn, where Raniere had been kept without bail throughout his 2019 trial. Frank Parlato, NXIVM's former publicist, claimed on video that he was able to identify actor Nicki Clyne and a few other former group members, whom he likens to the "brainwashed Manson girls." They even opened up a website that claimed they were dancing "for all the forgotten inmates." Raniere was the only one specifically named.

Parlato swears that NXIVM is still "absolutely active." He claimed that his "sources" told him the Society of Protectors was still holding meetings virtually on the messaging app Telegram. He started a website called the Frank Report, which reports on NVIXM and all the legal trials that stemmed from it.

Raniere, of course, is in prison, serving a 120-year sentence while being treated as a sex addict. It is doubtful that he is in control any longer. One can only wonder what former victims are feeling.

SULLIVANIANS: SEX AS A WAY OF LIFE

From the late 1950s to the early 1990s, the Sullivanians were a sex cult on New York City's Upper West Side for couples who were sick of their kids, tired of the traditional American family structure, bored with their sex life, and searching for a nontraditional experience. Their goal was to provide an alternative to the average nuclear family, and for more than 30 years, they did just that.

A typical commune offers members work and communal life, usually in a rural environment. Not the Sullivanians. They commandeered three uptown apartment buildings and didn't give a hoot about sustainable living. All they wanted was to suspend the idea of the traditional family unit, and get it on.

The guru of this convivial mix was a man named Bernard Cohen. He had fought in the Spanish Civil War and World War II, and with those experiences behind him, he was ready for peace and harmony. He studied psychotherapy and how the human brain worked. By 1957 he had changed his name to Newton and, with his wife, Dr. Jane Pearce, founded the Sullivan Institute for Research in Psychoanalysis.

The institute's name came from their mentor, Harry Stack Sullivan, with whom they both worked at the William Alanson White Institute. There is some argument about how closely they followed his teaching at their new institute.

The therapy sessions they provided became a fertile recruitment field for their sex cult. What eventually evolved was a small group of people who were cut off from the world at large even though they lived right in the middle of New York City. Members believed that the source of most of the anxiety in the world was a distorted view of the nuclear family. A "Mom, Dad, and the kids" family unit was the expected experience. If that experience could be avoided, the world would be far less stressful.

When patients came to see this, they usually cast off their family ties and moved in with the Sullivan Institute folks, whose apartment building became the base of their whole life.

In this environment, any system of professional boundaries quickly broke down. Therapists and patients slept together regularly, and they were cautioned

The Sullivan Institute attracted numerous artists and intellectuals to its East Village enclave, including singer-songwriter Judy Collins.

not to develop attachments that went too deep. As a former Sullivanian later said, "Everyone slept with everyone." The more people they attracted, the more buildings they acquired.

> **A communal bulletin board advertised who the next sexual partners would be.**

Life changed for all of them. Men and women occupied separate apartments to discourage the development of permanent attachments and the concept of the couple at the head of typical families. A communal bulletin board advertised who the next sexual partners would be. If children were born—as, of course, they were—they were usually separated quickly from their parents, given to a caretaker of some kind, and shipped off to boarding schools as soon as possible. Anything smacking of a traditional family structure was seen as oppressive, and harmony in the world could only be found when the whole idea of the family "unit" was completely destroyed.

It was this part of the Sullivanian way of life that eventually destroyed the cult. The members' parents, who no longer saw their children, began to file lawsuits. This brought about negative publicity.

When Pearce left the group in the 1970s and Newton brought in a second wife, members immediately noticed a change. Leadership became much more authoritarian and cult-like.

When a theater company, for instance, who owned the lease on a building the Sullivanians had agreed to occupy, refused to leave the premises, Newton and some of his followers rampaged through the building, destroying equipment and tearing down entire sets. Police soon arrived, and Newton barricaded the doors, seemingly enjoying the whole confrontation.

Needless to say, tempers were wearing thin. The anxiety the members had sought to alleviate with their alternative lifestyle simply morphed into a different type of stress.

Former members later expressed the opinion that Newton was falling into a state of dementia and becoming paranoid. He began to suspect the FBI of spying on the group, so he installed metal bunkers to foil the agency's ability to interfere with private films he was showing. After the Three Mile Island nuclear melt-down in March 1979, he became convinced that Manhattan Island was next, so he led the group to Orlando, Florida, on a so-called relocation trip.

At one point the organization numbered some 500 people, but membership eventually dropped off. Newton died in 1991, and that pretty well ended the whole experiment. Some former members still keep in touch through social media. Others want nothing more than to bury their memories. Some see their Sulli-vanian experience as the best years of their life. Others are em-barrassed. Some remember those years with old-fashioned nostalgia. Others are filled with regret. Some still agree with the premise and hope the old group, or at least something very much like it, will reunite someday. Others consider it to have been a con from the very beginning and want to see it swept under the rug.

CONCLUSIONS: WHAT'S AHEAD FOR INDIVIDUAL FREEDOM?

In the end, life always wins. Maybe that's why we come crying and screaming onto its stage in the first place. Somehow, we know we have entered a rigged game. The winner is already determined. Life chips away at us 24/7 for however many years we compete.

Oh, we may fight the good fight anyway. We all have our own ways of coping. We may try to insulate ourselves by accumulating creature comforts, money, power, or physical strength and stamina. Some of us diet and exercise or, as a last resort, buy insurance policies. We may meditate or medicate. Some of us have a doctor on speed dial. Others turn to religion. Many just enter the room called denial and never come out. But deep down inside, we know. We have always known. We're never going to change the outcome. Physically, mentally, emotionally, and spiritually, we're fighting a losing battle. In the end, life always wins.

Maybe that's what makes cults appealing. We come across someone with charisma, who seems to have it all together. We discover a new group of friends who welcome us into their family. They seem to share our fears—and hopes. They offer a light in the darkness. They recognize the inevitability of the final curtain but convince us that another act will follow this one in the great play in which we are all actors. Meanwhile, they tell us

For people seeking answers and guidance in the darkness, sometimes any light will do.

how to live as a way to stave off most of the hurt we experience every moment of every day. It sounds enticing. And in a moment of weakness, we sign on the dotted line.

In the end, are we all members of one kind of cult or another?

We began this survey with our own definition of the word "cult." Here is what has guided our quest:

♦ Cults don't always have bad intentions, but the ones we are going to study, for the most part, do.

♦ Cults begin with a founder who is at least narcissistic and usually psychopathic.

♦ Cults develop a top-down hierarchy.

♦ Cults tend to separate followers from the world that exists outside the group.

♦ The easiest way to spot a cult is to identify an obsession with crystal balls and conspiracies.

As we have seen, not all these points need to be ticked off in order to suspect that we are in the presence of a cult. Perhaps it is sufficient to follow the rule set down by Supreme Court justice Potter Stewart when he was asked about what obscenity was: "I know it when I see it!"

But maybe we need to dig a little deeper. Could it be that human beings are somehow genetically programed to form cults? Is it true that there are primarily two kinds of people—those who lead and those who follow? If so, cults are almost guaranteed to be with us for a long, long time.

IS EVERY ORGANIZATION A CULT?

And if we follow this kind of logic, virtually every human organization is, to at least some degree, a cult.

Most churches have pastors and parishioners—leaders and followers. A political party is often called "the party of (whomever)" who sets the tone and becomes the spokesperson. Social clubs elect presidents or chairpersons who represent the group. The point is that *ideas* don't necessarily shape our opinions. Someone who is a gifted speaker and communicator, who can attractively *present* those ideas, does that. Often, that person is not qualified for leadership beyond his or her particular area of expertise, but they end up leading anyway. Take the following examples:

Colin Kaepernick was a gifted athlete who had a successful football career as an NFL quarterback. He developed a following of fans who liked to see him play. Then he used that fan base to express his ideas about civil rights, beginning by kneeling during the National Anthem at football games. Was he qualified to become a civil rights spokesperson? Probably, considering the experiences he grew up with. But the point is that he was *first* famous as a football player. That's where he developed his fan base, who soon, for right or wrong, began a nationwide debate that didn't have much to do with football but featured strong, divisive rhetoric on both sides of the issue. Are celebrities such as Kaepernick allowed to speak out on social issues? Are they obligated to do so? Is there any reason, at least, that they shouldn't?

Cliven Bundy, a Nevada rancher who defied the federal government by letting his cattle graze on public land and neglected to pay the proper fees, established an almost cult-like following of people who supported his individual sense of freedom. Then, with the cameras rolling, he began a speech by saying, "Let me tell you what I know about the Black man," and proceeded to give his opinion of slavery. What did that have to do with grazing rights?

Ronald Reagan, Arnold Schwarzenegger, Sonny Bono, Clint Eastwood, and even Donald Trump were successful entertainment stars who used their popularity to fuel political campaigns that eventually saw them win respected positions in government. Were these men qualified to become leaders? Most of them were, but that's not the point. Without their fame and name recognition—in other words, without a cult-like following of people who believed in them—they probably would not have had the political success they did.

That's the way the world works. A lot of people (some of them unqualified) achieve success, despite their shortcomings, simply because people recognize their names from a different context. Other, more qualified people strive in obscurity because they start out unknown and remain that way.

The problem lies not in the fact of celebrity, or lack of it. It lies in how that recognition is used.

But that, in itself, doesn't even explain cults. It is easy to say that cult leaders manipulate people, and that's bad. But even good leaders manipulate people, albeit in a positive way.

Politicians manipulate people because, hopefully, they honestly believe they support good policies that they think will improve the lives of their constituents.

Church pastors, hopefully, believe they know God offers a way to live in love rather than the deceit that is so prevalent in a particular culture.

Parents manipulate their children because, hopefully, they want to protect them from harm and prepare them for life.

Manipulation is not a bad thing, necessarily. We all do it, and often with the very best of intentions.

The entire foundation of an ancient but long-lived religion and people was built upon the word of Moses, a man who said he spoke with G-d.

But that's the key: "with the very best of intentions."

What happens in cults is that even if they begin "with the very best of intentions," something goes wrong somewhere along the way. We don't know exactly where or how, but when it happens, to paraphrase Justice Stewart, "We know it when we see it!"

Most major world religions began as cults.

A cult followed Moses into the desert, accepting rules of conduct and instructions that were handed down to him by a god they couldn't even see. But Moses said he could, so that was sufficient. Some of these rules and instructions were good ones that anyone could understand. "Don't murder." Simple and direct. Everyone could agree with that. But "circumcise your sons"? And later, "murder all the Canaanites"? That sounds so cult-like that people are still trying to explain it.

A cult gathered around Jesus. They claimed they saw him after he died. No one else did. But in cult-like fashion, they all declared a reality that others still question. According to the book of Acts, "They devoted themselves to the apostles' teaching and to fellowship, to the breaking of bread and to prayer. Everyone was filled with awe at the many wonders and signs performed by the apostles. All the believers were together and had everything in common. They sold property and possessions to give to anyone who had need. Every day they continued to meet together. They broke bread in their homes and ate together with glad and sincere hearts." Sounds like a cult to me!

A cult grew up around the prophet Muhammad. Mecca was home to two widely venerated polytheistic cults whose gods were thought to protect their lucrative trade. After working for several years as a merchant, Muhammad was hired by Khadija, a wealthy widow, to ensure the safe passage of her caravans to Syria. They eventually married. But when he was about 40 years old, he began having visions and hearing voices. Searching for clarity, he would sometimes meditate at Mount Hira, near Mecca. On one of these occasions, the Archangel Gabriel appeared to him and instructed him to "recite in the name of [your] lord." This was how the Qur'an came to be.

Siddhartha Gautama meditated and claimed to have found enlightenment. He soon gathered a band of followers to him and began to teach. In cult-like fashion, they adopted practices including dietary, sexual, and clothing restrictions.

Confucius and Lao Tzu, along with many more spiritual leaders of old, were identified with similar movements.

The point is this. Today, none of those religions are called cults. They are all respected and accepted religious traditions. But traditions all start somewhere, and at the root of every major tradition lies an original cult.

If this is the case, how do we determine which cults are dangerous? All of the above were dangerous when they began. All of them, to some degree, changed the world. Most were even associated with violence and bloodshed, both in their formative years and throughout world history. So when did they stop being cults?

We probably need to examine the way we bandy about the word "cult." By doing so, we might even come to a better understanding about why people join cults in the first place and how we can better interact with them when they do. It might help us build a few uniting bridges of connection, rather than separating walls of division.

So, why do people join cults? Well, why do people join anything? Why do people join churches, clubs, or political parties? Why do they gather at the water cooler at the office? Why do they stop off at the local pub after work or invite their neighbors to weekend barbeques? Why do they gather on social media platforms or join special-interest groups online?

To answer those questions with the seriousness they require, we have to venture into the realm of spirituality. Perhaps even the realm of religion and metaphysics. Many people are not comfortable with a mental excursion such as this, because they fear we will explore, in the open, the very subject that makes them so uncomfortable that they spend a good deal of their lives avoiding it.

What follows is, of course, a departure from the research methods we have followed up to this point. We have so far consulted published reports, conducted interviews, and read numerous accounts in order to report our results as accurately as possible. We have regularly supplied dates, names, times, and sources in order to ensure accuracy.

But when it comes to *reasons*, the answers are less clear. So let the reader beware. What follows will undoubtedly veer off into personal opinion. I justify it only by assuring you that the opinions to follow are based on a lot of research and more than 40 years of counseling experience. Nevertheless, they are opinions. So proceed with caution.

In a recent interview, Dr. Zack Bush, a physician who has logged extensive time in hospital intensive care units, recalled a racking 36-hour stint he endured during which he revived three people who had all been declared clinically dead. He had done all the heroic things doctors are trained to do, including pumping chemicals into veins, administering electric shocks, and even exposing hearts for manual massage. The patients were about as far removed from each other socially as one could imagine. One was a popular African American pastor who had logged some 200 visitors in the days before his clinical death. One was a lonely patient with HIV/AIDS. One was a child who had been born with birth defects.

Every one of them, in that same, harrowing, 36-hour time period, without any contact with each other, and having "died" after experiencing completely different medical and social experiences, asked the same question: "Why did you bring me back?"

To say the least, that was an unexpected response to a doctor who had just "resurrected" them. He might have expected thanks. Instead, their question, multiplied by three, set him back. It was almost as if they were accusing him rather than congratulating him.

When further questioned, they all told the familiar story of a tunnel, a bright light, and all the rest we have come to expect from accounts of near-death experiences (NDEs). But they de-

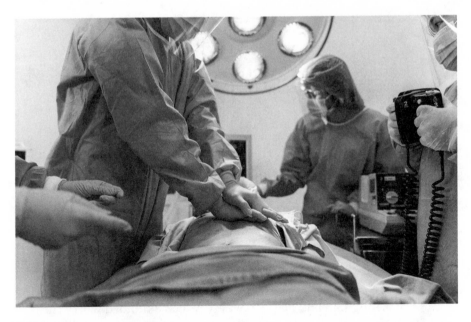

The stress and sensory overload of an emergency room stand in stark contrast to the peaceful immersive experience many patients describe after revival from a near-death experience.

scribed something even more significant. For the first time in their lives, they recounted, they had felt totally accepted, welcomed, and loved.

When asked what he made of this all this, Dr. Bush could only conclude that, whatever had happened, whether it was a biochemical experience or a metaphysical one, these people, and by extension maybe even *all* people, were incredibly lonely. Even the best of relationships are full of tension. Even the happiest times are tinged with sadness. Even during the times we feel physically at our very best, we know it won't last.

The Buddha said it best. His very first Noble Truth, uttered in the Deer Park discourse, which was his first teaching after he reached enlightenment, stated simply and elegantly, "All life is suffering."

We all like solitude. We all like a solitary walk on the beach or an evening run after work. We all long to "get away from it all" from time to time. But we always come back. We all crave relationships.

> **Why do we join things?**
> **Because we long for companionship.**

Why do we join things? Because we long for companionship.

Usually, in the great majority of cases, that's not a bad thing. But there are times in all human conditions when good things can go too far. When that happens, we call it pathology.

When a relaxing drink in the evening turns to four or five and the time extends to more than an hour or two, we notice the warning sign and begin to worry. When extended worry turns to chronic anxiety, we seek help. When an occasional ache or pain turns into excessive trips to the doctor, we begin to wonder about either chronic illness or hypochondria.

On and on it goes. This is common to the human condition and can usually be resolved. But sometimes it crosses an imaginary line that we didn't see was there. That's when pathology sets in.

LEADERS, FOLLOWERS, AND PATHOLOGY

Cults need two things to operate:

First, they need a leader who has passed through the stages of healthy confidence, then narcissism, and finally pathology. His or her sense of self-worth can only be nurtured by complete devotion and adoration. Such leaders need to be venerated. In severe cases, they need a group to offer continual assurance that they are, indeed, a god.

Second, if leaders need followers, followers also need a leader. Even more important, they need a community. Their sense of self-worth can only be encouraged by others. Such followers, either because of life experience or genetic reality, are often unable, except with a lot of psychological help, to trust their own opinions of themselves. Their support comes from outside, not inside. They need to be needed, love to be loved, and want to be wanted.

When that happens, it doesn't do any good to simply blame them, tell them to pick themselves up by their own bootstraps, and snap out of it. Cults are ruled by pathology—that of the leader and that of the followers. They are different but codependent pathologies.

Leaders and followers need each other. The more they are cut off from the simple releases that people traditionally have employed—the church, the civic club, the political party, the book club, the water cooler, or the local pub—the more the pathology nurtures itself, feeds on itself, and eventually consumes itself. It is an ever-expanding, widening gyre that grows as it circles above, waiting. The victims somehow come to even enjoy the experience. Knowing nothing different, having forgotten who they once were, they spiral downward into what can become a bottomless abyss.

That's why cult atrocities always seem to get worse over time. That's why behaviors gradually compound themselves.

That's why leaders gradually get away with more and more, and members allow it. Perhaps they even encourage it. Sadism and masochism go hand in hand. And the results can be, as we have seen throughout this book, both terrifying and unimaginable.

WHAT'S AHEAD FOR INDIVIDUAL FREEDOM?

With that insight, we can return to the question that heads up this section: What's ahead for individual freedom?

The answer now takes on some clarity. It isn't going to be as easy to answer as it first appeared.

Despite hundreds of years of the American experiment, despite the fact that we have tried to acknowledge that we are a nation of laws, one fact remains: We can't legislate morality. We will never close every loophole, cross every t, and dot every i. We will never be able to outlaw cults as long as people are people. We can watch closely, and we can step in as soon as unlawful pathology rears its ugly head. We can offer police protection to those who are the victims of cult-style intimidation. We can do our best to come to the aid of innocent victims. All that goes without saying. We can, and must, place an umbrella of social protection over those who might become victims of a cult's prejudice. We can, and must, open dialogues of understanding and help. We can, and must, shine a light into the darkness of cult activity. That's what this book is all about.

> **Can we eliminate cults from society?
> I seriously doubt it.**

But can we eliminate cults from society? I seriously doubt it. Not until we grow up spiritually, mentally, and emotionally. And that condition, although we hate to admit it, is a long way off.

We're good at technology. The sky's the limit when it comes to gadgets and gizmos. We're good at building things. No project seems too big for us to handle.

But spirituality, emotional stability, and social dialogue about morality and ethics? We are far from maturity when it comes to things like that. Some of us try. But far too many don't. When push comes to shove, "Look out for number one!" is our default position. Racism is here to stay for the foreseeable future. Exploitation is not going away any time soon. The need for some people to bully is a fact of life for now. We can't legislate these things away. All we can do is hope to protect the innocent and alleviate the fear.

There may be no good institutional solutions to the risks of culthood, but as individuals we can make a big difference in the lives of those near to us.

So like many other social problems, I'm afraid the answer to what's ahead for personal freedom, at least when it comes to cult activity, is that we have to keep muddling on. But the good news is that cults eventually either die out or learn to become respectable.

Meanwhile, there are things we can do. We may not be able to stamp out cults, just like we can't stamp out crime or war. But we can, perhaps, help a few individuals along the way—people who have become ensnared and want to get out.

That is at least a measure of hope, and it is why we can't close this book without one more word.

EPILOGUE

HOW DO I GET OUT?

Having seen how and why people join cults, the final thing we need to consider is this: How can they get out? What if you are involved in a group—it might be anything from a church to a civic organization, an MLM to a political party—that is beginning to display attitudes or attributes that tip off your internal radar that something is a bit "off"?

Or—and this might be even trickier—what if a close friend or acquaintance seems to be getting involved too deeply in such a cult? What should you do? Can you do anything? What is your best way forward?

There is no "one size fits all" solution, but we can suggest some guidelines. I've been involved on both sides of this trouble, and it is a very difficult situation in which to find yourself.

First, what if you are worried about yourself? You are beginning to sense that something is wrong with a group that once seemed very inviting and may have even helped you through a difficult time. Maybe a church that once seemed to have all the answers you were looking for has become a bit too pushy or controlling. Perhaps a political party that your family has supported for generations now exhibits traits of being controlled by a cult-like leader. Maybe you even have grown to suspect that your life is being controlled too much by an organization that promised you economic freedom and unlimited growth. Nothing is really wrong, but something seems a little different, a little too authoritarian.

First of all, trust your instincts. Honor your feelings. Something within you has sensed a change in the air. Believe it. Your instincts and feelings are yours. They don't belong to anybody else. They are all you have. You were born with them. They have made you who you are. Bring them out into the open and do not—repeat, *do not*—ignore them.

Chances are, you will be sorely tempted to talk about them with another member of the group. If you do, don't be surprised if they turn their back on you, insisting that you are being silly or naïve.

As a matter of fact, if this happens, run, do not walk, for the nearest exit. This is a classic cultic response. It is a textbook technique to combat doubt and apprehension. If you need to talk to someone, consult a person *outside* the group, preferably someone who has some training, or at least a knowledge, of the particular group you are dealing with.

Second, don't be afraid to use the word "cult." Say it out loud. See how it sounds. There is power in the spoken word. Something within you will caution you not to even use the word lest you find yourself guilty of tarnishing what you had hoped was an answer to the question that had led you to the group in the first place.

Third, you will probably start to feel a little ashamed of yourself. Not wanting to waste the time, and perhaps the money, you have already invested, you will want to stay the course, hoping against hope that your initial decision to join up was right and that things will yet turn out okay.

This is just like a gambler who loses his stake and then doubles down, hoping to win it back. It never works. It always turns bad, and he winds up losing even more.

Something in you will try to convince you that you have received something good from the group. It would be unfair, and demonstrate misplaced loyalty, to leave them now, after they have helped you so much.

Well, *of course* they helped you. You wouldn't have stayed this long if you hadn't received some benefit. When you read their literature in the first place, nowhere was there a line that read, "Join this group because it will mess you up for life!" It enticed you with an initial offer, and the group probably made good on that offer because they wanted you to hang on. It's just like a drug dealer who gives free samples to kids. He knows the kids will want more because their first experience gave them something enjoyable. Then he's got them right where he wants them, and to keep the good thing going, they will have to pay.

Understanding the sunk cost fallacy might help keep some disillusioned cult members from doubling down on their losing streak. But with the lure of cult-belonging just as addictive as gambling, it can be hard to escape the vicious cycle that pulls members back in.

EXTRICATING YOURSELF

Brandy Zadrozny offered some sage advice in her article "Escape from QAnon: How Jan. 6 Changed One Person's Path." She outlines a simple, three-step process that helped some people. I caution, however, that only the process is simple. The work is extremely difficult.

1. *The "Come to Jesus Moment":* There has to come a defining moment in which you approach the river, stare deeply into its depths, and then decide to cross. This is extremely important. You don't "slide" out of a cult's embrace. You have to want it.

2. *The Support Group:* Once you decide to leave, you need something to replace what you are giving up. It's not so much the product the group initially promised; it's all the rest. It's the reception, the friendship, the supposed support and feeling of acceptance. It's the feeling of family. Cults offer all this. They make you feel as though you *belong* someplace—that you are *wanted.*

When you decide to leave, you need to replace the source of these feelings. Eventually, and ideally, you will discover this source of strength within yourself. But for the short term, look for a support group of some kind. It might consist of friends, family, or acquaintances of some kind.

This step will take work because the cult has probably convinced you that these very people are the ones who are dragging you down. You might worry that because you rejected them, they will not be there for you now when you need them. You might be afraid of the "I tried to warn you!" or "I told you so!" responses. But risk it. Usually, they will be relieved that you got out, and they will want to help you.

3. *Do the Work:* This usually means therapy of some kind. You will no doubt be glad to have a trusted and experienced counselor to monitor your progress. Someone, somewhere, is out there. It might be an experienced therapist. It might be the pastor or staff member of a church. It might even be a gifted friend. But that person is out there, somewhere. Find them! You are not alone. Good luck!

EXTRICATING A FRIEND

Moving on to the second scenario: What if the one snagged by the cult was not you but a friend. What then? Can you help?

The simple answer is yes. But again, nothing in life is simple. Disentangling someone from a cult is hard and delicate work. You need to be extremely careful. Blunder in too quickly, and you might make things worse.

Malia Wollan, who writes for the *New York Times Magazine*, wrote an excellent article, published on September 26, 2018, entitled "How to Get Someone Out of a Cult." In it, she reports on her interview with cult expert Janja Lalich, whose advice includes the following:

"Do everything you can to stay in touch," says Janja Lalich, a sociology professor and consultant who studies cults and their coercive influence and control. If you're trying to persuade someone to leave a cult, supply reminders of the world beyond it by calling, emailing, writing letters, sending photographs and maybe even visiting, although Lalich warns that anyone can get lured into a cult. You should visit "only if you feel strong enough to resist," she says.

Don't try to forcibly remove someone, even if you're gravely concerned. In the 1960s, '70s and '80s, families often hired so-called deprogrammers to kidnap and hold cult members against their will. While that often worked, abduction is illegal, and the technique was discredited after a Washington man successfully sued his deprogrammer in 1995. Today's preferred method is "exit counseling," and it requires persuasion by therapists, lawyers, friends and family members.

Try to get one-on-one time, and if you do, don't use it to harp. Instead, ask questions and make sure you've already collected anti-cult evidence like news articles or memoirs. "Video testimonials from former cult members can be particularly persuasive," says Lalich....

Give some thought to working with a team of friends or family to set up a good-cop, bad-cop dynamic in which one of you is more forceful and another is warmer and more willing to listen. Make sure the inductee knows there is a safe and nonjudgmental place to come home to.

This is all good advice, to be sure. But remember that things rarely go by the book when dealing with emotions. When physical freedom is secured, the hard work is just beginning. It can take years for a person to trust their own instincts and return to even a semblance of their old self. Maybe they never will. Be gentle, be persistent, and be patient.

If you decide to take on a project as difficult as this, you need to remember a few things.

First and foremost, people who have fallen victim to a cult are not dumb. Maybe the reason they got involved in the first place is because they are smart enough to see the dangers and dark energies of life that many of us ignore through fear and ignorance. These are things some people aren't smart enough to see on their own. Life is tough! Life is dangerous! Life is discouraging!

Many of us may know this on a level we are not brave enough to bring out into the open and admit. We deal with it by pretending it's not true or that we are somehow superior beings who can ride above it.

But don't kid yourself. I have stood at the bedside of hundreds of people who were about to die, and only at the end did many of them admit they had never prepared for this moment because they had pretended it was never going to happen.

People do irrational things. We all do. We fall in love with the wrong people. We pretend we are stronger than we are. We believe things we know are not true, or we don't believe things we know *are* true. That's just the way we are. It's what people do. All people.

The cult member you are trying to help just fell in love with the wrong person, that's all. They fell hook, line, and sinker. If it was a rare occurrence, divorce wouldn't be so prevalent. There

If you're trying to help a loved one cope with cult entanglement, the best tool you can bring is radical empathy.

must have been something that attracted them. The initial fall wasn't the problem as much as what came after. Don't belittle it. Honor it. Making fun of the group, or criticizing it without fully understanding it, is like criticizing someone's dog. It's always a bad idea. It may be a dumb mutt, but it's *their* dumb mutt.

Psychologists learn a technique called "strategic and personal oriented dialogue," also called "motivational interviewing." The idea is to emphasize only positive statements. The technique behind it is to have someone express these statements out loud so they really *hear* them, rather than just *think* they know what they are. Expressing statements in this way can eventually lead a person to question whether they are really true rather than just assumed to be true. It takes dialogue. You have to keep talking. It's hard work. But sometimes good results depend on effort.

If you stick to it and are successful, the person might suddenly hear themselves for the first time. Perhaps they might even come to the conclusion that they were not really having a good experience at all. It is not uncommon to hear someone exclaim, "What was I thinking?"

When that happens, you are 90 percent of the way home. Healing has begun. The prodigal child is on their way back.

Cults are a fact of American life, and they will be for the foreseeable future. We need to deal with that fact and prepare for it. Until life itself universally supplies what a cult offers, there will be people who are willing to sign up.

When you, or someone you care about, steps out of a deep darkness into the bright light of renewal and begins to look around, you—or they—might feel the weight of depressing shame. You may feel somehow unworthy to continue on. At such a time, it might be helpful to remember this poem, written by John Clare. It's called "The Instinct of Hope."

> E'en the small violet feels a future power
>
> And waits each year renewing blooms to bring,
>
> And surely man is no inferior flower
>
> To die unworthy of a second spring?

FURTHER READING

Bombardieri, Marcella. "Street Smart." *Boston Globe*, June 23, 2002.

Bugliosi, Vincent, and Curt Gentry. *Helter Skelter: The True Story of the Manson Murders.* New York: Norton, 1974.

Cheetham, Erika. *The Final Prophecies of Nostradamus.* New York: Perigee, 1989.

Cline, Emma. *The Girls: A Novel.* New York: Random House, 2018.

Cowan, Douglas E., and David G. Bromley. *Cults and New Religions: A Brief History.* Malden, MA: Wiley, 2015.

Durant, Will, and Ariel Durant. *The Lessons of History.* New York: Simon & Schuster, 1968.

Edmondson, Edna, with Kristine Gaspar. *Scarred: The True Story of How I Escaped NXIVM, the Cult That Bound My Life.* San Francisco: Chronicle Books, 2019.

Glader, Paul, and Michael Ray Smith. "God and Guns: Why American Churchgoers Are Packing Heat." *Religion Unplugged*, June 8, 2021. https://religionunplugged.com/news/2020/5/18/god-amp-guns-how-american-churchgoers-are-packing-heat-and-opening-a-new-era-in-christendom.

Gleis, Radhia. *The Followers: "Holy Hell" and the Disciples of Narcissistic Leaders: How My Years in a Notorious Cult Parallel Today's Cultural Mania.* Sage Card Publishing, 2021.

Hassan, Steven. *The Cult of Trump.* New York: Simon & Schuster, 2021.

Hewes, Hayden C., and Brad Steiger. *U.F.O. Missionaries Extraordinary.* New York: Pocket Books, 1976.

Hudson, Winthrop S. *Religion in America.* New York: Charles Scribner, 1965.

Jeffs, Rachel. *Breaking Free: How I Escaped Polygamy, the FLDS Cult, and My Father, Warren Jeffs.* New York: Harper Collins, 2017.

Jessop, Carolyn, with Laura Palmer. *Escape.* New York: Random House, 2007.

Jung, C. G.; R. F. C. Hull, translator. *Flying Saucers: A Modern Myth of Things Seen in the Skies.* Princeton: Princeton University Press, 1978.

Kauffman, Stuart A. *Reinventing the Sacred: A New View of Science, Reason, and Religion.* Philadelphia: Basic Books, 2008.

Koresh, David, and Ulysses G. Morrow. *The Cellular Cosmogony; or, The Earth, a Concave Sphere.* Kessinger Publishing, 2018.

———. *The Immortal Manhood: The Laws and Processes of Its Attainment in the Flesh.* Kessinger Publishing, 2015.

Lewis, James R. *Odd Gods: New Religions and the Cult Controversy.* Amherst, NY: Prometheus Books, 2001.

Lindsey, Hal. *The Late Great Planet Earth.* Grand Rapids, MI: Zondervan, 1970.

———. *There's a New World Coming.* Grand Rapids, MI: Zondervan, 1984.

Martin, Rachel. "Word of Faith's Pattern of Abuse 'Got Worse over Time,' Says 'Broken Faith' Author." NPR, February 17, 2020. https://www.npr.org/2020/02/17/806052660/word-of-faiths-pattern-of-abuse-got-worse-over-time-says-broken-faith-author.

Miller, Russell. *Bare-Faced Messiah: True Story of L. Ron Hubbard.* Sphere Books Limited, 1987.

Moon, Sun Myung. *Divine Principle.* Holy Spirit Association for the Unification of World Christianity, 1973.

Moriarty, Liane. *Nine Perfect Strangers.* New York: Flatiron Books, 2018.

Morris, Adam. *American Messiahs: False Prophets of a Damned Nation.* New York: Norton, 2019.

Murakami, Haruki. *Underground: The Tokyo Gas Attack and the Japanese Psyche.* New York: Random House, 2001.

"New from ADL: Leaked Oath Keepers' Membership List Reveals Hundreds of Current & Former Law Enforcement Officers, Members of Military, and Elected Officials." ADL Online. September 6, 2022. https://www.adl.org/resources/press-release/new-adl-leaked-oath-keepers-membership-list-reveals-hundreds-current-former.

Palmer, Susan J. *Aliens Adored: Raël's UFO Religion.* New Brunswick, NJ: Rutgers University Press, 2004.

Parloff, Roger. "The Conspirators: The Proud Boys and Oath Keepers on Jan. 6." *Lawfare*, January 6, 2022. https://www.lawfareblog.com/conspirators-proud-boys-and-oath-keepers-jan-6.

Pattison, E. Mansell. "Religious Youth Cults: Alternative Healing Social Networks." *Journal of Religion and Health* 19 (December 1980), 275–86. https://doi.org/10.1007/BF00996250.

Redfern, Nick. *Secret History: Conspiracies from Ancient Aliens to the New World Order.* Detroit: Visible Ink Press, 2015.

Ross, Rick Alan. *Cults Inside Out: How People Get In and Can Get Out.* North Charleston: Create Space Independent Publishing Platform, 2014.

Russell, Charles Taze. *Food for Thinking Christians: Why Evil Was Permitted and Kindred Topics.* Pittsburgh, PA: Watchtower and Bible Tract Society.

Shadel, Doug, Alicia Williams, Karla Pak, and Lona Choi-Allum. *A Moment's Notice: Recognizing the Stressful Life Events, Emotions and Actions That Make Us Susceptible to Scams. An AARP National Fraud Frontiers Report.* Washington, DC: AARP, October 2021. https://doi.org/10.26419/res.00484.001.

Smith, Erin A. "*The Late Great Planet Earth* Made the Apocalypse a Popular Concern." *Humanities* 38, no. 1 (Winter 2017). https://www.neh.gov/humanities/2017/winter/feature/the-late-great-planet-earth-made-the-apocalypse-popular-concern.

Stott, Rebecca. *In the Days of Rain: A Daughter, a Father, A Cult.* New York: Harper Collins, 2017.

Sykes, Joe. *Victims and Survivors: Escapees from the Eckankar Cult.* Georgia, 2020.

Toobin, Jeffrey. *American Heiress: The Wild Saga of the Kidnapping, Crimes and Trial of Patty Hearst.* New York: Random House, 2017.

Twitchell, Paul. *The Shariyat-Ki-Sugmad, Books One & Two.* Minneapolis: Ekenkar, 1970.

Walker, Jerald. *The World in Flames: A Black Boyhood in a White Supremacist Doomsday Cult.* Boston: Beacon Press, 2016.

Waziyatawin. *What Does Justice Look Like? The Struggle for Liberation in Dakota Homeland.* St. Paul, MN: Living Justice Press, 2008.

Weiss, Mitch, and Holbrook Mohr. *Broken Faith: Inside the Word of Faith Fellowship, One of America's Most Dangerous Cults.* Toronto: Hanover Square Press, 2020.

Willis, Jim. *The Religion Book: Places, Prophets, Saints, and Seers.* Detroit: Visible Ink Press, 2004.

Willis, Jim, and Barbara Willis. *Armageddon Now: The End of the World, A–Z.* Detroit: Visible Ink Press, 2006.

Wollan, Malia. "How to Get Someone Out of a Cult." *New York Times Magazine,* September 26, 2018. https://www.nytimes.com/2018/09/26/magazine/how-to-get-someone-out-of-a-cult.html.

Wright, Lawrence. *Going Clear: Scientology, Hollywood, and the Prison of Belief.* New York: Random House, 2013.

Zadrozny, Brandy. "Escape from QAnon: How Jan. 6 Changed One Person's Path." NBC News, January 18, 2022. https://www .nbcnews.com/tech/internet/qa non-jan-6-changed-one-per sons-path-rcna11276.

IMAGE CREDITS

Page 53: Jim Jones and Cecil Williams: Nancy Wong, via Wikimedia Commons

Page 55: Rep. Leo Ryan: Office of the Clerk, U.S. House of Representatives, via Wikimedia Commons

Page 59: Tammy Faye Bakker and Jim Bakker: Peter K. Levy, via Wikimedia Commons

Page 61: Jerry Falwell: Mark T. Foley, via Wikimedia Commons

Page 64: Jim Bakker studio: Arkivet, Thorvaldsens Museum, via Wikimedia Commons

Page 67: Papyrus sheet: Public Domain, via Wikimedia Commons

Page 70: Jerry Falwell and Moral Majority: Deborah Thomas, via Wikimedia Commons

Page 73: Second Amendment sign, "From My Cold Dead Hands": Anthony Crider, via Wikimedia Commons

Page 77: Book of Revelation vision: Phillip Medhurst, via Wikimedia Commons

Page 80: Osama bin Laden: Hamid Mir, via Wikimedia Commons

Page 81: C-4 explosive: U.S. Navy photo by Chief Mass Communication Specialist Kathryn Whittenberger, via Wikimedia Commons

Page 84: River Phoenix: Alan Light, via Wikimedia Commons

Page 86: Watchtower: Charles Taze Russell, via Wikimedia Commons

Page 89: Charles Russell: Mitchell, via Wikimedia Commons

Page 92: Westboro Baptist Church demonstration: JCWilmore, via Wikimedia Commons

Page 94: Westboro Baptist Church: Americasroof, via Wikimedia Commons

Page 96: Park Rules: ROI6/Shutterstock

Page 99: Abused child: Suzanne Tucker/Shutterstock

Page 103: Exorcism: LightField Studios/Shutterstock

Page 104: Ellen G. White: Orlandobrunet, via Wikimedia Commons

Page 107: Vernon Howell/David Koresh: McLennan County Sheriff's Office, via Wikimedia Commons

Page 110: Explosion at Mount Carmel, Waco, Texas: Federal Bureau of Investigation, via Wikimedia Commons

SCIENCE, POLITICS, ECONOMICS, AND METAPHYSICS

Page 115: Dr. Anthony Fauci: NIAID, via Wikimedia Commons

Page 118: Ibn al-Haytham, drawn by Adolph Boÿ, engraved by Jeremias Falck: Johannes Hevelius,

Selenographia, via Wikimedia Commons

Page 120: Carl Sagan: PBS, via Wikimedia Commons

Page 123: Donald Trump at St. John's Church: The White House, via Wikimedia Commons

Page 127: Pyramid scheme diagram: U.S. Security and Exchange Commission, via Wikimedia Commons

Page 132: Sun Myung Moon and Hak Ja Han: Unknown, via Wikimedia Commons

Page 136: Unification Church blessing ceremony: Cristinadeargentina, via Wikimedia Commons

Page 138: Richard Nixon and Sun Myung Moon: The White House, via Wikimedia Commons

Page 142: New Yorker Hotel: Bramstercate, via Wikimedia Commons

Page 144: Temple of ECK: Jonathunder, via Wikimedia Commons

Page 148: Creepy housemate/Eckankar: Motortion Films/Shutterstock

THE UNIVERSE AND BEYOND

Page 153: Arthur C. Clarke: ITU Pictures, via Wikimedia Commons

Page 155: The Rapture, by Jan Luyken: Bowyer's Bible, Bolton, England, via Wikimedia Commons

Page 158: Rachel Carson: U.S. Fish and Wildlife Service, via Wikimedia Commons

Page 163: L. Ron Hubbard: Los Angeles Daily News, via Wikimedia Commons

Page 166: Tom Cruise: Gage Skidmore, via Wikimedia Commons

Page 170: Raëlian mascot: Nesnad via Wikimedia Commons

Page 173: Vishnu demonstration of *maya*: Benjamín Preciado, via Wikimedia Commons

Page 175: Joseph Smith's first vision: Unknown, via Wikimedia Commons

Page 178: Brigham Young: Unknown, via Wikimedia Commons

Page 181: Mormon baptismal font: James E. Talmadge (1912), The House of the Lord, Salt Lake City/Deseret News

Page 184: Austin College: Michael Barera, via Wikimedia Commons

Page 186: Extraterrestrial ships: IgorZh/Shutterstock

Page 188: Comet Hale-Bopp: Mkfairdpm, via Wikimedia Commons

PROPHETS OF THE END TIMES

Page 192: Palmistry: Photology1971/Shutterstock

Page 194: Number 666 and false prophet: The William Blake Archive, via Wikimedia Commons

Page 198: Mesopotamian art: Andrea Izzotti/Shutterstock

Page 200: Hand (accepting Jesus): Jacob_09/Shutterstock

Page 202: Second Coming: IgorZh/Shutterstock

Page 205: *Jeremiah Lamenting the Destruction of Jerusalem* by Rembrandt: Rijksmuseum, Amsterdam, Netherlands, via Wikimedia Commons

Page 208: Jesus entering Jerusalem: *The Bible Panorama, or The Holy Scriptures in Picture and Story,* William A. Foster, 1891, via Wikimedia Commons

Page 211: Nostradamus, portrait by César de Notre-Dame: Sasha I, via English Wikipedia/Wikimedia Commons

Page 215: *The Prophecies* by Nostradamus: Zereshk, via Wikimedia Commons

Page 217: Edgar Cayce: Unknown, via Wikimedia Commons

Page 221: Doomsday Clock: Dimitrios Karamitros/Shutterstock

Page 224: Brandon Carter: Brandon Carter, via Wikimedia Commons

Page 225: Revelation: Isaiah Shook/Shutterstock

Page 229: Dorchester Penitentiary: Verne Equinox, via Wikimedia Commons

THE RISE OF RACIAL RELIGION CULTS AND SOCIAL MEDIA

Page 232: John, King of England: Unknown, via Wikimedia Commons

Page 235: Trump worship: Johnny Silvercloud, via Wikimedia Commons

Page 237: Bust of Nathan Bedford Forrest by Christopher Amrich: DSC_0191, via Wikimedia Commons

Page 242: January 6, 2021, Capitol invasion: TapTheForwardAssist, via Wikimedia Commons

Page 245: United Nations General Assembly Hall: Patrick Gruban, via Wikimedia Commons

Page 250: Proud Boys: Anthony Crider, via Wikimedia Commons

Page 253: Three Percenters: Elvert Barnes, via Wikimedia Commons

Page 255: Antifa at Juggalo March: Amaury Laporte, via Wikimedia Commons

Page 257: *Constitution of the United Nuwaubian Nation of Moors,* by Dr. Malachi Z. York: Nuwaubianfacts.com, via Wikimedia Commons

Page 260: Nuwaubian Nation compound: Kenneth C. Budd, via Wikimedia Commons

Page 263: Paul Revere: Internet Archive Book Images, via Wikimedia Commons

Page 266: World Wide Web: Coolcaesar, via Wikimedia Commons

Page 269: "Birds Aren't Real": Ismael Olea, via Wikimedia Commons

Page 272: QAnon adaptation of Gadsden flag: RootOfAllLight, via Wikimedia Commons

Page 274: "QAnon Shaman" Jacob Angeli Chansley: TheUnseen011101, via Wikimedia Commons

SEX IN THE CITY

Page 278: Bhagwan Shree Rajneesha and disciples: Redheylin, via Wikimedia Commons

Page 281: Air Rajneesh: Ted Quackenbush, via Wikimedia Commons

Page 283: Keith Raniere: U.S. Government, Eastern District of New York, via Wikimedia Commons

Page 285: Raniere brand: U.S. Attorney's Office of the Eastern District of New York, via Wikimedia Commons

Page 289: Judy Collins: ABC Television, via Wikimedia Commons

CONCLUSIONS

Page 294: Light in a tunnel: Marco Barone/Shutterstock

Page 296: *Moses with the Tables of the Law* by Guido Reni: Web Gallery of Art, via Wikimedia Commons

Page 299: Near-death experience: RONNACHAIPARK/Shutterstock

Page 303: Support group: G-Stock Studio/Shutterstock

EPILOGUE

Page 307: Sunk cost fallacy: Real Deal Photo/Shutterstock

Page 310: Helping a loved one: chainintorn.v/Shutterstock

INDEX

Note: (ill.) indicates photos and illustrations

A

AARP, 7

AARP: The Magazine [magazine], 6

Abraham, Book of, 174

Abraham [biblical], 137, 179, 260

Abú Tálib, 185

Abyss, 185

acceptance as cult-joining factor, 2, 5, 114, 300, 307

Acts, Book of, 15, 154, 176, 297

Adam [biblical], 135–37, 198, 259

Adventism, 15, 88, 104–7, 157, 225

Afghanistan and Afghans, 91

Africa and Africans, 97, 247

Age of Apocalypse (Age of Revelation), 169–70

Age of Aquarius, 160

Agenda 21, 245

Agricultural Revolution, 197–99

Ahn, Ché, 235

Air Rajneesh, 281 (ill.)

Alabama, 71, 238–39

Aladdin [movie], 249

Alamo Christian Foundation, 262

Albany, New York, 282, 286

Alcoholics Anonymous, 4

al-Dajjāl, 78

Ali [biblical], 259

Ali, Muhammad, 258

Ali Tálib, 185

Ali, Yashar, 167

Aliens Adored: Raël's UFO Religion (Palmer), 173

All in the Family [TV show], 71

Allah, 259

Allen, Will, 20–21

Alley, Kirstie, 161

al-Madhi (Muhammad Ahmad Ibn Abdullāh), 258–59

Almanachs (Nostradamus), 212

Alpha, 77

al-Qaeda, 79

Amazon, 156

"America the Beautiful" [song], 235

American Dream, 20

Americanism, 45

Amorites, 78

Amunnubi Rooakhptah. See York, Michael

Amway, 125

Ancient Mystic Order of Melchizedek, 257, 260–61

Anderson, Jamey, 100

Anderson, Sir Robert, 207–8

Anointed One. See Jesus Christ

Ansaar Pure Sufi, 257–58

Ansaaru Allah Community, 257, 259

Ant Hill Kids [cult], 224–30

Antarctic, 219

Antelope, Oregon, 278

Antichrist

    Christian Rapture, Carl Jung, and flying saucers, 155, 158

    Joshua, Jesus, Muhammad, and the implications of *jihad*, 78

    Nostradamus, 214

    prophets of the End Times, 195, 199–200, 202, 209

    spoofing cults, 269

Anti-Defamation League, 91

Anti-Defamation League Center on Extremism, 248

Antifa [cult], 241, 244–45, 248, 254–57, 255 (ill.)

Antifa: The Anti-Fascist Handbook (Bray), 254

anti-Semitism, 50, 239, 249, 272–73

Apocalypse, 107, 109, 155, 157, 225

Appalachian State University, 97

Applewhite, Marshall Herff, 183–90

Appomattox, 236

Aquarius, 160

Arctic, 219

Argentina and Argentinians, 41, 140

Aristotle, 118 (ill.)

Arizona, 178, 194, 234, 274, 276, 282

Arkansas, 81–82, 236, 269

Arkelian, Krikor, 50

Armageddon

America as cult fertile field, 32

Jim Bakker, *The PTL Club*, and the return of Jesus, 64

Jim Jones and the Peoples Temple Full Gospel Church, 47

Nostradamus, 214

prophets of the End Times, 195, 197, 199–202, 209

Watchtower Society and Jehovah's Witnesses, 89

Armed Conflict Location and Event Data Project, 252

Army, U.S., 134, 159, 242

Army Signal Corps, U.S., 183

Arnold, Kenneth, 159

Artaxerxes [biblical], 207

Aryan Nations, 81, 239

As Siddid Al Imaan Isa Al Haahi Al Madhi. See York, Michael

Asia and Asians, 239

Ask.com, 266

Assemblies of God, 48–52, 55–56

Associated Press, 103, 174, 249

Association for Research and Enlightenment, 218

Assyria and Assyrians [historical], 77, 178

ATF (Bureau of Alcohol, Tobacco, and Firearms), 107–8

Atlanta, Georgia, 237

Atlantic Council, 251

Atlantis, 219

Auburn Theological School, 196

Audible Life Current, 144

Austin College, 183, 184 (ill.)

Australia and Australians, 162

Avignon, France, 211

Avon, 125

Azusa Street Revival, 48

B

Babylon and Babylonians [historical], 195, 205, 208

Baha'i, 185

Bahamas, 219

Baker, George (Father Divine), 41–47, 53, 65

Baker, Peninnah (Mother Divine), 43, 46–47

Bakker, Jim, 56–65, 59 (ill.), 72, 97

Bakker, Lori, 63–64

Bakker, Tammy Faye, 57–58, 59 (ill.), 63, 97

Baltimore, Maryland, 42

Bantam, 157

Baptism

Evangelical church, politics, and the NRA, 68, 70, 72

Father Divine and the Peace Mission, 42

Jim Jones and the Peoples Temple Full Gospel Church, 49

Westboro Baptist Church, 91, 93

Word of Faith Fellowship, 97–98

Baptist World Alliance, 91

Bare-Faced Messiah: The True Story of L. Ron Hubbard (Miller), 164

Barrytown, New York, 142

Bates, Joseph, 104

Battlestar Galactica [TV show], 174

Bay Area News Group, 166

Baylor University, 86

Beam, Jack, 48

Beam, Louis, 239

Belo Horizonte, Brazil, 98

Beloit, Wisconsin, 252

Belvedere, 142

Berg, David (Moses David), 83–85

Berg, Maria, 85

Bergman, Ingrid, 9

Berkeley, California, 256

Berners-Lee, Tim, 266

Bernstein, Rachel, 1, 5–6, 9

Bertino, Jeremy, 251

Bethlehem [historical], 201

Beyond Human—The Last Call [video series], 188

Bible

America as cult fertile field, 16–17, 33

Christian Rapture, Carl Jung, and flying saucers, 154, 156–57, 160

David Berg and the Family International, 84

David Koresh and the Branch Davidians, 104–8

Edgar Cayce, 217

Evangelical church, politics, and the NRA, 67, 71, 73–75

Heaven's Gate, 184, 186

Jim Bakker, *The PTL Club*, and the return of Jesus, 58

Jim Jones and the Peoples Temple Full Gospel Church, 49, 54

Joshua, Jesus, Muhammad, and the implications of *jihad*, 79, 81

Latter-day Saints and the colonization of the cosmos, 177–78

metaphysics as a cult, 130

Nostradamus, 210–11, 214, 216

Nuwaubian Nation, 259

possibility of cults, 2

prophets of the End Times, 191–205, 207, 210

Raëlians and the Elohim, 169

Roch Thériault and the Ant Hill Kids, 225

Sun Myung Moon and the Unification Church, 135–37

Watchtower Society and Jehovah's Witnesses, 87–89

Westboro Baptist Church, 93

Word of Faith Fellowship, 98–99, 103

Biden, Joe, 122

Bierut, Michael, 220

Biggs, Joe, 27

Billy Graham Evangelistic Association, 69

bin Laden, Osama, 79, 80 (ill.), 83

"Birds Aren't Real" campaign, 268–71, 269 (ill.)

Birmingham, Alabama, 71, 238

Black Lives Matter (BLM) movement, 243–44, 248, 255

BlackBerry, 284

Blackstone, William Eugene, 156

Blodgett, Jen, 148

Boilard, Solange, 228–29

Boisselier, Brigitte, 171

Bond, Julian, 258

Bono, Sonny, 295

The Book of Mormon [play], 173

Bopp, Thomas, 183

Borg, Marcus, 195

Boston, Massachusetts, 69, 263

Bowman, Matthew, 174

Boy Scouts, 66

Branch Davidians [cult], 3, 32, 103–11

Branham, William, 50 (ill.), 50–51

Branson, Missouri, 64

Bray, Mark, 254

Brazel, W. W. "Mac," 159

Brazil and Brazilians, 96, 98

Brennan, Frederick, 276

Britain and the British. See England and the British

British Israelism, 50

Broadway, 173

Brock, Jane. See Whaley, Jane

Broken Faith: Inside the Word of Faith Fellowship, One of America's Most Dangerous Cults (Weiss and Mohr), 98

Bromley, David G., 143

Bronfman, Clare, 284, 286–88

Bronfman, Edgar Jr., 284

Bronfman, Edgar Sr., 286

Bronfman, Sara, 288

Brooklyn, New York, 43, 257–58, 287–88

Brown, Jerry, 222

Brown Shirts, 248

Buddha (Siddhartha Gautama), 169, 297, 300

Buddhafield [cult], 21

Buddhism, 75, 146

Buffett, Warren, 20

Buies Creek, North Carolina, 73

Bulgaria and Bulgarians, 105

Bulgarian Orthodoxy, 105

Bulletin of the Atomic Scientists [bulletin], 220–22

Bundy, Cliven, 295

Bundy Ranch, 242

Bunker, Archie [character], 71

Bunyasi, Tehama Lopez, 240

Bureau of Alcohol, Tobacco, and Firearms (ATF), 107–8

Burnt River, Canada, 227

Bush, George H. W., 72, 133, 151

Bush, Zack, 298, 300

C

California

America as cult fertile field, 21

Antifa, 256

Christian Rapture, Carl Jung, and flying saucers, 157

Church of Scientology, 162–63

Cyrus Teed and the Koreshan Unity, 39

David Berg and the Family International, 83–84

David Koresh and the Branch Davidians, 105–6

Eckankar, 144–45, 148

Evangelical church, politics, and the NRA, 71

Father Divine and the Peace Mission, 43

Heaven's Gate, 188

Jim Bakker, *The PTL Club*, and the return of Jesus, 60

Jim Jones and the Peoples Temple Full Gospel Church, 48–51, 53–54

Latter-day Saints and the colonization of the cosmos, 178

Proud Boys, 252

racial religion and social media cults, 233, 235

Raëlians and the Elohim, 168

social media and the rise of hate groups, 264

spoofing cults, 270

Calvinism, 93

Campbell, Alexander, 182

CAN (Cult Awareness Network), 24

Canaan and Canaanites [biblical], 78, 259–60, 297

Canada and Canadians

David Koresh and the Branch Davidians, 106

Father Divine and the Peace Mission, 46

Keith Raniere and NXIVM, 282, 284, 287

Latter-day Saints and the colonization of the cosmos, 178

Raëlians and the Elohim, 168, 171

Roch Thériault and the Ant Hill Kids, 225–29

Westboro Baptist Church, 93

Capitol, Tennessee, 237

Capitol Building, U.S.

America as cult fertile field, 27–28

Evangelical church, politics, and the NRA, 75

Oath Keepers, 241–42, 249

politics as a cult, 124

possibility of cults, 10

Proud Boys, 250–51

QAnon, 274

racial religion and social media cults, 234

social media and the rise of hate groups, 264

Three Percenters, 253

Capitol Hill, 133

Carnegie family, 20

Carson, Rachel, 158, 158 (ill.)

Carter, Brandon, 223, 224 (ill.)

Carter, Jimmy, 72

Carter Principle, 224

Carthage, Illinois, 178

Cartwright, Nancy, 161

Catherine de' Medici, Queen, 212

Catholicism

America as cult fertile field, 17

Eckankar, 147

Evangelical church, politics, and the NRA, 68, 71

Ku Klux Klan and White Nationalism, 237

Nostradamus, 211

racial religion and social media cults, 233, 235

Roch Thériault and the Ant Hill Kids, 225–26

Westboro Baptist Church, 94

Cayce, Edgar, 216–20, 217 (ill.)

Cayce, Gertrude, 218

The Cellular Cosmogony; or, The Earth, a Concave Sphere (Teed), 37

Centers for Disease Control and Prevention, U.S. (CDC), 114–15

Central America and Central Americans, 176

Central Intelligence Agency (CIA), 270

CERN, 266

Champaign, Illinois, 254

Chaney, James, 238

Chanhassen, Minnesota, 144–45

Chansley, Jacob Angeli, 274, 274 (ill.)

Chariots of the Gods? (von Däniken), 157–58

Charlotte, North Carolina, 57

Charlottesville, Virginia, 253, 256

Chastain, Jessica, 63

Chauvin, Derek, 243

Chavigny, Jean-Aymes de, 213

Cheetham, Erika, 211–14

Chicago, Illinois, 36, 39, 71

Chicago Atomic Scientists, 220

Chief Black Eagle. See York, Michael

Childhood's End (Clarke), 152

Children of God (COG) [cult], 84

Children's Aid, 228

China and the Chinese, 79, 215, 231, 248, 272

Choi, Sun Kil, 134

Christ for Greater Los Angeles, 51

Christchurch, New Zealand, 239

Christensen, Erika, 161

Christian Assembly, 51

Christian Identity, 81

Christian Jesus [cult], 21

Christian Science, 42

Christianity

America as cult fertile field, 14–18, 32–33

Christian Rapture, Carl Jung, and flying saucers, 154–61

David Berg and the Family International, 83

David Koresh and the Branch Davidians, 103–4, 107

Eckankar, 147, 149

Edgar Cayce, 216, 218–19

Evangelical church, politics, and the NRA, 67–71, 73

Father Divine and the Peace Mission, 45

Heaven's Gate, 185

Jim Bakker, *The PTL Club*, and the return of Jesus, 57–58, 62

Jim Jones and the Peoples Temple Full Gospel Church, 48–51

Joshua, Jesus, Muhammad, and the implications of *jihad*, 75, 77–80, 82–83

Latter-day Saints and the colonization of the cosmos, 177–78, 182

metaphysics as a cult, 130

Nostradamus, 210–11, 216

possibility of cults, 2

prophets of the End Times, 193, 195, 200–201, 203, 209

QAnon, 274

racial religion and social media cults, 234–35

spoofing cults, 269

Watchtower Society and Jehovah's Witnesses, 86–88, 90–91

Westboro Baptist Church, 92–93

Word of Faith Fellowship, 98, 101

Christianity Today [magazine], 69

Christmas, 90

Christology, 135

Chronis, Claire, 271

Church Age, 154, 209

Church of Jesus Christ of Latter-day Saints. See Mormonism [cult]

Church of Scientology, 161–67

CIA (Central Intelligence Agency), 270

Cincinnati, Ohio, 269

Civil Rights movement

    Evangelical church, politics, and the NRA, 71

    Father Divine and the Peace Mission, 42, 45, 47

    Jim Jones and the Peoples Temple Full Gospel Church, 47, 53

    Ku Klux Klan and White Nationalism, 238

    Nuwaubian Nation, 258

    organizations always as cults, 295

    social media and the rise of hate groups, 264

Civil War, Spanish, 289

Civil War, U.S., 18, 233, 236–37, 241, 243

Clare, John, 311

Clarke, Arthur C., 31, 152, 153 (ill.)

Clinton, Hillary, 272

Clonaid, 171

Clyne, Nicki, 288

COG (Children of God) [cult], 84

Cohen (Newton), Saul Bernard, 289–91

Cold War, 158, 242

Collins, Judy, 289 (ill.)

Colombia and Colombians, 219

Colorado, 74, 178

Columbus, Christopher, 177

Columbus, Indiana, 50

Combatting Cult Mind Control (Hassan), 124

"Come, Ye Thankful People, Come. Raise the Song of Harvest Home," 14

The Coming Prince (Anderson), 207

Communist Party, 134

community as cult-joining factor

    America as cult fertile field, 21, 31

    Cyrus Teed and the Koreshan Unity, 39, 41

    Keith Raniere and NXIVM, 284

    leaders, followers, and pathology, 301

    MLMs as cults, 128

    possibility of cults, 4–5

    Proud Boys, 252

    QAnon, 273

    Word of Faith Fellowship, 103

Community Preparedness Teams (CPTs), 246–47

Concord, Massachusetts, 66, 263

Confederate States of America, 236–37, 240

Confucianism, 75

Confucius, 138, 297

Congregationalism, 88, 93

Congress, U.S., 15, 75, 133, 140, 233, 276

Connecticut, 17, 24, 91, 140

conspiracies as cult-joining factor

    America as cult fertile field, 27, 29–31, 34

future of individual freedom, 294

Keith Raniere and
NXIVM, 288

new militia movement,
240–41

Oath Keepers, 243

prophets of the End
Times, 194

Proud Boys, 252

QAnon, 271–72, 274–75

science, politics, eco-
nomics, and meta-
physics as
codependent, 113

social media and the rise
of hate groups, 265

spoofing cults, 269–71

Sun Myung Moon and
the Unification
Church, 140

Watchtower Society and
Jehovah's Witnesses,
90

Constitution, U.S.

America as cult fertile
field, 15, 17, 22, 24

Evangelical church, pol-
itics, and the NRA, 71–
73

Jim Jones and the Peoples
Temple Full Gospel
Church, 56

metaphysics as a cult, 130

Oath Keepers, 241–42,
244–45

Proud Boys, 250

Raëlians and the Elohim,
172

Word of Faith Fellow-
ship, 103

Constitution of the United
Nuwaubian Nation of
Moors, 257 (ill.)

Consumers' Buyline Inc., 283

Continental Congress of
1774, 17

Copeland, Kenneth, 97

Copernicus, 38

Corea, Chick, 161

Corinthians, Book of, 67–68

Cosby, Bill, 133

Cosmos [TV show], 120

Covenant, Sword, and the
Arm of the Lord (CSA),
80–82

COVID-19

America as cult fertile
field, 30

Antifa, 255

Church of Scientology,
166–67

Evangelical church, pol-
itics, and the NRA, 73

Jim Bakker, The PTL
Club, and the return
of Jesus, 64

MLMs as cults, 128

Oath Keepers, 243, 245,
247

Proud Boys, 252

QAnon, 274, 276

racial religion and social
media cults, 235

science, politics, eco-
nomics, and meta-
physics as
codependent, 114–15

scientism as a cult, 118

Watchtower Society and
Jehovah's Witnesses,
87

Word of Faith Fellow-
ship, 102

Covidites, 167

Cowan, Douglas E., 143

CPTs (Community Prepared-
ness Teams), 246–47

Crawford, Jerry, 65

Cronkite, Walter, 29

Crossan, Dominic, 195

Crucifixion, 200

Cruise, Tom, 161, 166 (ill.),
166–67

Crystal Palace, 59–60

CSA (Covenant, Sword, and
the Arm of the Lord), 80–
82

Cuba and Cubans, 164

Cuban Missile Crisis, 158

Cult Awareness Network
(CAN), 24

The Cult of Trump (Hassan),
121, 124

Cults and New Religions: A
Brief History (Cowan and
Bromley), 143

Cumberland, Rhode Island,
18

Cush [historical], 77

D

Daily Beast [website], 167

Daily Courier [newspaper],
99

Daily Mail [newspaper], 232

Dalai Lama, 286

Dallas, Texas, 188

Dallas Seminary, 157

Damascus [historical], 78–79

Danbury Baptist Association
of Connecticut, 17

Daniel, Book of, 204–5, 209

Daniel [biblical], 204–6, 209

Daoism, 76

Dap Ren. See Gross, Darwin

Darby, John Nelson, 154–56

Dark Web, 265, 267–68, 273

Daughters of the Confederacy, 237

David, House of, 262

David, Moses (David Berg),
83–85

David [biblical], 179, 183

Davidian Seventh-day Ad-
ventism, 106–7

Davies, Clem, 50

d'Avignon, BridgeAnne, 232

Davis, Danny, 133

Dawkins, Richard, 120

Dayton, Ohio, 273

Dead Reckoning [movie], 166

Dean of the Universe (George Baker). See Baker, George (Father Divine)

Death Valley, California, 188

Deep State, 240–41, 248, 271

Deep Web, 265–67

Deer Park, 300

Delaware County, New York, 35

Delusions: An Analysis of the Book of Mormon (Campbell), 182

Democratic Party
  America as cult fertile field, 29
  Evangelical church, politics, and the NRA, 72
  metaphysics as a cult, 130
  Oath Keepers, 244–45
  prophets of the End Times, 196
  QAnon, 271
  racial religion and social media cults, 233
  spoofing cults, 269
  Sun Myung Moon and the Unification Church, 133

DePalma, Louie [character], 8

Department of Health, New York, 287

Department of Justice, U.S., 110

Desmond-Harris, Jenée, 240

Desolation (Great Tribulation), 209

destruction as cult-joining factor
  America as cult fertile field, 31–34

Dark Web, 267

Doomsday Clock, 220

Joshua, Jesus, Muhammad, and the implications of *jihad*, 78, 83

MLMs as cults, 124

Oath Keepers, 242, 248

prophets of the End Times, 192, 199–200, 202, 204

Proud Boys, 250

social media and the rise of hate groups, 265

spoofing cults, 269

Sullivanians, 290

Watchtower Society and Jehovah's Witnesses, 90

Word of Faith Fellowship, 99

Deuteronomy, Book of, 78–79

Devil, the, 159

Devils in Deliverance, 102

DeVito, Danny, 8

Dharma, 146

Dianetics (Hubbard), 163–64

Dias, Elizabeth, 234

Digital Forensic Research Lab, 251

Direct Selling Association, 128

DirectTV, 63

Dirksen Senate Office Building, 133

DISH Network, 63

Disney World, 59

Disneyland, 59–60

Distributed Denial of Secrets, 248

Divine Principle (Moon), 135, 137–38

Dominus Obsequious Sororium (DOS), 286–87

"Don't Tread on Me" slogan, 272

Doomsday, 221

Doomsday Clock [cult], 220–24, 221 (ill.)

Doomsday Clock Symposium, 221

Dorchester Penitentiary, 229 (ill.)

DOS (Dominus Obsequious Sororium), 286–87

Doyle, Sir Arthur Conan, 182

DuckDuckGo, 266–67

Duke, David, 239

Dylan, Bob, 32

E

Early Jesus [cult], 31

East Asia and East Asians, 239

East Side Baptist Church of Topeka, 92

East Side, New York, 44

East Village, New York, 289

Easter, 90, 132

Eastwood, Clint, 74, 295

Ebola, 247

Ecclesiastes, Book of, 58

ECK, 143–45, 149

Eckankar [cult], 143–49

Edmondson, Sarah, 287

Egypt and Egyptians [historical], 77, 79, 185, 260

Egypt and Egyptians [modern], 194

8chan, 273, 276

8kun, 273, 276

Einstein, Albert, 130

El Paso, Texas, 273

Elam [historical], 77

Eldorado, Texas, 179

Eldredge, Ira, 23

Elizabeth, New Jersey, 163

Ellison, James, 80–81, 83

Elohim, 168–73

Emanuel African Methodist Episcopal Church, 239

Emerson, Ralph Waldo, 36

THE END, 31–33, 152, 194, 222

England and the British
    Cyrus Teed and the Koreshan Unity, 35
    Jim Bakker, *The PTL Club*, and the return of Jesus, 60
    Jim Jones and the Peoples Temple Full Gospel Church, 50
    Nuwaubian Nation, 258
    prophets of the End Times, 207
    racial religion and social media cults, 232–33
    social media and the rise of hate groups, 263
    Three Percenters, 252

entrepreneurship as cult-joining factor, 20–21, 33, 35

Ephesians, Book of, 199

Episcopalianism, 68

Epoch Media Group, 272

Equal Rights Amendment (ERA), 71

Erie Canal, 175

"Escape from QAnon: How Jan. 6 Changed One Person's Path" (Zadrozny), 307

Estero, Florida, 39

Eternal Mountain, 226

Europe and Europeans, 45, 50, 79, 209, 213, 215

European Common Market, 158

Evangelicalism, evangelism, and televangelism [cult]
    America as cult fertile field, 33

Christian Rapture, Carl Jung, and flying saucers, 154, 156–57

David Berg and the Family International, 84

Edgar Cayce, 217

Evangelical church, politics, and the NRA, 65–75

Heaven's Gate, 185

Jim Bakker, *The PTL Club*, and the return of Jesus, 57, 61, 63

Jim Jones and the Peoples Temple Full Gospel Church, 47, 49–51

prophets of the End Times, 195, 205, 207

QAnon, 274

racial religion and social media cults, 234

social media and the rise of hate groups, 263

Sun Myung Moon and the Unification Church, 141

Watchtower Society and Jehovah's Witnesses, 86

Eve [biblical], 135–36, 138, 198, 259

Eve [clone], 171

"Eve of Destruction" [Barry McGuire song], 32

"Event" ("Storm") Day, 272–73

Evers, Medgar, 258

The Evolutionary Level Above Human (TELAH), 186

Executive Success Programs Inc, 283–85

Exo/Eso, 286

Les extraterrestres m'ont amené sur leur planète (Raël), 168

The Eyes of Tammy Faye [2021 movie], 63

Ezekiel, Book of, 88

F

Facebook, 25–26, 247, 265, 274–75

"the Fall," 136, 284

Falun Gong, 272

Falwell, Jerry, 61 (ill.), 61–62, 70 (ill.), 70–72

Falwell, Trey, 62

The Family [cult], 84–85

Family International [cult], 83–85

Family of Love [cult], 84

Father Divine (George Baker), 41–47, 53, 65

Father Jehovia (Samuel Morris), 42–43

Fatima [biblical], 259

Fauci, Anthony, 115

Fayette, New York, 177–78

Federal Bureau of Investigation (FBI), 81, 107–10, 165, 272, 284, 291

Federal Emergency Management Agency (FEMA), 246

Federal Trade Commission (FTC), 7, 127

Fermi, Enrico, 153–54

Fermi paradox, 154

Fifth Initiation, 146

The Final Prophecies of Nostradamus (Cheetham), 211–14, 215 (ill.)

Finished Work Pentecostals, 48

First Amendment, U.S. Constitution, 24, 103

First Baptist Church, 73

Fish and Wildlife Service, U.S., 158

Five Passions, 146

The Flaming Sword [newspaper], 38, 41

Flavor Aid, 55

Florida
America as cult fertile field, 27
Church of Scientology, 165
Cyrus Teed and the Koreshan Unity, 39, 41
Jim Bakker, *The PTL Club*, and the return of Jesus, 59–60
Proud Boys, 249
racial religion and social media cults, 235
Raëlians and the Elohim, 168
Sullivanians, 291

Floyd, George, 243

flying saucers. See UFOs

Flying Saucers: A Modern Myth of Things Seen in the Skies (Jung), 159

Flynn, Michael, 275

Food for Thinking Christians: Why Evil Was Permitted and Kindred Topics (Russell), 88

Forbes [magazine], 286

Ford, Gerald R., 133

Ford [company], 20

Forest City, 99

The Forgotten Ones, 288

Forrest, Nathan Bedford, 237, 237 (ill.)

Fort Myers, Florida, 41

Fort Sumpter, 241

Founding Fathers, 15–16, 56, 130, 263

Fox News, 122–23

France and the French, 22, 144, 162, 168, 170, 210–12, 215

Franco da Rocha, Brazil, 98

Frank Report, 288

Franklin, Benjamin, 16–17

FREECOG (Parents' Committee to Free Our Children from the Children of God), 84

Freedman, Michael, 286

Freedom of Mind (Hassan), 124

Freeman, Morgan, 31

French Inquisition, 210

Frenkel, Sheera, 251–52

Freudians, 130

Friedman, Thomas, 28

The Friend. See Wilkinson, Jemima (Publick Universal Friend)

Friend's Settlement, 19

FTC (Federal Trade Commission), 7, 127

Full Gospel and Pentecostal Holiness revivals, 48

Full Gospel Businessmen's Association, 50

Fuller Brush, 86

Fundamentalism
America as cult fertile field, 23
Bhagwan Shree Rajneesh, 280
Christian Rapture, Carl Jung, and flying saucers, 156
Eckankar, 147
Evangelical church, politics, and the NRA, 68–71
Latter-day Saints and the colonization of the cosmos, 179
prophets of the End Times, 194
Watchtower Society and Jehovah's Witnesses, 86

Furber, Paul, 276

G

Gab, 265

Gabriel, Archangel, 204–8, 297

Gadsden flag, 272

Gage Park, 94

Gaither, Bill, 33

Gaither, Gloria, 33

Galilee, 176

Garden of Eden, 198, 201

Garencières, France, 215

Garfield, Andrew, 63

Gas Light [1938 play], 9

Gaslight [1944 movie], 9

gaslighting as cult-joining factor, 9–10

Gaspésie, Canada, 226

Gates, Bill, 20

Gaydos, Connor, 270

Gen Z, 271

General Association of Davidian Seventh-day Adventists, 105

General Electric, 20

General Motors, 20, 196

Genesis, Book of, 90, 198, 259–60

Geneva, Switzerland, 168

la Geniocratie, 170

George Washington University, 162

Georgia, 42, 236–37, 260–61, 275

Germany and Germans, 41, 162, 180, 231

Ghana and Ghanans, 96

G.I. Bill, 68

Gilguere, Samuel, 226–27

Glader, Paul, 73–74

Go Topless protest, 172

God
aliens as a cult, 151–52
America as cult fertile field, 13–16, 18, 32–33

Bhagwan Shree Rajneesh, 281

Church of Scientology, 164

Cyrus Teed and the Koreshan Unity, 37–38

David Berg and the Family International, 84

David Koresh and the Branch Davidians, 104, 106–9

Eckankar, 143–47, 149

Edgar Cayce, 217–18, 220

Evangelical church, politics, and the NRA, 65, 74–75

Father Divine and the Peace Mission, 42, 45–47

Jim Bakker, *The PTL Club*, and the return of Jesus, 58, 60–61

Jim Jones and the Peoples Temple Full Gospel Church, 48–49, 53–55

Joshua, Jesus, Muhammad, and the implications of *jihad*, 76–78, 81, 83

Latter-day Saints and the colonization of the cosmos, 174–77, 175 (ill.), 179, 181, 183–86

metaphysics as a cult, 130–31

Nuwaubian Nation, 260

organizations always as cults, 296

prophets of the End Times, 191–93, 197–99, 201–2, 204, 206–8, 210

racial religion and social media cults, 234–35

Raëlians and the Elohim, 168–69

Roch Thériault and the Ant Hill Kids, 224–26, 229

science, politics, economics, and metaphysics as codependent, 114

social media and the rise of hate groups, 262–63

Sun Myung Moon and the Unification Church, 132, 135–37, 139, 141

Watchtower Society and Jehovah's Witnesses, 86–90

Westboro Baptist Church, 91

Word of Faith Fellowship, 96–99, 101

"God and Guns: Why American Churchgoers Are Packing Heat" (Glader and Smith), 73

Going Clear: Scientology and the Prison of Belief [TV documentary], 163

Going Clear: Scientology, Hollywood, and the Prison of Belief (Wright), 161

Golden Plates, 176–77, 182

Goldsmith, Hyman, 220

Gomez, Selena, 28

Goodman, Andrew, 238

Google, 266, 273

GOP, 10, 122

Gorbachev, Mikhail, 133

Gospel, 67–68, 88, 154, 176–77, 201, 208

Graham, Lindsey, 122

Graham, Rev. Billy, 51–53, 69

Granieri, Solange, 98

Great Britain. See England and the British

Great Commission, 73

Great Depression, 43, 45–46, 105

Great Migration, 238

Great Tribulation (Desolation), 209

Greece and Greeks, 116, 140

Greene, Marjorie Taylor, 275

Gross, Darwin, 145, 148

"The Growing Religious Fervor in the American Right: 'This Is a Jesus Movement'" (Dias), 234

growth as cult-joining factor, 3–5, 146, 200, 279

Guinness Book of World Records, 161

Gulf of Mexico, 40

Guyana and Guyanans, 24, 47, 54–55, 259

H

Hagin, Kenneth, 98

Hagopian, Avak, 50

Hahn, Jessica, 60, 64

Haight-Ashbury, California, 264

Hale, Alan, 183

Hale-Bopp comet, 188, 188 (ill.)

Ham [biblical], 259–60

Hamath [historical], 77

Hampden-Sydney College, 174

Han (Moon), Hak Ja, 132 (ill.), 137, 143

Hancock, Graham, 158

Happiness Academy, 172

Hare Krishna, 141

Hari, Emily Claire (Michael B.), 254

Harlem, New York, 43

Harnesser of Atomic Energy (George Baker). See Baker, George (Father Divine)

Harvest Rock Church, 235

Harvey, Hurricane, 247

Hassan, Steven, 121–22, 124–25

Hawaii, 168

Hearst, William Randolph, 51

Heavenly Sanctuary, 104

Heaven's Gate [cult], 32, 183–90

Hebrews, Book of, 104

Hebrews [biblical]. See Israel and Israelites [biblical]

Hegseth, Pete, 122

Henry II, King, 212

Herbalife, 125

Heritage USA, 59, 61

Hewes, Hayden C., 187

Heyer, Heather, 256

Hill Cumorah, 176–77, 181

Hinduism, 146–47, 149, 172, 279–80

Hinn, Benny, 97

Hiroshima, Japan, 169, 220

Hitchens, Christopher, 120

Hitler, Adolf, 25, 52, 134, 138

Hittites, 78

HIV/AIDS, 213, 299

Hivites, 78

Hochman, John, 285

Holiness Movement, 42, 48

Holley, Vernal, 182

Hollywood, 72, 139, 167, 269

Holmes, Sherlock [character], 182

Holocaust, 180

Holt, Jared, 251

Holy Ghost, 33, 177

Holy Hell [movie], 20

Holy Land, 182

Holy Spirit, 42, 48, 96, 144, 154–55

Holy Tabernacle Ministries, 257, 260–61

Holy Wine Ceremony, 137

Holy Writ, 195

homosexuality. See LGBTQ

Hoon Dok Hae (Moon), 139

Hoover, Herbert, 51

Hoover Dam, 275

Hopedale Community [cult], 36

Hopkinsville, Kentucky, 216–17

Houari, 172

House of Representatives, U.S., 17

Houston, Texas, 184

Houteff, Florence, 106

Houteff, Victor T., 105–7

"How to Get Someone Out of a Cult" (Wollan), 308

Howell, Vernon. See Koresh, David

HTTP (hypertext transfer protocol), 266

Hubbard, L. (Lafayette) Ronald "Ron," 161–65, 163 (ill.)

Hudson River, 142

Huffington Post [newspaper], 167

Huntington Beach, California, 83

Hutchinson Island, Georgia, 42

hypertext transfer protocol (HTTP), 266

I

IBM, 20

Ibn al-Haytham, Hasan, 118

Idaho, 178

Illinois, 24, 36, 39, 71, 133, 178, 254

The Immortal Manhood: The Laws and Processes of Its Attainment in the Flesh (Teed), 40

Inchon [movie], 139

Independent Assemblies of God, 52

India and Indians, 79, 144, 278–81

Indian Removal Act, 233

Indiana, 47–50, 53, 55, 237

Indianapolis, Indiana, 48–50

Indianapolis Human Rights Commission, 53

Infinitechan (Infinitychan), 273

Inner Light, 143

Inner Sound, 143

Inside Edition [TV show], 99

Insider [magazine], 1

Instagram, 26, 28, 270

"The Instinct of Hope" (Clare), 311

Institute for Studies of Religion, Baylor University, 86

Institute for the Study of American Religion, 86

Intelligent Design (Raël), 168

Internal Revenue Service (IRS), 165, 202

International Bible Students, 88

International Hotel, 49

International Raëlian Movement (IRM), 168

internet protocol (IP), 267

Interreligious and International Federation for World Peace, 133

Iran and Iranians, 50

Iraq and Iraqis, 91

Ireland and the Irish, 154, 231

IRM (International Raëlian Movement), 168

Irvington, New York, 142

Isa. See Jesus Christ

Isaac [biblical], 179, 260

Isaiah, Book of, 76–77, 90, 105, 183, 192–93

Ishmael [biblical], 260

Ishmaelites, 260

Islam
  Heaven's Gate, 185
  Joshua, Jesus, Muhammad, and the implications of *jihad*, 75, 77–80, 83
  Nuwaubian Nation, 259
  Oath Keepers, 244
  Proud Boys, 249
  Sun Myung Moon and the Unification Church, 137
  Three Percenters, 254
  Westboro Baptist Church, 92
Israel and Israelis [modern], 71, 170
Israel and Israelites [biblical]
  David Koresh and the Branch Davidians, 106
  Jim Jones and the Peoples Temple Full Gospel Church, 50
  Joshua, Jesus, Muhammad, and the implications of *jihad*, 81
  Latter-day Saints and the colonization of the cosmos, 178, 182
  Nuwaubian Nation, 260, 262
  prophets of the End Times, 204
  Roch Thériault and the Ant Hill Kids, 226
Italy and Italians, 153, 162
"It's the End of the World as We Know It (and I Feel Fine)" [REM song], 32

J

Jacob [biblical], 179, 260
Jaggers, Rev. Orval Lee, 51
Jain, Chandra Mohan. See Rajneesh, Bhagwan Shree (Acharya Rajneesh, Chandra Mohan Jain, Osho)

Jamaica and Jamaicans, 259
Jambres [biblical], 193
James [biblical], 68
Jannes [biblical], 193
January 6 Capitol insurrection
  America as cult fertile field, 27–28
  Antifa, 256
  Oath Keepers, 241, 242 (ill.), 243, 248–49
  politics as a cult, 124
  possibility of cults, 10
  Proud Boys, 250–52
  QAnon, 274
  racial religion and social media cults, 234
  social media and the rise of hate groups, 262
  Three Percenters, 253 (ill.)
Japan and the Japanese
  Church of Scientology, 162
  Doomsday Clock, 220
  Edgar Cayce, 219
  racial religion and social media cults, 231
  Raëlians and the Elohim, 168–70
  Sun Myung Moon and the Unification Church, 134, 139–40, 143
Japheth [biblical], 259–60
Jebusites, 78
Jefferson, Thomas, 16–17
Jeffersonians, 130
Jeffersonville, Indiana, 50
Jehovah. See God
Jehovah's Witnesses [cult], 14, 22–23, 42, 85–91
Jenkins, Jerry B., 195
Jeremiah, Book of, 205
Jeremiah [biblical], 205 (ill.)

Jeremiah Lamenting the Destruction of Jerusalem [painting], 205 (ill.)
Jerusalem [historical], 77, 79, 155, 176, 204–9
Jerusalem [modern], 209
Jerusalem Township, 19
Jesse [biblical], 76
Jesus Christ
  America as cult fertile field, 15, 17, 25, 31, 33
  Christian Rapture, Carl Jung, and flying saucers, 154–56, 160
  David Koresh and the Branch Davidians, 104–7
  Eckankar, 147
  Evangelical church, politics, and the NRA, 67–68
  getting out of a cult, 307
  Heaven's Gate, 186, 188
  Jim Bakker, *The PTL Club*, and the return of Jesus, 56–65
  Jim Jones and the Peoples Temple Full Gospel Church, 48–49
  Joshua, Jesus, Muhammad, and the implications of *jihad*, 75–83
  Latter-day Saints and the colonization of the cosmos, 175 (ill.), 175–78, 183–84
  MLMs as cults, 126
  Nuwaubian Nation, 259
  organizations always as cults, 297
  possibility of cults, 2–3
  prophets of the End Times, 195–96, 199–205, 207–8, 208 (ill.)
  racial religion and social media cults, 233, 235

Raëlians and the Elohim, 169–70

social media and the rise of hate groups, 262–63

Sun Myung Moon and the Unification Church, 132, 137–38, 141

Watchtower Society and Jehovah's Witnesses, 88–90

Jesus Christ Light and Power Company, 157

Jesus Is Coming (Blackstone), 156

Jesus People, 83, 85, 157

jihad [cult], 75–83, 244

The Jim and Tammy Show [TV show]. See *The PTL Club* [TV show]

The Jim Bakker Show [TV show], 63

Jim Crow laws, 237

Jness, 285

Jobs, Steve, 20

Joel, Book of, 49

John, Book of, 67, 176, 199

John of England, King, 232, 232 (ill.)

John of Patmos (John the Revelator) [biblical], 32, 43, 77, 77 (ill.), 107

John the Baptist [biblical], 137

Jones, Rev. James "Jim," 32, 47–56, 49 (ill.), 53 (ill.), 65, 72

Jonestown, Guyana, 24, 47, 54–55

Joshua, Book of, 49

Joshua [biblical], 75–83

Joshua son of Joseph. See Jesus Christ

Journal of Religion and Health [journal], 26

Judaism
America as cult fertile field, 15

David Koresh and the Branch Davidians, 104

Evangelical church, politics, and the NRA, 68, 71

Father Divine and the Peace Mission, 45

Joshua, Jesus, Muhammad, and the implications of *jihad*, 75–76, 78–83

Ku Klux Klan and White Nationalism, 237

Latter-day Saints and the colonization of the cosmos, 180

Nostradamus, 210–11

Oath Keepers, 242

prophets of the End Times, 192, 200, 206, 208–9

QAnon, 272

racial religion and social media cults, 231, 233

Raëlians and the Elohim, 169

Watchtower Society and Jehovah's Witnesses, 91

Westboro Baptist Church, 92, 94

Jude, Book of, 33

Juggalo March, 255

Jung, Carl, 154–61

Jungians, 130

K

Kaepernick, Colin, 295

Kahl, Gordon, 81

Kahn, David, 218

Kansas, 91–92, 94

Kansas City, Missouri, 80

Kardashian, Kim, 50

Kardashian, Tatos "Thomas," 50

Karma, 146–47

Katrina, Hurricane, 247

Kemp, Jack, 133

Kent, Clark [character], 283

Kentucky, 38, 144, 216–17

Kevin's House, 60

Khadija, 297

Khartoum, Sudan, 258

Kidman, Nicole, 167

Kim Il-sung, 138

Kim Jong-un, 222

King, Martin Luther Jr., 258

Kingdom of God, 89, 106, 186, 235

Kirk, Captain [character], 262

Kirpal Singh, 144

Klemp, Harold, 144–45

Knights of the Ku Klux Klan, 239

Kobol [fictional planet], 174

Kolob [fictional planet], 174

Konnikova, Maria, 30

Kool-Aid, drinking the, 24, 47, 55

Korea and Koreans, 132, 134, 136–37, 139–40, 142, 222

Korean Peninsula, 134

Korean War, 139

Koresh (Cyrus Reed Teed), 35–41, 36 (ill.)

Koresh, David, 103–11, 107 (ill.)

Koreshan Unity [cult], 35–41

Koreshan Unity Settlement Historic District, 41, 41 (ill.)

Koreshanity, 36, 39–41

Ku Klux Klan [cult], 50, 236–40, 262

Kuchwada, India, 279

Kwang-Ya Church, 134

L

LaHaye, Tim, 195

Lalich, Janja, 308–9

Lamb of God, 109

Lammers, Arthur, 218

Langsdorf, Martyl, 220

Lansbury, Angela, 9

Lao Tzu, 297

Laodicea [historical], 196

Las Vegas, Nevada, 145

The Late Great Planet Earth (LGPE) (Lindsey), 156–57

Latinos for Trump, 249

Latter Rain, 49–52

Latter-day Saints. See Mormonism [cult]

Laurel Street Tabernacle, 48, 50–51

Lavallée, Gabrielle, 228

Law of Attraction, 129

Law of Detachment, 146

Law of "Dharma" or Purpose in Life, 146

Law of Giving, 146

Law of Intention and Desire, 146

Law of "Karma" or Cause and Effect, 146

Law of Least Effort, 146

Law of Pure Potentiality, 146

Lawfare [blog], 27

Lee, Ann, 14

Lehi [prophet], 176

LEM (Living Eck Master), 144–45, 148

Lenin, Vladimir, 134

Leslie, John, 223

Leviticus, Book of, 90

Lewis, James R., 187, 189

Lewis, John, 258

Lexington, Massachusetts, 263

LGBTQ

Antifa, 254

Evangelical church, politics, and the NRA, 71

Jim Bakker, *The PTL Club*, and the return of Jesus, 61

Joshua, Jesus, Muhammad, and the implications of *jihad*, 80–82

Proud Boys, 249

Raëlians and the Elohim, 171

Sun Myung Moon and the Unification Church, 141

Westboro Baptist Church, 92, 94–95

Word of Faith Fellowship, 99

LGPE (The Late Great Planet Earth) (Lindsey), 156–57

Libertarianism, 242

Liberty University, 62

Library of Congress, 13

Life Force, 144

Life with Lori [TV show], 63

LifeBridge Church, 274

LifeWay Research, 73

Light and Sound of God, 144

Lincolnians, 130

Lindell, Mike, 65

Lindsey, Hal, 156–58, 195

lip-service religion as cult-joining factor, 15–18, 33, 130, 233

Live Word (Ministerio Verbo Vivo), 98

Living Eck Master (LEM), 144–45, 148

Le Livre qui dit la verité (Raël), 170

London, England, 60

Long Island, New York, 43

Longfellow, Henry Wadsworth, 263

Lopez, Robert, 173

Lord. See God

Lord's Prayer, 17, 203

Los Angeles, California, 48, 51, 71, 105, 157, 162–63

Los Angeles County, California, 235

Lost Tribes of Israel, 50, 182

Louisiana Purchase Exposition, 263–64

love as cult-joining factor

Eckankar, 149

getting out of a cult, 310

Joshua, Jesus, Muhammad, and the implications of *jihad*, 78

leaders, followers, and pathology, 301

organizations always as cults, 296, 300

possibility of cults, 2, 5

prophets of the End Times, 200

Raëlians and the Elohim, 168

Sun Myung Moon and the Unification Church, 135–36

Word of Faith Fellowship, 101

Love Charter, 85

Lowry, Michael, 99

Lucifer, Archangel, 135–36

Luciferians, 186, 285

Luke, Book of, 58, 67, 88, 154, 208, 214

Lynchburg, Virginia, 62

M

MacArthur, Douglas, 139

Mack, Allison, 283–84, 287–88

MADECH (*Mouvement pour l'Accueil des Elohim, Créateurs de l'Humanité*), 170

Madison, James, 16

Madison Square Garden, 139

MAGA (Make America Great Again), 122

MagnifyMoney.com, 127

Mahanta. See Living ECK Master (LEM)

mahdis, 146

Maine, 73

Major Jealous Divine, Rev. (George Baker). See Baker, George (Father Divine)

Make America Great Again (MAGA), 122

Manchester, New York, 176

Manhattan Center, 139

Manhattan Island. See New York, New York

Manhattan Project, 220

Manifest Destiny, 233

Manson girls, 288

Mark, Book of, 67, 214

Mars, 214

Martel, Charles, 79

Martin, John, 98

Martin, Rachel, 100

Martin Luther King Jr. Humanitarian Award, 53

Marxism, 15, 243–44, 248

Mary [biblical], 205

Mary Kay, 125–26

Maryland, 42

Masons, 261

Massachusetts, 36, 66, 69, 263

Matthew, Book of, 67, 89, 141–42, 214

maya, 172–73

Mayas, 32

Mayflower [ship], 14, 233

McGuire, Barry, 32

McIndoe, Peter, 268–71

McInnes, Gavin, 249

McLamb, Jack, 242

McVeigh, Timothy, 110

Meathead [character], 71

Mecca, Saudi Arabia, 297

Mediterranean Sea, 165, 176

Melton, J. Gordon, 86

Memphis, Tennessee, 268

Menlo Park, California, 145

Mesopotamia, 197–98

Messenger (George Baker). See Baker, George (Father Divine)

Messiah
    Cyrus Teed and the Koreshan Unity, 36
    David Koresh and the Branch Davidians, 105, 107
    Father Divine and the Peace Mission, 42
    Latter-day Saints and the colonization of the cosmos, 176
    Nuwaubian Nation, 259
    prophets of the End Times, 208
    rebelliousness as cult-joining factor, 18–19
    Sun Myung Moon and the Unification Church, 132, 134–35, 137, 141

Messianism, 140

Messner, Roe, 60, 64

Methodism, 42, 47, 49–51, 68, 70, 86, 175

Metropolitan Detention Center, 288

MeWe, 265

Mexico and Mexicans, 162, 178, 233, 282, 284, 287

Michigan, 235

Middle East, 79, 209, 215

Middle East Times [newspaper], 140

Midtown Manhattan, 139

Milky Way, 152

Millennial Dawnists, 88

Millennium and Millennialism, 154–55, 203

Miller, Russell, 164

Millerites, 14, 32

Milwaukee, Wisconsin, 274

Ministerio Evangelico Comunidade Rhema (Rhema Community Evangelical Ministry), 98

Ministerio Verbo Vivo (Live Word), 98

Minneapolis, Minnesota, 145, 243

Minnesota, 144–45, 243, 254

Minute Men, 66

Miscavige, David, 165, 167

Mission: Impossible [movie series], 166

Mississippi, 238

Missouri, 64–65, 80, 82–83, 89, 186, 264

Mitochondrial Eve, 153

MLMs (Multi-Level Marketing) [cult], 114, 124–30, 283, 305

Mo Letters, 84

Modernism, 68

Mohammad (Muhammad) [biblical], 75–83, 138, 169, 185, 205, 259, 297

Mohr, Holbrook, 98, 100–101

A Moment's Notice: Recognizing the Stressful Life Events, Emotions and Actions That Make Us Susceptible to Scams (Shadel et al.), 7

Monroe, James, 16

Montaigne, David S., 214–15

Montana, 242

Moody, Dwight L., 217

Moon, Sun Myung, 121, 132 (ill.), 132–43, 138 (ill.)

Moonies, 121, 142

Moorish Science Temple of America, 257

Moral Majority, 62, 70–72

Mormon, Book of, 176–78, 182, 210

Mormon [prophet], 176

Mormon Pageant, 181

Mormon Tabernacle Choir, 181

Mormonism [cult], 14, 23, 42, 71, 94, 173–83, 185

Morningside, Missouri, 64–65

Moroni, Angel, 176–77

Morris, Samuel (Father Jehovia), 42–43

Morrow, Ulysses Grant, 38–41

Moses [biblical], 78, 175, 179, 193, 296, 296 (ill.)

Mother Divine (Peninnah Baker), 43, 46–47

Mount Carmel, 105–6

Mount Hira, 297

Mount of Olives, 141

Mount Rainier, 159

Mouvement pour l'Accueil des Elohim, Créateurs de l'Humanité (MADECH), 170

MSNBC, 123

Mueller, Robert, 272

Muhammad (Mohammad) [biblical], 75–83, 138, 169, 185, 205, 259, 297

Muhammad Ahmad Ibn Abdullāh (al-Madhi), 258–59

Multi-Level Marketing (MLMs) [cult], 114, 124–30, 283, 305

Muslims. See Islam

MyPillow, 65

N

Nagasaki, Japan, 220

Nation of Islam, 257

National Academy of Scienes, 117

National Anthem, 295

National Endowment for the Humanities, 156

National Football League (NFL), 295

National Fraud Frontiers Report, AARP, 7

National Institutes of Health (NIH), 115

National Mall, 139

National Register of Historic Places, 41

National Rifle Association (NRA) [cult], 65–75

Native Americans, 177, 182, 231, 233, 240, 261

Navy, U.S., 162

Navy Reserve, U.S., 162

Nayya Malachizodoq-El. See York, Michael

Nazareth [historical], 200

Nazism, 239–40, 253, 255, 273

near-death experiences (NDEs), 299

Nebraska, 74, 219

Nebuchadnezzar [biblical], 205

Nehemiah, Book of, 207

neo-Nazism, 239–40, 273

Nero, 195

Nettles, Bonnie Lu, 184–90

Nevada, 145, 178, 242–43, 295

New Age, 139

New Brunswick, Canada, 229

New England, 13, 19, 235

The New Good News [periodical], 84

New Jersey, 36, 163

New Jerusalem, 39, 39 (ill.), 178

New Laurel Street Tabernacle, 51

New Light Baptist, 18

New Mexico, 36, 159, 178

New Mount Carmel Center, 106–7, 109, 110 (ill.)

New Order of the Latter Rain, 49–50

New Testament
America as cult fertile field, 33

Christian Rapture, Carl Jung, and flying saucers, 154

David Koresh and the Branch Davidians, 104

Heaven's Gate, 186

Latter-day Saints and the colonization of the cosmos, 177

prophets of the End Times, 193, 195–96, 201

New Thought, 42

New World Order, 242, 244–45

New York
America as cult fertile field, 19, 24

Cyrus Teed and the Koreshan Unity, 35

Father Divine and the Peace Mission, 43–44, 46

Heaven's Gate, 184

Keith Raniere and NXIVM, 282–84, 286–88

Latter-day Saints and the colonization of the cosmos, 175–78, 181–82

Nostradamus, 215

Nuwaubian Nation, 257–59

prophets of the End Times, 196

Sullivanians, 288–89, 291

Sun Myung Moon and the Unification Church, 139–40, 142–43

New York City Tribune [newspaper], 139

New York Daily News [newspaper], 232

New York Magazine [magazine], 167

New York, New York, 139, 184, 196, 288–89, 291

New York Times [newspaper]

America as cult fertile field, 28

Christian Rapture, Carl Jung, and flying saucers, 156

Edgar Cayce, 217

Keith Raniere and NXIVM, 287

politics as a cult, 123

Proud Boys, 251

QAnon, 276

racial religion and social media cults, 234

Sun Myung Moon and the Unification Church, 132

The New York Times Magazine [magazine], 308

New Yorker Hotel, 139, 142 (ill.)

New Zealand and New Zealanders, 239, 273

Newsom, Gavin, 235

Newsweek [magazine], 109

Newton (Cohen), Saul Bernard, 289–91

Newton, Sir Isaac, 38, 130

Newtown, Connecticut, 91

NFL (National Football League), 295

Nichols, Terry, 110

NIH (National Institutes of Health), 115

Nike, 96

Nile Valley, 261

9/11, 91, 143, 215

Nineteen Eighty-Four (Orwell), 10

Nissan, 207

Nixon, Richard M., 71, 138 (ill.), 139

Noah [biblical], 259–60

Noble, Kerry, 80–83

Noble Truth, 300

Nollag, Catherine na, 30

NORC, University of Chicago, 7

North Africa and North Africans, 79

North America and North Americans, 261

North Carolina, 57, 73, 96–98, 251

North Dakota, 81

North Korea and North Koreans, 132, 134, 222

Northrup (Hubbard), Sara, 162–64

Nostradamus (Michel de Nostredame), 32, 210–16, 211 (ill.), 220

Noticias del Mundo [newspaper], 139

NRA (National Rifle Association) [cult], 65–75

Nubian Islaamic Hebrew Mission, 257

Nubian Islamic Mission, 258

Nubians, 259–61

Nuclear Age, 153

Nuwaubian Nation of Moors [cult], 257–62

NXIANs, 283

NXIVM [cult], 282–88

O

Oath Keepers [cult], 28, 241–49, 251, 262

Obama, Barack, 247, 269, 272

Occupy Wall Street, 254

Ockenga, Harold, 69

Odd Gods: New Religions and the Cult Controversy (Lewis), 188

Ohio, 24, 36, 269, 273

Oklahoma, 97, 110

Oklahoma City, Oklahoma, 110

Old Jerusalem, 60

Old North Church, 263

Old Testament, 78, 87, 177

Oliveira, Juarez De Souza, 98

Olivier, Laurence, 139

Omega, 77

"On the Job" [*Taxi* episode], 8

Ontario, Canada, 227

Ophir [historical], 193

Orange County, California, 252

The Order, 81–82

Order of Angels, 171

Ordo Templi Orientis, 162

Oregon, 24, 187, 255–56, 278, 280–81

Orlando, Florida, 291

Orwell, George, 10, 80

Osho. See Rajneesh, Bhagwan Shree (Acharya Rajneesh, Chandra Mohan Jain, Osho)

Osho Institute, 282

Osho International Meditation Resort, 282

Osho Meditation Center, 282

Osteen, Joel, 97

Ozarks, Missouri, 64

P

Pacific Ocean, 162

Paducah, Kentucky, 144

Pakistan and Pakistanis, 79

Pale Rider [movie], 74

Palm Springs, California, 50

Palm Sunday, 207

Palmer, Susan, 173

Palmyra, New York, 175–76, 181–82

Parents' Committee to Free Our Children from the Children of God (FREE-COG), 84

Paris, France, 144

Park Chung-hee, 140

Park Street Church, 69

Parker, Trey, 173

Parlato, Frank, 288

Parler, 27, 265

Parloff, Roger, 27

Parsons, Jack, 162–63

Pasadena, California, 235

Passover, 106

Pathros [historical], 77

Patriot Prayer, 255–56

Pattison, E. Mansell, 26

Pau [historical], 213

Paul, Apostle, 15, 67, 175, 186, 193, 199

Paul, Ron, 242

Paulji (Paul Twitchell), 144–45, 148

Peace Mission [cult], 41–47, 44 (ill.)

Pearce, Jane, 289–90

The Pearl of Great Price (Smith), 174

Pennsylvania, 19, 24, 46, 271

Pentagon, U.S., 143

Pentateuch, 169

Pentecost, 154

Pentecostalism, 22, 42, 50–51, 98

Peoples Temple Full Gospel Church [cult], 3, 47–56

Peoria, Arizona, 274

Perizzites, 78

Persia [historical], 79, 205

Peter, Apostle, 176

Peter [biblical], 68

Pew Research Center, 118–19

Pharisees, 208

Phelps, Fred Waldron, 92–95

Phelps-Roper, Shirley, 94–95

Philadelphia, Pennsylvania, 19, 46

Phoenix, Arizona, 234

Phoenix, River, 84 (ill.)

Picard, Jean-Luc [character], 271

Pilgrims, 233

Pisces, 160

pistis, 115–16

Pittsburgh, Pennsylvania, 271

Plandemic [film], 274

Planetary Court, 40

Playboy [magazine], 60

Pledge of Allegiance, 17

Police Against the New World Order, 242

Ponzi schemes, 124–30

Portland, Oregon, 255–56

Post-Disaster Responses, 246

Potter, Robert "Maximum Bob," 61

Potter, William, 19

Powell, Sidney, 275

Prairie Home Community [cult], 36

Presbyterianism, 93, 132, 140, 175, 184

Price, Rev. John, 51–52

Primitive Baptism, 93

Prognostications (Nostradamus), 212

Promised Land, 78, 81

The Prophet (Jim Jones). See Jones, Rev. James "Jim"

Protestant Reformation, 93

Protestantism

David Koresh and the Branch Davidians, 104

Eckankar, 146

Evangelical church, politics, and the NRA, 70, 73

Father Divine and the Peace Mission, 42, 44

Jim Jones and the Peoples Temple Full Gospel Church, 47–48

Ku Klux Klan and White Nationalism, 237

Latter-day Saints and the colonization of the cosmos, 178, 180

Nostradamus, 211

racial religion and social media cults, 232

Proud Boys [cult], 27, 241, 249–53, 250 (ill.), 255–56, 262

Psalms, Book of, 74, 208

Psychology Today [magazine], 124

The PTL Club [TV show], 56–65, 97

PTL ministry [cult], 58, 61–63

PTL Satellite Network (PTL Television Network), 57, 63

Publick Universal Friend (Jemima Wilkinson), 18–19, 19 (ill.)

Publishers Weekly [magazine], 157

Puerto Rico and Puerto Ricans, 247, 259

Pulaski, Tennessee, 236

Pulitzer Prize, 98

Pune, India, 278, 280

Puritanism, 13–14, 177, 235

Pusan, South Korea, 134

Pyongyang, North Korea, 134

pyramid schemes, 124–30, 127 (ill.), 282–84, 286–87

Q

Q [character], 271–76

Q drops, 273–76

QAnon [cult], 29, 271–76

QAnon Super PAC, 276

Quakerism (Society of Friends), 18–19, 35, 42, 233

Quayle, Dan, 151

Québec, Canada, 171, 225–26

Quora, 148

Qur'an, 77–80, 137, 205, 210, 259, 297

R

Raël (Claude Vorilhon), 168–73

Raëlism [cult], 168–73

Raël's Sensual Meditation (Raël), 172

Raipur Sanskrit College, 279

Rajneesh, Bhagwan Shree (Acharya Rajneesh, Chandra Mohan Jain, Osho), 278 (ill.), 278–82

Rajneeshpuram, Oregon, 278, 280–81

Rally of Hope, 143

Rancho Rajneesh, 280

Rancho Santa Fe, California, 188

Raniere, Keith, 282–88, 283 (ill.)

Rapture, 154–61, 201–3, 209

Raritarian Bay Union [cult], 36

Rather, Dan, 121

RATs (remote access trojans), 267

Reagan, Ronald, 72, 151, 295

Rebazar Tarzs, 144

rebelliousness as cult-joining factor, 18–21, 33, 244, 252, 279

Reconstruction, 42, 236

Reddit, 275

Reformation, Protestant, 178

Religion Unplugged [magazine], 73

religious freedom as cult-joining factor, 15, 22–24, 34, 233

Religious Right, 70–72

REM, 32

Rembrandt, 205

remote access trojans (RATs), 267

Republican Party, 10, 72, 121–22, 130, 196, 234–35

"Rev. Sun Myung Moon, Self-Proclaimed Messiah Who Built Religious Movement, Dies at 92" (Wakin), 132

"Revealed! Who Gets Scammed" (Shadel), 6

Revelation, Book of
  America as cult fertile field, 32
  Christian Rapture, Carl Jung, and flying saucers, 158
  David Koresh and the Branch Davidians, 105, 107–9
  Evangelical church, politics, and the NRA, 75
  Heaven's Gate, 184–85
  Joshua, Jesus, Muhammad, and the implications of *jihad*, 77
  Nostradamus, 214, 216
  prophets of the End Times, 194–97, 200
  Sun Myung Moon and the Unification Church, 137
  Watchtower Society and Jehovah's Witnesses, 90

Revere, Paul, 263, 263 (ill.)

Revolutionary War, 19, 177, 241, 252

Rhema Bible Training College, 97–98

Rhema Community Evangelical Ministry (Ministerio Evangelico Comunidade Rhema), 98

Rhode Island, 18–19

Rhodes, Stewart, 28, 242–43, 248

Richmond, Virginia, 250

Riddle, Ruth, 109

"Righteous Government Platform" [document], 45

Rinder, Mike, 166–67

Ritchings, Edna Rose (Sweet Angel), 46

Robertson, Pat, 72

Rockefeller family, 20

Roe v. Wade, 71

Rogerians, 130

Roku, 63

Rolls Royce, 282

Roman Catholicism, 211, 226

Rome and Romans [historical], 79, 195, 200

Roof, Dylann, 239

Rose City Antifa, 255

Ross, Martha, 166

Rostand, Michel, 21

Roswell, New Mexico, 159

Rothschild family, 272

Ruby Ridge, 110

Ruhani Satsang movement, 144

Russell, Charles Taze, 14, 88–89, 89 (ill.)

Russell, Kathy, 284

Russellites, 88

Russia and Russians, 28, 215, 272–73, 284

Rutherford, Joseph Franklin, 89

Rutherford County, North Carolina, 96

Rutherfordites, 88

Ryan, Leo, 54–55, 55 (ill.)

S

Sabbath, 104

Sacred Grove, 175

Sagan, Carl, 31, 120, 120 (ill.)

Sagan Standard, 120

Saint-Rémy-de-Provence, France, 210

Salon-de-Provence, France, 212

Salt Lake City, Utah, 23, 178, 219

Salt Lake Temple, 181 (ill.)

Salt Lake Valley, 178

Salzman, Lauren, 284

Salzman, Nancy, 283–84, 288

San Francisco, California, 39, 49, 53, 264, 270

sannyasins, 280

Santa Monica, California, 157

Saragossa [historical], 213

Satan, 90, 140, 202

Saudi Arabia and Saudi Arabians, 297

Savannah, Georgia, 42

Sayville, New York, 43

Scaramucci, Anthony, 121

Schwarzenegger, Arnold, 295

Schwerner, Michael, 238

scientism [cult], 114, 117–21, 130

Scientology [cult], 22, 161–67

Scotland and the Scottish, 96

Scripture

David Koresh and the Branch Davidians, 104

Evangelical church, politics, and the NRA, 68

Joshua, Jesus, Muhammad, and the implications of jihad, 78, 83

Latter-day Saints and the colonization of the cosmos, 174

prophets of the End Times, 192–93, 204–5

Watchtower Society and Jehovah's Witnesses, 87–89

Sea Organization (Sea Org), 165

Seagram's, 284

Seattle, Washington, 49

Second Advent, 137

Second Amendment, U.S. Constitution, 72–73, 244–45, 250

Second Coming, 195, 201–3, 216

Second Initiation, 146

Secondary Separationism, 69

Security and Exchange Commission, U.S., 127

Sekai Nippo [newspaper], 140

Senate, U.S., 17, 262

Seneca Lake, 19

Seoul, South Korea, 134, 136

Separationism, 69

Separatism, 233

September 11, 2001. See 9/11 [nine eleven]

Seven Sisters, 39

Seventh-day Adventism, 15, 104–6, 225

Seymour, William J., 48

Shadel, Doug, 6–7

Shakerism, 14, 35–36, 42, 233

Shalam Colony [cult], 36

Shem [biblical], 259–60

Shepard, Matthew, 95

The Shepherd's Rod (Houteff), 105

Shinar [historical], 77

Siddhartha Gautama (Buddha), 169, 297, 300

Silent Spring (Carson), 158

Silver Solution, 64

666, 194–95, 197

16th Street Baptist Church, 238

Sixtus V, Pope, 212

Small Arms Treaty, UN, 245

Smallville [TV show], 283

Smith, Candis Watts, 240

Smith, Erin A., 156

Smith, Hyrum, 185

Smith, Joseph, 14, 169, 174–79, 175 (ill.), 182, 185

Smith, Michael Ray, 73–74

Smothers Brothers Comedy Hour [TV show], 71

Snell, Richard Wayne, 82

social media as cult-joining factor and as cult

America as cult fertile field, 24–29, 34

Latter-day Saints and the colonization of the cosmos, 182

MLMs as cults, 128

organizations always as cults, 298

possibility of cults, 7

racial religion and social media cults, 262–76

Sullivanians, 291

Social Security, 194, 198

Society of Friends (Quakerism), 18–19, 35, 42, 233

Society of Protectors (SOP), 286, 288

Society of Universal Friends [cult], 19

Sodom [biblical], 185

Solomon [biblical], 179

Somerset, Indiana, 47

Somerset Methodist Church, 51

SOP (Society of Protectors), 286, 288

Soros, George, 272

Source, the, 218–19

South America and South Americans, 219, 282

South Carolina, 59, 122, 239

South Dakota, 74

South Korea and South Koreans, 134, 136, 139–40, 142

Southern Baptist Convention, 73, 91

Southern Poverty Law Center, 91, 249

Soviet Union and Soviets, 133, 158, 221

Sowers, Rev. Mike, 73

Space Age, 153

Spain and the Spanish, 79

Spock, Commander [character], 262

Spur, Texas, 183

St. Jogues, Canada, 226

St. Louis, Missouri, 186, 264

St. Louis World's Fair, 263–64

Stalin, Joseph, 134, 138

Star of David, 171

Star Trek [TV show], 31, 154

Star Trek: The Next Generation [TV show], 271

Star Wars [movie], 31

State Capitol Commission, Tennessee, 237

Stay Woke: A People's Guide to Making All Black Lives Matter (Bunyasi and Smith), 240

Steiger, Brad, 187

Stern, Marlow, 167

Stewart, Potter, 294, 296

Stockholm syndrome, 285

Stone, Matt, 173

Stonehenge, 201

"Storm" ("Event") Day, 272–73

A Study in Scarlet (Doyle), 182

Sudan and the Sudanese, 258, 260

Sudar Singh, 144

Sugmad, 143

Sullivan, Chloe [character], 283

Sullivan, David, 31

Sullivan, Harry Stack, 289

Sullivan Institute for Research in Psychoanalysis, 289

Sullivanians [cult], 288–91

Summer of Love, 264

Sundance Film Festival, 20

Sunday school, 3, 72

Sunshine Cab Company, 8

Supernatural (Hancock), 158

Supreme Court, Texas, 180

Supreme Court, U.S., 23–24, 71, 86, 93, 238, 294

Swaggart, Jimmy, 72

Sweden and the Swedish, 96

Sweet Angel (Edna Rose Ritchings), 46

Swinton, Rozita "Sarah," 179–80

Switzerland and the Swiss, 159, 168

Sykes, Joe, 147–48

Syria and Syrians, 297

T

Tampa Bay Times [newspaper], 167

Tarrant, Brenton, 239

Tarrio, Enrique, 27, 249–50, 250 (ill.), 252

Tarrytown, New York, 142

Tate, David, 82–83

Taxi [TV show], 8

TCP/IP (transmission control protocol/internet protocol), 266

Teed, Cyrus Reed (Koresh), 35–41, 36 (ill.)

Teens for Christ [cult], 83–84

TELAH (The Evolutionary Level Above Human), 186

Telegram, 251, 265, 288

televangelism. See Evangelicalism, evangelism, and televangelism [cult]

Temple of ECK, 144 (ill.), 145

Ten Commandments, 78

"10 Orders We Will Not Obey" [list], 245–46

Ten Tribes of Israel, 178

Tennessee, 236–37, 268

Tennessee State Museum, 237

Texas

America as cult fertile field, 16, 24

David Koresh and the Branch Davidians, 105–6, 110

Evangelical church, politics, and the NRA, 73

Heaven's Gate, 183–84, 188

Latter-day Saints and the colonization of the cosmos, 179–80

Oath Keepers, 248

prophets of the End Times, 194

QAnon, 273

racial religion and social media cults, 233

Watchtower Society and Jehovah's Witnesses, 86

Thanksgiving, 14

Thériault, Roch "Moïse," 224–30

Thetans, 165

Third Blessing, 135

Thirteen Articles of Faith, 178

Thomas Rhode Baptist Church, 62

Thoreau, Henry David, 36

Thorngate, Rev. Jon, 274

Thornton, Rev. W. L., 51–52

Three Mile Island, 291

Three Percenters [cult], 241, 252–54, 253 (ill.)

Through the Wormhole [TV show], 31

Tibet and Tibetans, 144

Tiempos del Mundo [newspaper], 140

Tierra del Fuego, 219

TikTok, 270

Times Union [newspaper], 287

Timothy, Book of, 193

"'Tis a Gift to Be Simple" [hymn], 35

TitleMax, 125

Topeka, Kansas, 91–92, 94

Tor, 267

Toronto, Canada, 228

Tours, Battle of, 79

Trail of Tears, 231, 233

transmission control protocol/internet protocol (TCP/IP), 266

Travolta, John, 161

Tribulation, 155, 202–3, 209

Trilateral Commission, 158

Trinidad and Tobago and Trinis, 259

True Parents, 137

Trump, Donald J.

America as cult fertile field, 28

Antifa, 256

Doomsday Clock, 222

Evangelical church, politics, and the NRA, 72

Jim Bakker, *The PTL Club*, and the return of Jesus, 65

Oath Keepers, 242–44, 247–48

organizations always as cults, 295

politics as a cult, 122, 123 (ill.), 124

Proud Boys, 249–50

QAnon, 271–75

racial religion and social media cults, 234–35

social media and the rise of hate groups, 262

spoofing cults, 268

Sun Myung Moon and the Unification Church, 143

Three Percenters, 254

Trumpism, 114, 121

Tulsa, Oklahoma, 97

Tupperware, 125

2030 Agenda for Sustainable Development, 245

Twin Towers, 143

Twitchell, Paul (Paulji), 144–45, 148

Twitter, 25, 30, 166, 243–44, 265, 270, 274–75

U

"UFO Cult Resurfaces with Final Offer," 188

U.F.O. Missionaries Extraordinary (Hewes and Steiger), 187

UFOs

Christian Rapture, Carl Jung, and flying saucers, 154–61

Heaven's Gate, 183, 187, 189

Jim Jones and the Peoples Temple Full Gospel Church, 51

Nuwaubian Nation, 257–62

Raëlians and the Elohim, 168, 173

Ukraine and Ukrainians, 28

Últimas Noticias [newspaper], 140

Unification Church Interfaith Seminary (Unification Theological Seminary), 142

Unification Church of the United States [cult], 121, 132–43

Unification Movement, 262

Union, the, 236–37

Unite the Right, 253, 256

United Church of Christ, 70

United Kingdom, 93

United Klans of America, 239

United Nations (UN), 134, 245, 245 (ill.)

United Nuwaubian Nation of Moors, 260–61

United Press International, 140

Universal Friends [cult], 19

The Universal Friend's Advice to Those of the Same Religious Society [prayerbook], 19

Universal Pictures, 284

University of Alabama, 184

University of Bridgeport, 140

University of Jabalpur, 279

University of Montpellier, 211

Upper West Side, New York, 288

Uruguay and Uruguayans, 140

US News and World Report [magazine], 123

USA Today [newspaper], 188

Utah, 23, 178, 180, 219

V

Valley Forge, 151

Veer, Guy, 226

Vermont, 175

Verne, Jules, 31

Verona [historical], 213

Vicenza [historical], 213

Victims and Survivors: Escapees from the Eckankar Cult (Sykes), 147–48

Vietnam War, 71, 239, 257

The Villages, 60

Virgin Mary, 43

Virginia, 62, 218, 250, 253, 256

Virginia Beach, Virginia, 218

Virginia Holocaust Museum, 92

Vishnu, 173 (ill.)

Voice of Healing [publication], 50

Voice of Healing community, 50, 52

von Däniken, Erich, 31, 157–58

Vorilhon, Claude (Raël), 168–73

Vox [website], 240

vulnerability as cult-joining factor, 4–5, 7–11, 25, 27, 245

W

Waco, Texas, 86, 105–6, 110

Waco Massacre (Waco Siege), 110

Wah Z. See Klemp, Harold

Wakin, Daniel J., 132

War of 1812, 19

The War of the Worlds [Welles radio broadcast], 31

The War of the Worlds (Wells), 31

Warren, Earl, 238

Warren, Joseph, 263

Waseda University, 134

Washburn University, 95

Washington, D.C.

America as cult fertile field, 27–28

Antifa, 255

Doomsday Clock, 221

Evangelical church, politics, and the NRA, 75

Ku Klux Klan and White Nationalism, 238

Oath Keepers, 241, 243, 248

prophets of the End Times, 196

Proud Boys, 251

social media and the rise of hate groups, 262

Sun Myung Moon and the Unification Church, 133

Washington, George, 16, 151

Washington Post [newspaper], 123, 276

Washington State, 49, 159, 309

Washington Times [newspaper], 140

WASPs (White, Anglo-Saxon, Protestant Americans), 232–33

The Watchtower [magazine], 90

Watchtower Bible and Tract Society [cult], 88

Watchtower Society [cult], 85–91

Waterford, New York, 284

Watergate, 71, 138–39

Watkins, Jim, 276

Watkins, Ron, 276

Watts, California, 71

WBC (Westboro Baptist Church) [cult], 91–96, 94 (ill.)

"We Gather Together to Ask the Lord's Blessing," 14

Weaver, John, 121

Weiss, Mitch, 98, 100–101

Welles, Orson, 31

Wells, H. G., 31

West Africa and West Africans, 247

West Freeway Church of Christ, 73

West Indies, 260

Westboro Baptist Church (WBC) [cult], 91–96, 94 (ill.)

Western Civilization, 197, 244

Whaley, Jane, 96–101, 103

Whaley, Robin, 97

Whaley, Sam, 96–99

Wheel of Samsara, 147

"Where we go one we go all" (WWG1WGA) slogan, 272 (ill.), 275

White, Anglo-Saxon, Protestant Americans (WASPs), 232–33

White, Ellen G., 14, 104, 104 (ill.)

White, James, 104

White House, 121, 138, 262

White Nationalism [cult], 235–40, 250, 257, 263, 265

White Rabbit Three Percent Illinois Patriot Freedom Fighters Militia, 254

WHO (World Health Organization), 114–15

Wien, Lacy, 100

Wilkinson, Jemima (Publick Universal Friend), 18–19, 19 (ill.)

William Alanson White Institute, 289

Williams, Rev. Cecil, 53 (ill.)

Wings of Deliverance, 52

Wink, Walter, 196, 199–200

Wired [magazine], 30

Wisconsin, 252, 274

Wollan, Malia, 308

Women's Equality Day, 172

Wood, Lin, 275

Woodruff, Wilford, 179

Word of Faith Fellowship [cult], 96–103

World Health Organization (WHO), 114–15

World Trade Center, 215

World War I, 89

World War II, 68, 162, 289

World Wide Web (WWW), 265–66

Wormwood, 109

Wright, Lawrence, 161

Wright, Matthew, 275

WWG1WGA ("Where we go one we go all") slogan, 272 (ill.), 275

Wyndham Hotels, 142

Wyoming, 95, 106, 178

X

Xenu, 166

Y

Yahoveh. See God

Yahweh. See God

Yamasee Native American Tribe. See Nuwaubian Nation of Moors [cult]

Yamasee Tribe, 261

Yankee Stadium, 139

Yearning for Zion Ranch, 179

Yeshua ben Yosef. See Jesus Christ

YHVH. See God

York, Malachi Z. See York, Michael

York, Michael, 257–61

Young, Brigham, 178 (ill.), 178–79

Young Living, 125

YouTube, 26, 73, 249, 269–70, 275

Z

Zabriskie Point, 188

Zadrozny, Brandy, 307

Zarephath-Horeb, 80–81

Zaskq, Peddar. See Twitchell, Paul (Paulji)

Zello, 265

Zion, 178

Zion's Watchtower Society, 88

Zondervan Publishing Company, 156